Scenic Driving

MINNESOTA

Phil Davies

FALCON®

HELENA, MONTANA

A FALCON GUIDE ®

Falcon® is continually expanding its list of recreational guidebooks. All books include detailed descriptions, accurate maps, and all the information necessary for enjoyable trips. You can order extra copies of this book and get information and prices for other Falcon® guidebooks by writing Falcon, P.O. Box 1718, Helena, MT 59624 or calling toll-free 1-800-582-2665. Also, please ask for a free copy of our current catalog. To contact us via e-mail, visit our website at http:\\www.falconguide.com.

All black-and-white photos by the author.
Front cover photo by G. Alan Nelson.
Back cover photo by Laurance B. Aiuppy.

Davies, Phil, 1958-
    Scenic driving Minnesota / by Phil Davies.
        p. cm.
    ISBN 1-56044-557-2 (pbk.)
    1. Minnesota—Tours. 2. Automobile travel—Minnesota—Guidebooks.
    I. Title.
    F604.3.D38 1997
    917.7604'53—dc21   97-10979
                                                            CIP

CAUTION

All participants in the recreational activities suggested by this book must assume the responsibility for their own actions and safety. The information contained in this guidebook cannot replace sound judgment and good decision-making skills, which help reduce risk exposure; nor does the scope of this book allow for disclosure of all the potential hazards and risks involved in such activities.

Learn as much as possible about the recreational activities in which you participate, prepare for the unexpected, and be cautious. The reward will be a safer and more enjoyable experience.

 Text pages printed on recycled paper.

Contents

Acknowledgments

My greatest thanks go to my wife Lydia, who prepared maps, lent me her laptop computer, and accompanied me—despite her best judgment—on many of the drives. I could not have completed this book without her moral support and willingness to carry more than her share of the load throughout a very long summer and fall. Thanks also to my parents, who instilled in me a love of exploration by dragging me all over the world as a child. I am indebted to countless people all over the state who took the time to share their knowledge of local geography, history and natural resources; they provided insights and nuggets of information that in many cases were unavailable in print. Particularly helpful were Judy Stringer, executive director of the Fergus Falls Convention and Visitors Bureau, who designed the Otter Tail Scenic Byway; Edwin Robb, an Afton resident who has written a book on the village's history; and G. B. Morey of the Minnesota Geological Survey, who gave me an 11th-hour crash course on Precambrian rocks.

Finally, thanks to Sarah Snyder of Falcon Press for giving me the opportunity to write this book.

Locator Map

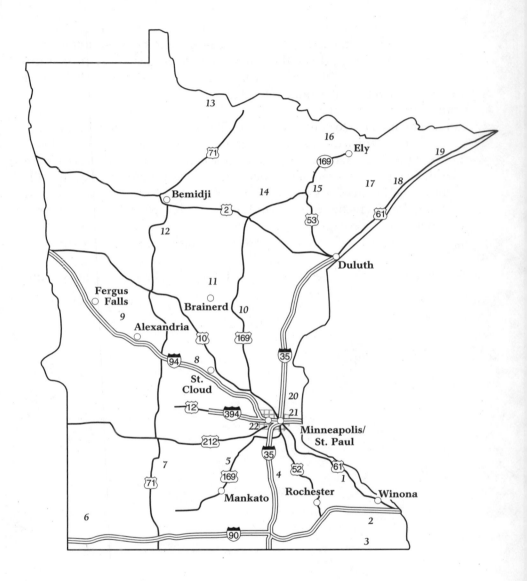

Map Legend

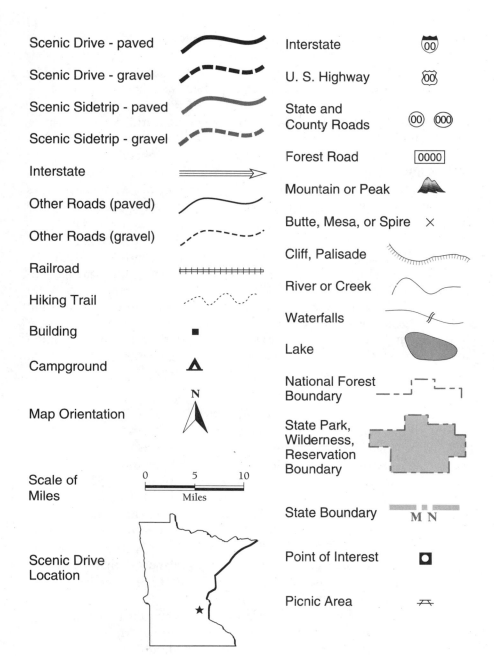

Scenic Drive - paved

Scenic Drive - gravel

Scenic Sidetrip - paved

Scenic Sidetrip - gravel

Interstate

Other Roads (paved)

Other Roads (gravel)

Railroad

Hiking Trail

Building

Campground

Map Orientation

Scale of Miles

Scenic Drive Location

Interstate

U. S. Highway

State and County Roads

Forest Road

Mountain or Peak

Butte, Mesa, or Spire

Cliff, Palisade

River or Creek

Waterfalls

Lake

National Forest Boundary

State Park, Wilderness, Reservation Boundary

State Boundary

Point of Interest

Picnic Area

Introduction

You won't find snow-capped mountains in Minnesota. Snow, sure; in keeping with the state's reputation for bone-numbing cold, the white stuff lies close at hand in streets, backyards, and cornfields from November through April. But mountains? Nada, unless you count the ancient, knobby ridges above the shore of Lake Superior. That said, the landscape of the North Star State offers motorists just about every other visual delight: waves crashing and foaming against the rocky shore of the world's largest freshwater lake; forests of pine, spruce, birch, and aspen dotted with lakes and wetlands; stately bluffs towering above red-brick river towns and apple orchards; lush, gently rolling farm country punctuated by corn silos and wooden barns.

Located at a geographic and ecological crossroads, Minnesota defies stereotypes. The state's 79,548 square miles encompass eye-stretching grassy plains and hills cloaked in oak, maple, and basswood, as well as lake-studded boreal forest. Intensely agricultural, Minnesota ranks among the top five producers of corn, soybeans, spring wheat, oats, barley, cheese, hogs, and turkeys; yet it's also a leading manufacturer of paper, industrial machinery, medical devices, and computer software. Yes, many Minnesotans live in small towns like Lake Wobegon, the Mayberry-on-the-tundra celebrated in *A Prairie Home Companion*, or even deeper in the country where the nearest hospital is an hour's drive away. But half of the state's 4.5 million population resides in cosmopolitan Minneapolis–St. Paul, the economic and cultural hub of the Upper Midwest.

The natural world

In the language of the Dakota (Sioux) Indians, Minnesota means cloudy waters, as in a turbid river at flood stage. Except for the dry southwest, water is omnipresent in the state, flowing powerfully in major rivers such as the Mississippi, Minnesota, and Red, coursing down innumerable streams, and pooling in tens of thousands of lakes and wetlands. The "Land of 10,000 Lakes" motto on the state's license plates is an understatement; there are actually more than 12,000 lakes at least 10 acres in size within Minnesota's borders. Not counting Lake Superior, the vast inland sea that Minnesota shares with Michigan, Wisconsin, and Ontario, and Lake of the Woods, the northernmost waters in the continental U.S.

All that water is a legacy of the last Ice Age, when a massive blanket of ice up to a mile thick smothered almost all of present-day Minnesota. Like a giant bulldozer, the Wisconsin Glaciation scooped out basins and depressions that filled with meltwater when the climate warmed about 11,000

Lovely Embarrass Lake outside Biwabik on Minnesota Highway 135.

years ago. Lake of the Woods and Upper and Lower Red lakes (the largest lakes entirely within the state), are remnants of Glacial Lake Agassiz, an inland sea that once covered an area the size of Texas and Colorado combined. Massive torrents rushing south from the retreating ice sheet cut the broad, bluff-lined Minnesota and Mississippi valleys, and the dramatic Dalles of the St. Croix River. The ice also shaped dry land, scraping bare the ancient granites and schists of the Canadian Shield in the northeast, depositing rich topsoil in the south, and forming distinctive topographical features such as kettle lakes, moraines and eskers. The state's southeastern corner, reminiscent of New England with its wooded hills and narrow stream-cut valleys, escaped the onslaught of the glaciers.

Of course, Minnesotans sometimes feel that they're still living in the Ice Age. Did you hear about the farmer who was informed that as a result of a land resurvey, he was now living in Iowa instead of Minnesota? "Thank God, no more cold winters," he wrote in his diary. Smack-dab in the middle of the continent, far from the moderating influence of the sea, Minnesota has a climate similar to Russia's. Daytime temperatures remain below freezing for five months of the year, and northern Minnesota regularly posts the lowest temperatures in the country. The tiny community of Tower reported an all-time official low of -60 degrees F. on February 3, 1996. That's 174 degrees cooler than the state's record high of 114 degrees F. at Moorhead on

July 6, 1936. No wonder that Minnesotans invented the snowmobile, and are among the nation's leading practitioners of ice fishing.

Three of North America's major ecological regions converge in Minnesota, supporting a startling variety of plant and animal life. Mixed coniferous forests of white spruce, balsam fir, red and white pine, aspen, and birch thrive in the northeastern third of the state—ideal habitat for white-tail deer, snowshoe hares, bald eagles, black bears, lynxes, and timber wolves. More than 2,000 wolves roam Minnesota, more than in any other state in the Continental U.S. In the west, once covered with tallgrass prairie, cottonwood groves, and wetland oases provide shelter and food for coyotes, gray foxes, prairie chickens, and migratory birds such as Canada geese, goldeneye ducks, and tundra swans. Pines and grass give way to sugar maples and acorns in the southeastern blufflands, the western edge of deciduous woodlands that stretch all the way to the Atlantic. Brown, brook, and rainbow trout swim in coldwater streams, while wild turkeys stalk wooded slopes and draws.

In the northwest, hundreds of square miles of coniferous bogs and peatland comprise a fourth ecosystem—a rich vegetative mosaic that includes rare orchids and many carnivorous and parasitic plants. This largely undisturbed area is a haven for sandhill cranes and gray owls, and the stomping ground of the moose, a shy herbivore that can weigh more than 2,000 pounds. In all, Minnesota is home to 2,010 different species of trees, shrubs, and plants, 403 species of breeding and migrant birds, 144 of fish, 81 of mammals, and 29 different species of reptiles.

Minnesota past and present

Burial mounds are found on riverbanks, blufftops, and in other undisturbed areas all over the state—mute testimony to ancient cultures that flourished here hundreds of years before French explorers penetrated the wilderness. Woodland and Mississippian peoples built large, permanent villages, crafted beautiful pottery and stone tools, and maintained a trading network that reached as far as St. Louis and the Rocky Mountains. In more recent times Minnesota was home to the Santee Dakota, an eastern branch of the powerful tribe that ruled the northern plains on horseback. In the 1700s and 1800s the Dakota were pushed out of the forest onto the prairie in a series of wars with the Ojibwe, who themselves had been forced west from the Great Lakes region by the Iroquois. Both the Ojibwe and Dakota led a semi-nomadic lifestyle, hunting and fishing, harvesting wild rice in birchbark canoes, and tending gardens of corn, potatoes, beans, and squash.

As it was throughout the West, that way of life was threatened and then swept aside by whites eager to exploit the region's rich resources of furs, lumber, iron, and prairie soil. French adventurers such as Pierre Esprit Radisson and Sieur Du Luth came first, searching for the fabled northwest passage to the Far East. In 1679, Sieur Du Luth, after whom the port on Lake Superior is named, rendezvoused with the Dakota at their principal village on Mille Lacs and promptly claimed the country for Louis XIV. His French and British successors found beaver, mink, and fox instead of a route to Cathay, and established outposts such as Fort Beauharnois near Red Wing and Grand Portage on Lake Superior for trade with Indian trappers.

After the Louisiana Purchase in 1803 a young, expansionist United States exerted its authority in the region. In 1805, U.S. Army Lieutenant Zebulon Pike negotiated the purchase of most of present-day Minneapolis-St. Paul from the Dakota for 60 gallons of liquor and $200 in trade goods, and in 1819 Fort Snelling rose atop the bluffs at the confluence of the Mississippi and Minnesota rivers. The new settlement grew rapidly. St. Paul, the practical head of navigation on the Mississippi, became a port of call for riverboats bringing settlers and vital supplies to the northwestern frontier. Farther upstream, the Falls of St. Anthony were harnessed to drive mills that would later make Minneapolis the flour-milling capital of the world.

The 1840s heralded the era of King Pine as lumbermen from New England moved into the St. Croix Valley to log immense tracts of virgin white pine, red pine, and spruce. The lumber camps, ever moving north and west to cut fresh timber, gave rise to the legend of Paul Bunyan and his Blue Ox, Babe, immortalized in statuary in the towns of Brainerd and Bemidji.

Drawn west by stories of fertile soil and a salubrious climate (it wasn't *that* cold, local boosters said), tens of thousands of European immigrants laid claim to a piece of Minnesota sod in the decade before the Civil War. Many of these farmers were from Germany, Norway, Sweden, and Denmark; today more than half of Minnesotans trace their ancestry to either Germany or Scandinavia. Four years after statehood in 1858, an Indian war temporarily stemmed the tide of white settlement. Confined to reservations along the Minnesota River and starving because of tardy federal annuity payments, the Dakota under Little Crow took to the warpath, killing dozens of settlers and laying siege to New Ulm and Fort Ridgely. The Dakota Conflict ended with a mass hanging of 38 warriors in Mankato on Dec. 26, 1862. The farmers returned, and new communities such as Willmar and Marshall sprang up along the railroads that continued to drive the frontier farther out onto the prairie. Recruited on the East Coast by agents for James J. Hill's Great Northern Railroad, settlers bought Minnesota railroad lands for $2.50 an acre.

The pace of immigration accelerated in the 1880s with the discovery of iron in northeast Minnesota. New arrivals from Italy, Poland, Slovakia, Croatia, Finland, and Greece flocked to the Mesabi, Vermilion, and Cuyuna ranges to toil in open-pit and underground mines that would yield billions of tons of iron over the next century.

The seemingly limitless forests were reduced to stumps by the 1920s, throwing lumbermen out of work and leading to ultimately disastrous homesteading in the "cutover" lands. The Iron Range suffered its own depression in the 1950s, when the high-grade ore that provided the steel for cars, skyscrapers, and the munitions expended in two World Wars ran out. Since then, Minnesota's economy has shifted from extractive industries to a diversified base that includes agriculture, pulp and paper, food processing, manufacturing, software design, medicine, and tourism. Roughly 60,000 farms cultivate everything from Red River Valley spring wheat, potatoes, and sugar beets, to Green Giant corn, sweet peas, and carrots. Duluth, accessible to seagoing freighters via the Great Lakes and St. Lawrence Seaway, is a major exporter of western coal, wheat, and iron derived from taconite (a low-grade iron ore). The Twin Cities and Rochester—home of the Mayo Clinic—are world-renowned for medical technology.

Inheritors of a progressive, populist tradition that nurtured former vice president Hubert H. Humphrey and U.S. Senators Eugene McCarthy and Paul Wellstone, Minnesotans insist on clean government and open debate of public issues. And they're committed to protecting an environment that gives them so much opportunity to indulge their love of the outdoors.

Minnesota's clean air and water laws are among the most stringent in the nation, and a "no net loss" policy protects wetlands that provide habitat for fish, amphibians, and waterfowl. Reforestation projects in the 1930s created Superior National Forest, Chippewa National Forest, and twenty state forests that together cover more than forty percent of the state. Itasca, Minnesota's first state park, was established by the Legislature in 1891; since then sixty-two more state parks have been created to preserve natural ecosystems and support activities such as camping, hiking, rock climbing, canoeing, cross-country skiing, and snowmobiling.

Other protected, unique places include the Boundary Waters Canoe Area Wilderness (BWCA), the largest federal wilderness east of the Mississippi; rocky, island-studded Voyageurs National Park, the only national park that contains more water than dry land; and Blue Mounds State Park, a patch of rocky prairie roamed by a herd of bison. Minnesotans—and increasingly, outdoors enthusiasts from all over the country—make the most of these wild, beautiful places. More boats are registered in the state than in Florida, and on many summer weekends and holidays city streets seem deserted, forsaken for a lakeshore, river bank, or blufftop—whichever one is most convenient.

Enjoying the drives

Whether you're a native, a recent transplant, or a vacationer, the twenty-two drives in this book will open your eyes to Minnesota's ever-changing landscape, colorful history, and natural wonders. Not to mention a few unnatural wonders, such as the awesome Hull Rust Mahoning Mine in Hibbing and Garrison's giant fiberglass walleye. The drives, designed as daytrips or weekend outings with overnight lodging or camping, are by no means comprehensive. Feel free to explore alternate state and county routes that meander all over the countryside, especially in the agricultural south and west.

Wherever the road takes you, try to stop long enough to explore Minnesota under your own power. Stroll along a forest trail or the levee in a historic river town; toss a line in the water from a boat dock or rented canoe; admire a prize dairy cow or pumpkin at a county fair. Folks you encounter aren't likely to say "howdy" and slap you on the back; remember that German and Scandinavian heritage. But they open up after a few minutes of conversation. The weather is a sure-fire conversation starter, whatever the situation: *"Cold enough for you?"*

"You betcha."

Welcome to Minnesota.

Before you go

The maps in this book are intended only as rough guides to the drives. In addition to a state map, it's a good idea to have along a topographical atlas or set of county maps before hitting the road. U.S. Forest Service maps, available at ranger stations or through the mail, are particularly helpful for drives in the Chippewa and Superior national forests. Other pointers for a safe, hassle-free trip:

■ You'll need a car permit to enter Minnesota state parks. The annual sticker, available at any park, is the best deal—about $20 for unlimited access through the year.

■ The speed limit on Minnesota highways is 55 mph, and 65 mph on rural interstates.

■ When driving in northern or western Minnesota, especially in the winter, carry extra clothing, emergency food, and jumper cables. It can be a long haul to the nearest gas station or town.

■ Keep a sharp lookout for white-tailed deer dashing across the road. Mutually destructive collisions are particularly frequent at dusk, when deer become more active.

Drive 1: The Great River Road:

Red Wing to La Crescent via U.S. Highway 61

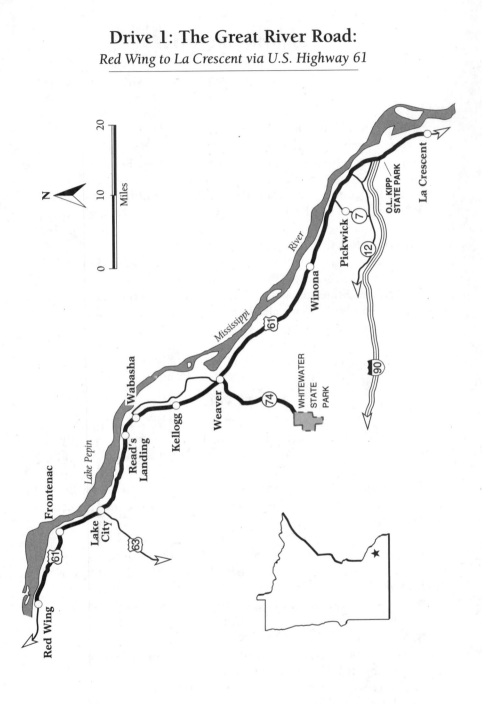

1

The Great River Road

Red Wing to La Crescent via U.S. Highway 61

General description: Squeezed between the Mississippi River and towering, forested bluffs, the Great River Road (U.S. Highway 61) passes through handsome nineteenth century river towns, sleepy villages, and natural areas rich in wildlife. The 107-mile segment from Red Wing to La Crescent offers two optional excursions off US 61: one loops through lush meadows and wetlands in the Mississippi's floodplain, the other scales the bluffs, offering breathtaking views of the river valley and hillside apple orchards.

Special attractions: Strolling, dining, and antique shopping in the historic towns of Red Wing, Lake City, Wabasha, and Winona; Frontenac, a village where little has changed since the 1880s; hiking and birdwatching at Frontenac and O. L. Kipp State Parks; biking on county roads and the Cannon Valley Trail; bald eagle watching at Read's Landing; spectacular views along the shore of Lake Pepin and from the blufftops on Apple Blossom Drive.

Drive route numbers: US 61; Wabasha County Roads 30, 184; Winona County Roads 7, 12, 1.

Location: Southeast Minnesota, in and around the Mississippi River Valley about 50 miles south of the Twin Cities.

Travel season: Year-round, but special seasonal attractions include apple blossoms in the spring, vivid leaf color and fresh apples in the fall, and bald eagle watching in late winter.

Camping: RV and tent camping at Frontenac and O. L. Kipp state parks; Hay Creek Valley Campground on US 61 south of Red Wing; Pioneer Camp south of Wabasha; Winona KOA south of town on US 61.

Services: Plentiful gas, food, and lodging in major river towns such as Red Wing, Wabasha, Winona, and La Crosse, Wisconsin, La Crescent's big sister across the river.

Nearby attractions: Scenic sidetrips through woods, farmland, and small towns in the uplands west of US 61 (see Drives 2, 3); the Root River Trail, a bike route linking Rushford, Lanesboro, Preston, and other towns in the Root River Valley; historic river town of Hastings (see Drive 20); pretty villages of Alma, Maiden Rock, and Stockholm on the Wisconsin side of river; Laura Ingalls Wilder birthplace in Pepin, Wisconsin; river cruises and Granddad Bluff Overlook in La Crosse, Wisconsin.

 # The drive

Mark Twain captured the essence of the Upper Mississippi River Valley in *Life on the Mississippi*:

> *The majestic bluffs that overlook the river, along through this region, charm one with the grace and variety of their forms, and the soft beauty of their adornment. . . . And then you have the shining river, winding here and there and yonder, its sweep interrupted at intervals by clusters of wooded islands threaded by silver channels; and you have glimpses of distant villages, asleep upon capes; and of stealthy rafts slipping along in the shade of forest walls; and of white steamers vanishing around remote points. And it is all as tranquil and reposeful as dreamland. . . .*

The stealthy rafts and white steamers have gone, but the rest of the sights that enchanted Twain are still there along the Mississippi south of Red Wing. Those "majestic bluffs," as high as 500 feet in some places, were formed by an overwhelming torrent of meltwater that rushed east and south after the retreat of the glaciers. The broad floodplain is a boater's paradise and a refuge for bald eagles, trumpeter swans, canvasback ducks, beavers, and muskrats.

Long before Twain steamed up the Mississippi (the name comes from an Algonquin word meaning "great water,") the Dakota Indians relied on the river to trade with and make war on neighboring tribes; in his time river towns such as Red Wing, Wabasha, and Winona sprang up, important export centers for Minnesota lumber and wheat. Today these towns, with their superb nineteenth century architecture, restful river views, and home-style cooking, offer succor to travelers on one of the most stunning drives in the United States.

You know you're in bluff country as soon as you reach Red Wing, the starting point for the drive. US 61 seems to run right into Barn Bluff, a massive formation of sandstone and dolomite rising nearly 350 feet above the town. Henry David Thoreau listed wildflowers growing atop the bluff in 1861; you can follow in his footsteps by parking at the end of East Fifth Street and ascending steep trails to the mountain's broad, grassy top. The passage of more than 130 years has not diminished the view.

Beautifully restored buildings downtown include the Beaux Arts-style T. B. Sheldon Memorial Auditorium on Third Street and the stately St. James Hotel on Main Street, built in 1875. The tourism office hangs its shingle in a 1905 railroad depot in Levee Park—a great place to watch cabin cruisers and slow-moving barges plying the river. If your tastes run more to the material, browse for antiques on Main Street, or visit the Pottery District north of downtown. Outlet stores selling everything from galoshes to gargoyles have taken over the old Red Wing Stoneware Company factory, famous for its bluish, salt-glazed crockery. Potters still use local clay to turn out replicas of the traditional designs. The Pottery District is also the eastern terminus for the Cannon Valley Trail, a 19.5-mile bike path along the deep, wooded valley of the Cannon River.

Leave town on US 61, skirting the stratified flanks of Barn Bluff and swinging south at the foot of a chain of hills that rise in a wall of green above the rooftops. Unbroken hardwood forest drapes the steep slopes; at the top, outcrops of limestone poke out like the battlements of a gigantic castle. Where there's room between the bluffs and the road, corn grows in neat rows. Just over 10 miles brings you to Frontenac Station, a whistle stop on the St. Paul to Milwaukee rail line that consists of little more than a cafe, a gas station, and a few houses.

But the place is a thriving hub of commerce compared with Frontenac, a village two miles to the east that has managed to escape the twentieth century entirely. To get there, turn left on Goodhue County Road 2 (at the State Park sign) and follow it through marshland and pasture past the entrance to Frontenac State Park. A summer resort for America's elite in the 1870s, Frontenac is a tranquil relic today. There are no shops, offices, or streetlights on the gravel streets, just elegant 1860s-vintage homes, well-tended gardens and stunning views of Lake Pepin, a 2.5-mile-wide bulge in the river caused by natural damming of the Mississippi downstream.

Frontenac State Park, a sanctuary for migratory warblers and bald and

Lake City Marina, Lake Pepin.

golden eagles, completely encircles the village. Hiking trails lead to a high ridge overlooking the valley and In-Yan-Teopa, a giant boulder that was sacred to the Dakota and Fox Indians. CR 2 makes a right-angle turn in Frontenac and passes Villa Maria, a secluded conference and retreat center, on the return loop to US 61. At the junction a historical marker commemorates Fort Beauharnois, a French fur-trading post built nearby in 1727.

It's only 4 miles to Lake City, past inspiring views of the body of water the Dakota called *Pem-vee-cha-mday* ("Lake in the Mountains") and the distant bluffs of Wisconsin. On summer weekends white sails flit back and forth across the lake, chasing the fickle breeze. The town is known for its Haralson apples—roadside stands overflow with the crisp, tart variety in late September and October—and as the birthplace of water-skiing. Yes, it was on the shores of Lake Pepin, not Key Biscayne or Santa Monica Bay, that an 18-year-old boy wonder named Ralph Samuelson strapped a couple of 8-foot pine boards to his feet and sped into sporting lore in 1922. His feat is celebrated annually during Water Ski Days on the last weekend in June. The action revolves around the marina downtown, home to hundreds of powerboats and sailboats moored in perfect array.

For the next 10 miles the road clings to the shore of Lake Pepin, offering splendid vistas of the water—calm and brilliant on cloudless days—and advancing headlands cloaked in oak, basswood, hickory, and maple. Just past the fishing resort of Camp Lacupolis you can pull off the road and take in views of wooded islands, fishing boats, and perhaps a barge, toiling upstream with a load of gravel or coal.

Read's Landing, a cluster of houses long removed from its glory days as a staging area for huge rafts of northern pine headed to sawmills, marks the beginning of the Upper Mississippi River National Wildlife and Fish Refuge—nearly 194,000 acres of floodplain stretching south to Rock Island, Illinois. A labyrinth of islands, sandbars, backwater sloughs, and marshes, the refuge provides food and shelter for more than 270 species of birds, including great blue herons, common egrets, rails, bitterns, white pelicans, bald eagles, and trumpeter swans. Bald eagles frequent Read's Landing in the late winter, diving for fish and nesting in trees along the shore.

Just south of Read's Landing turn left on 5th Grant Boulevard West, cross the railroad tracks, and continue past a riverside cemetery and cornfields into Wabasha, a town of 2,400 that gained fame as the setting of the movie *Grumpy Old Men*. The film and its sequel were actually shot in Stillwater and the Twin Cities, but Wabasha, named for a dynasty of Dakota chiefs who once ruled the area, is well worth a visit. Turn right on Bridge Street to reach the town's classic Main Street, a parade of brick-and-sandstone facades dating to the 1850s. The Anderson House at 333 West Main is the oldest operating hotel in the state; the rambling three-story building opened for business in 1856. Specialties on the menu include roast mallard, Mississippi catfish, and double Dutch fudge pie.

Turn right on Minnesota Highway 60 and left on Wabasha County Road 30 (Hiawatha Drive) to leave town via the back door, through rich cropland in a section of the river where the bluffs veer away to the west. After 4 miles the road intersects with US 61 just north of the dusty hamlet of Kellogg. Here you have a choice: stay on US 61, skirting the bluffs inland, or strike out into the bottomlands, much of which is managed as a refuge for natural vegetation and wildlife. To take the low route, turn left on Wabasha County Road 18 into Kellogg, then bear left on Wabasha County Road 84. Sprawling fields of corn give way to prairie grass, wildflowers, and stands of pine and spruce, then to undulating sand dunes sparsely covered with grass and scrub. Otters, sandhill cranes, and Blanding's turtles—watch for the "Rare Turtle Crossing" sign—live in nearby McCarthy Lake Wildlife Management Area, a 2,800-acre expanse of floodplain forest, marsh, and sand dunes.

After 9 miles you're back on US 61 and heading toward Weaver Bottoms, a magnet in spring and fall for migratory birds such as trumpeter swans, great egrets, and blue-winged teals. At Weaver Landing there's an observation platform with interpretive displays that explain how the Bot-

View of 500-foot-high Sugar Loaf Bluff from Lake Park in Winona.

toms, while still rich in wildlife, have become degraded by dam construction and repeated floods. For a sidetrip into the heart of bluff country, take Minnesota Highway 74 from Weaver to Whitewater State Park. The river has cut a dramatic path through heavily wooded limestone hills—prime habitat for ring-necked pheasants, wild turkeys, and white-tailed deer. Brown and rainbow trout can be tempted onto a hook in the Middle Branch of the Whitewater River. Otherwise, continue on US 61 to Winona past soaring, crenellated bluffs and Lock and Dam number 5—the structure responsible for high water levels in Weaver Bottoms.

Winona's name breathes romance. We-no-nah was a legendary Dakota maiden who, rather than accept an arranged marriage with a man she didn't love, leapt to her death from a high crag near Maiden Rock, Wisconsin. The city enjoys an idyllic setting on bottomlands between the river and Lake Winona, a reflecting pool for 500-foot Sugar Loaf Bluff. Winona invites strolling and bicycling in Lake Park, with its bandshell, rose gardens, and downtown streets graced with grand buildings such as Winona National & Savings Bank, a rare example of Egyptian Revival style, and the lavishly decorated Watkins mansion. The helpful folks at tourist information (turn left on Huff Street, a causeway spanning the lake into downtown) can direct you to the sights. For an eagle's perspective on the city and its surroundings, drive up Garvin Heights Road, accessible from Lake Boulevard west of US 61. The views from a wayside park at the top extend for 50 miles, up and down the river valley and deep into Wisconsin.

The journey to La Crescent on US 61 and Interstate 90 is fast and scenic, with yet more vistas of islands in the stream and rock-turreted hills. An alternate route, part of which has been designated a state scenic byway, takes a more circuitous path up narrow, stream-cut valleys and along the blufftops. To head for the hills, turn right on Winona County Road 7 (9 miles south of Winona), and follow it through a lovely valley hemmed in by steep bluffs to the village of Pickwick.

Here, next to Big Trout Creek, stands a wonderful relic of Minnesota's industrial past: a six-story grist mill, built from native limestone in 1858. During the Civil War the mill's machinery, powered by a 25-foot water wheel, ground non-stop to feed Union troops. Much of that machinery, a Rube Goldbergian assemblage of chutes, metal cogs, belts, and pulleys, still resides in the cool interior. Pickwick Mill is being restored by local citizens, who are on hand to show you around from May through October.

Continue on CR 7 past some farmsteads to the head of the valley, where the road abruptly climbs the densely wooded bluffs and intersects with Winona County Road 12. The next 3 miles parallel I-90 over open, flat terrain; keep straight and bear left on Winona County Road 3 to reach O. L. Kipp State Park, a 3,000 acre preserve with magnificent views of the Mississippi River Valley from trail overlooks. The main route to La Crescent turns right on CR 12, crosses the freeway and heads due south to Nodine, a tiny place that revolves around a white clapboard general store with a single gas pump. Turn left at the gas pump; you're on Apple Blossom Drive, a state scenic byway that rides the ridgetops through countryside that rivals New England in its verticality and pastoral appeal. You'll have a hard time keeping your eyes on the road as the ground to the left drops away, revealing the immense Mississippi coursing 400 feet below. A warm snowfall of apple blossoms covers the hillsides in the spring, and in the fall, wooded ravines burn with russet, gold, and crimson.

Apple Blossom Drive continues on Winona County Road 1, eventually spiraling down sheer limestone cliffs into La Crescent, a town of 4,300 that bills itself as the Apple Capital of Minnesota. All those orchards up the hill bear fruit in the fall, providing the raw material for the La Crescent Apple Festival, held during the third week in September. The drive ends here; you can return to Red Wing and the Twin Cities on US 61, or pick up Drive 2, from La Crescent west along the Root River Valley.

2

The Root River Valley
*La Crescent to Forestville/Mystery Cave
State Park on MN 16*

General description: This 70-mile excursion down a river gorge in the bluff country of southeast Minnesota winds past cornfields and dairy pastures and through picturesque, historic towns hewn from native limestone. Few drives in the Midwest—or anywhere, for that matter—can match the Root River Valley's combination of visual splendor and rustic tranquillity.

Special attractions: Outstanding views of forested bluffs, river bottom and lush, rolling farmland; nineteenth century limestone buildings in Rushford, Lanesboro, Preston, and other towns; Scenic Valley Winery in Lanesboro; biking on the Root River Trail; restored Meighen General Store; Forestville/Mystery Cave State Park; trout fishing, canoeing, hiking, birdwatching.

Drive route numbers: Minnesota Highways 16, 44, 76; Fillmore County Roads 11, 12, 5.

Location: Southeast Minnesota. The drive begins in La Crescent on the Mississippi River and ends at Mystery Cave in Forestville State Park.

Travel season: Year-round with early to mid-October best for leaf color, and spring and winter if you want to escape the crowds in Lanesboro.

Camping: Rushford Municipal Campground; Sylvan Park in Lanesboro; The Old Barn Resort, 5 miles north of Preston on Fillmore County Road 17; Hidden Valley Campground in Preston; Forestville/Mystery Cave State Park; Maple Springs Campground just outside park.

Services: Gas, food, and lodging in Rushford, Lanesboro, and Preston. Hokah, Houston, Peterson, and Whalan have more limited facilities.

Nearby attractions: Old Order Amish colony near Harmony; Niagara Cave south of Harmony; Norwegian community of Spring Grove; Beaver Creek Valley State Park and Schech's Mill; Apple Festival in La Crescent; Pioneer Home Museum in Spring Valley, home of Laura Ingalls Wilder's husband Almanzo; Upper Mississippi River National Wildlife and Fish Refuge; river cruises and Granddad Bluff Overlook in La Crosse, Wisconsin.

Drive 2: The Root River Valley
La Crescent to Forestville/Mystery Cave State Park on MN 16

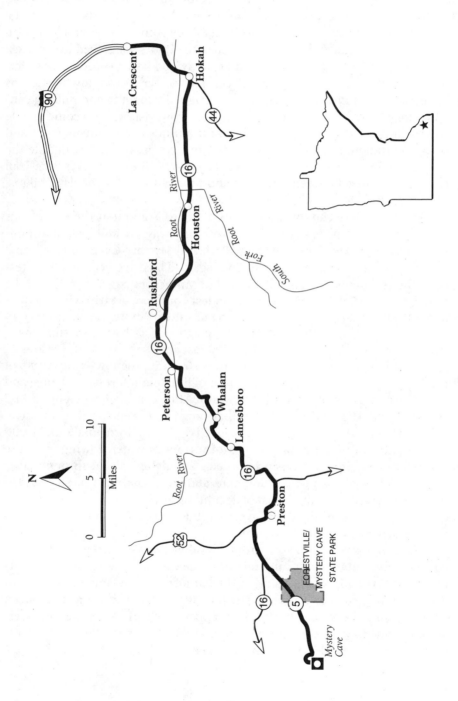

The drive

The Root River slashes through the blufflands of southeast Minnesota in dramatic fashion, flowing eastward to the Mississippi at the bottom of a deep, wide gorge cut by glacial meltwater. Limestone buttresses cloaked in oak, maple, walnut, and juniper—much of the Root's watershed lies in the 2 million-acre Richard J. Dorer Memorial Hardwood Forest—tower above fertile bottomland planted in corn, soybeans and hay. River towns such as Lanesboro, Rushford, and Preston were originally logging and milling centers; today they derive much of their income from visitors who come to ogle ante-bellum limestone buildings, hunt for antiques and Amish crafts, and savor the tranquillity and beauty of the countryside. In the last decade the Root River Valley has been "discovered" by bikers (the Root River Bike Trail runs for 40 miles between Fountain and Money Creek), canoeists, hikers, and trout anglers.

You'll understand what all the excitement is about at the end of this 70-mile drive up the valley on Minnesota Highway 16, and beyond on minor county roads to Forestville State Park and Mystery Cave. In fact, you'll probably want to turn around and do it again. The drive begins in La Crescent, the self-proclaimed Apple Capital of Minnesota (see Drive 3). Up the hill from U.S. Highway 61, there's a modest commercial strip with a supermarket, gas station, bank, and several retail stores. But the town, founded in the 1850s as an agricultural center, long ago lost its battle for supremacy with La Crosse, a booming city of 52,000 just across the river in Wisconsin.

Head south on Minnesota Highway 16, along the low-lying banks of the Mississippi River Valley—a vast quilt of floodplain forest, wetlands, and backwater lakes rolling toward Wisconsin. After 2 miles, bear right on MN 16/Minnesota Highway 44 into another broad valley enclosed by massive, trapezoid-shaped hills. This is the Root River Valley, formed about 11,000 years ago by an unimaginably powerful torrent of water flowing from the edge of the melting Wisconsin Ice Sheet. The deluge sliced through layer upon layer of shale, sandstone, dolomite, and limestone, creating steep-sided bluffs that later grew a thick coat of deciduous forest. Glacial meltwater also cut deep channels for the Root River's various forks and tributaries, spreading like dendrites farther upstream.

The highway carries you across the valley floor—a melange of woods, cow pasture, cattail marsh, and miniature lakes—and the surprisingly narrow Root River. MN 16 splits off to the left just outside Hokah, a village of 600 souls tucked into a narrow stream valley. Follow it up a long, steep incline, riding the edge of the bluff. An expanse of corn, soybeans, and wetland, threaded by the thin, green ribbon of the Root, stretches to 150-foot-high, heavily wooded bluffs in the distance.

After a few miles MN 16 descends into the valley, hugging the foot of the bluff, draped in white oak, maple, basswood, butternut, shagbark hickory, and other hardwoods. The relatively warm, moist forests of the southeast harbor many species of trees and shrubs uncommon in the rest of the state. Look across the valley as you approach Houston and you'll notice that not all the bluffs are richly timbered; "goat prairies"—extremely steep, south-facing slopes dotted with juniper and juneberry—are the home of prairie plants such as blazing star, coneflower, wild indigo, and Indian paintbrush, along with the elusive timber rattlesnake, Minnesota's only poisonous serpent.

Houston, once a port for small steamboats carrying freight and settlers from Germany, Ireland, and Scandinavia, received a shot in the arm when plans were announced to extend the Root River Trail eastward in 1998. Restaurants and antique stores have enlivened the town's red-brick main street, and business has picked up for Addie's Attic, a bed and breakfast in a turn-of-the-century house on Jackson Street. A nearby stone church is well worth a 3-mile side trip through rolling farmland on Minnesota Highway 76 (turn left just before you get to Houston). The simple church, shaded by cedars and pines, was built in 1866 of local, chamois-hued limestone by Norwegian settlers. They obviously stayed and prospered; virtually every headstone in the graveyard bears a Norwegian name. Many of the older, lichen-encrusted inscriptions are in Norwegian.

MN 16 continues up the valley, flanked by tall, overlapping headlands marching into the haze. Tidy farms with red wooden barns—an item that could be ordered, precut and ready to assemble, out of the Sears catalog in the 1890s—nestle against the tree line, on the shore of an ocean of corn. Small streams tumble out of the hollows toward the Root, meandering through a corridor of ash, cottonwood, sugar maple, and willow.

White letters stenciled on a grassy blufftop announce that you've reached Rushford; MN 16 hangs a sharp right and crosses the river into town, passing a two-story, 1867-vintage railroad depot on the left. The depot, a popular starting point for bikers on the Root River Trail, also serves as a tourist information center. A one-room schoolhouse next door has been restored to its turn-of-the-century appearance, complete with tiny wooden desks and a stoneware water cooler. Rushford, once called "Trail City" because so many Indian foot trails and pioneer-era wagon routes converged here, boasts a number of old limestone buildings, including the Mill Street Inn, a restaurant at Mill and Grove Streets, and Tews Mill on the banks of Rush Creek. Across the highway there's a park with a picnic pavilion and a large children's playground.

The broad valley, still carpeted with crops, begins to narrow a few miles west of Rushford. Near the village of Peterson opposing headlands close in like pincers, and the river swings all the way across the valley to squeeze through the gap near the highway. A side road spans the stream into Peterson, a cluster of nineteenth century houses and shops shoehorned into the bluffs. The Wenneson Hotel, a Colonial-style hostelry built in 1904 and restored in 1993, caters to bikers on the Root River Trail.

For the next 10 miles the river caroms from one side of the gorge to the other, first running close beside the road, fringed with evergreens and hardwoods, then veering away across the open cornfields, only to return around the next bend. Large stands of white pines with gracefully upswept branches darken the almost vertical slopes of the bluffs, towering 200 feet above the road. To the right, outcrops and pinnacles of limestone loom over the river like the battlements of a gigantic medieval fortress. This section of the river is popular with trout fishermen, and with canoeists and kayakers making their way downstream to takeout points in Peterson, Rushford, and Houston.

Whalan, just across the river on Fillmore County Road 36, was just another fading hamlet until the bike trail came through in the early 1980s. These days the Overland Inn packs 'em in with homemade pies and ice cream in the summer and fall, and Besta's Norwegian bed and breakfast caters to winter romantics as well as the two-wheel crowd. Back on the main route, MN 16 clambers up the bluff and sweeps around an endless curve to the left, breaking away from the main channel of the Root toward Lanesboro. Fillmore County Road 8, a right turn near the top of a hill, takes you along the banks of the Root's South Branch into the town's historic heart.

Lanesboro's charming setting—a bowl-shaped valley, surrounded by limestone crags—and its remarkably well preserved nineteenth century architecture have made the town the hub of bluff country. Two-story limestone and brick buildings dating to the 1860s line Parkway Avenue, retooled into cafes, bed and breakfasts, restaurants, antique shops, art galleries, and bike rental stores. The Commonweal Theatre Company puts on plays year-round in an 1883 vaudeville house, and Scenic Valley Winery produces wines from locally grown fruit in a former creamery on Coffee Street. When the crowds and constant bike traffic get a bit much, relax in Sylvan Park, a lovely patch of greenery with trout ponds and picnic facilities down the hill from Brewsters Red Hotel; or take a walking tour of the town's residential district. A map is available at the tourist information office, one block off Parkway on the bike trail.

Leave town on Parkway, passing Sylvan Park, then turn right on MN 16. The highway corkscrews up a steep-sided valley, nudging outcrops of fissured limestone overhung with sumac, pin oak and hackberry. Eventually the road emerges into open cropland hundreds of feet above the Root River Valley; there's a pull-off to the left where you can park and take in a

Parkway Avenue in Lanesboro, the hub of bluff country.

glorious view of Lanesboro, its limestone and white, wood-frame buildings gleaming against the backdrop of forest and field. The builders of Union Prairie Lutheran Church, on the crest of the hill, must have wanted to be as close to Heaven as possible on Sunday. Starkly beautiful with its soaring, white-washed walls and tall belltower, the church occupies a ridge over-looking two valleys. To the right, dairy cows graze in a hillside meadow fringed with oaks. In the distance, on the valley floor, contoured cropland swirls around dark wedges of woodland.

More images from a Grant Wood painting fly by as the highway crosses a rolling tableland dissected by swift streams. Cornfields alternate with open pasture dotted with groves of oak, maple, basswood, and other hardwoods. After about 2 miles MN 16 joins U.S. Highway 52 at a T-junction. Turn right; the road ascends a ridge, passing Preston Apple and Berry Farm, then winds down into a valley that spreads out for miles, a tableau of green and gold punctuated by scattered corn silos and barns.

Fillmore County Road 12 splits off to the left into Preston, a town that's bigger than Lanesboro, with a year-round population of 1,500, but doesn't come close to matching its cuteness. The buildings on Courthouse Square are made of brick, not limestone, and they sit on the valley floor, denied a dramatic bluff backdrop. But Preston does have its share of historic buildings, most notably the Jailhouse Inn, a two-story edifice of white-trimmed brick at 109 Houston. Formerly the county jail, the 127-year-old main building and carriage house have been converted into a 12-room bed and breakfast where guests are invited to "spend the night behind bars." An extension of the Root River Trail scheduled to be completed in late 1997 will connect the town to the Amish community of Harmony, 20 miles to the south (see Drive 3).

Return to US 52 and follow it up the hill and out of the valley. In less than a mile MN 16 veers off to the left, crossing steeply rolling cornfields and dairy pasture. In about 3 miles, turn left at a sign for Forestville State Park. Fillmore County Road 11, a gravel road, wends its way through dairy pasture and down a narrow stream valley framed by wooded bluffs. After 1 mile turn right on Fillmore County Road 118 and follow it along the edge of a wider valley carpeted with corn. A green belt in the middle marks the course of the South Fork of the Root, the same stream that flows through Lanesboro. Overhung by oaks, elms and maples, the road winds along the valley, passing Sunnyside Farm, a dairy operation that could have been the setting for the TV show *Green Acres*. A picture of a Holstein cow graces the big white barn, its paint peeling from the onslaught of sun, rain, and snow. A nearby guest house is available for overnight stays.

The village of Forestville, a couple of miles farther on, has a *Brigadoon*-like quality; its tranquil setting on the banks of the Root evokes the past so perfectly that you expect it to vanish into thin air, sucked back to an era

14

before cars, microwaves, and women's suffrage. Forestville is a ghost town that comes to life during the summer, inhabited by costumed guides who carry on as though it's still 1899. A thriving trade center with two general stores, a grist and saw mill, a school, and two hotels in the 1860s, the village went into a slow decline after the railroad bypassed it in 1868. For more than 40 years Thomas Meighen kept the town alive by employing the 50 remaining residents on his farm; in return they received housing, board, and credit in his store, built of hand-pressed brick in 1856-58. The store closed in 1910, and the weeds took over until 1963, when the state park was established.

Today you can tour the store—stocked with original merchandise from the 1890s—Meighen's brightly painted house next door, and adjacent farm buildings. Hiking, horseback, cross-country, and snowmobile trails wind through the rest of the heavily wooded park, a haven for wild turkeys, red and gray foxes, beavers, and timber rattlesnakes. Three spring-fed streams are rated among the best brown-trout waters in the state.

Mystery Cave, one of the largest limestone caverns in the Upper Midwest, is also part of the park. To get there, cross the 107-year-old bridge at the end of the gravel and follow Fillmore County Road 12 along the bluffs above pretty Forestville Creek. You pass Maple Springs Campground on your right, then climb out of the valley, coming to a T-junction in 1.5 miles.

Sunnyside Farm, approaching Forestville/Mystery Cave State Park on Fillmore County Road 11.

Leaving the Meighen Store in Forestville/Mystery Cave Park.

It's 3 more miles to the cave; turn left on Fillmore County Road 5, descending once again into the valley of the Root, and follow the signs. A maze of linear passageways formed over millions of years by seeping water, Mystery Cave has 12 miles of tunnels and domed caverns. Highlights of the hour-long tour include a turquoise lake with rafts of calcite, translucent "draperies" of flowstone, and more stalactites and stalagmites than you can shake a flashlight at.

The drive ends here; CR 5 will take you back to MN 16, which connects Preston with Spring Valley (home of the Wilder family, of *Little House on the Prairie* fame), 10 miles to the west.

3

Amish Country

St. Charles–Harmony–La Crescent

General description: A 77-mile ramble through the wooded hills and intimate hollows of southeast Minnesota's "bluff country." Crossing the great rift valley of the Root River at Lanesboro, the drive passes through Amish farm country near Harmony and loops north and east through small towns and secluded valleys to the Mississippi River.

Special attractions: Storybook vistas of wooded bluffs and lush farmland in Minnesota's unglaciated zone; Old Order Amish farms near Harmony and Canton; antique shopping in historic towns of Lanesboro, Harmony, and Spring Grove; Niagara Cave south of Harmony; Norwegian community of Spring Grove; Schech's Mill, an operating grist mill built in 1876; hiking, fishing, and cross-country skiing at Beaver Creek Valley State Park; biking on the Harmony-Preston and Root River State trails.

Drive route numbers: U.S. Highway 61; Minnesota Highways 74, 250, 30, 44, 139; Fillmore County Roads 11, 21, 115, 30, 103; Houston County Roads 4, 10, 1.

Location: Southeastern Minnesota. The drive begins in St. Charles on Interstate 90 east of Rochester and ends in La Crescent on the Mississippi River.

Travel season: Year-round with mid-May through June ideal for wildflowers, mid-October best for leaf color. Spring Grove's Syttende Mai festival is held on the weekend closest to May 17, and Mabel celebrates Steam Engine Days on the weekend after Labor Day.

Camping: Whitewater and Beaver Creek Valley State Parks; Sylvan Park municipal campground in Lanesboro; Old Barn Resort near Preston; Big Woods Campground near Canton; Dun Romin' Park Campground south of Caledonia.

Services: Gas stations, restaurants, and motel/B&B accommodations in Lanesboro, Harmony, Spring Grove, and La Crescent.

Nearby attractions: Historic Pickwick Mill and O.L. Kipp State Park off U.S. Highway 61 (see Drive 1); hiking and fishing at Whitewater State Park; restored Meighen General Store and Mystery Cave at Forestville/Mystery Cave State Park (see Drive 2); Pioneer Home Museum in Spring Valley; Upper Mississippi River National Wildlife and Fish Refuge; river cruises and Granddad Bluff Overlook in La Crosse, Wisconsin.

The drive

Southeast Minnesota is a feast for the senses, a land of steep hills covered with hardwood forest and intimate valleys lush with dairy pasture and corn. Somehow the region escaped the scouring and planing of the last Ice Age; when glaciers just to the west halted their advance and began to melt, torrents of water rushed east to the Mississippi River, carving deep channels in the sandstone and limestone bedrock. In time a fine, wind-blown soil called loess covered the hills, and a thick forest of maple, oak, black walnut, shagbark hickory, and other hardwoods took root soon after.

Drawn to the area by its fertile soils and beauty, farmers from New England, Germany, and Scandinavia homesteaded the valleys in the 1850s, building churches and mills out of native limestone. More recently, Amish families have moved to the rolling countryside around Harmony; their black, horse-drawn buggies are a common sight on quiet backroads and in town on market day. This 77-mile drive meanders through the heart of bluff country toward the Mississippi, crossing the spectacular Root River Valley and stopping in historic towns such as Lanesboro, Harmony, and Spring Grove.

The drive begins at the St. Charles exit (Minnesota Highway 74) off Interstate 90. The town, consisting of a couple of motels, several eateries, and shops aligned along a typical turn-of-the-century Main Street, lies 1 mile to the north, on the banks of the Whitewater River. The Victorian Lace Inn bed and breakfast at 1512 Whitewater Avenue serves lunch and, on Wednesdays from May through December, afternoon tea at 3 P.M.

MN 74 crosses the freeway and descends into a narrow valley enclosed by forested bluffs on both sides. To the right, on the valley floor, cornfields swirl around red wooden barns and corn silos with checkered crowns. Over the next 7 miles the valley gradually opens up, with fewer trees and more corn and pasture spreading to distant bluffs. At the sign for Troy, turn left on Winona County Road 43; the road passes a farm and ascends a steep, bare-rock hillside onto a ridge that winds through dairy pasture and hills thick with red and white oak, maple, basswood, and ash.

Within 2 miles CR 43 becomes Fillmore County Road 11; bear left on Fillmore County Road 103, passing an abandoned one-room schoolhouse, and drop down once again into a deep, shaded valley. Trout Creek, a remnant of the vast river of meltwater that carved out the valley thousands of years ago, percolates through the woods beside the road. You can pull off in a county park and watch the clear, cold water cascade over an old concrete dam. The road crosses the creek and descends the narrow, winding course of another to Pilot Mound, a ghost-hamlet with a derelict general store and a graceful wooden church.

At the bottom of the hill, Minnesota Highway 30 clambers out of the

Drive 3: Amish Country
St. Charles–Harmony–La Crescent

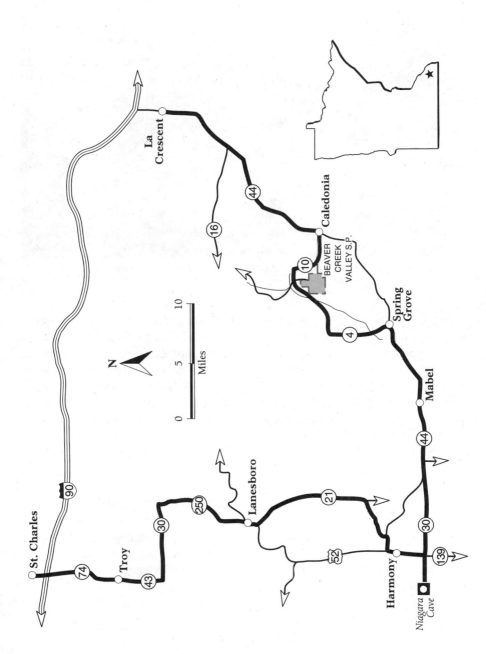

Entering the ghost village of Pilot Mound on Fillmore County Road 103.

valley into billowing, largely treeless uplands covered with corn, soybeans, and dairy pasture. Naked, chalky patches gleam in the turf where rainstorms have ripped away the topsoil; unwise farming practices in the nineteenth century devastated much of the region, and erosion is still a problem. After 5 miles, turn right on Minnesota Highway 250. You're on top of a steeply rolling tableland dissected by wooded draws draining to river valleys on both sides. Prosperous-looking farms ringed by groves of pines and hardwoods rule over mile after mile of rich cropland.

Suddenly, the land opens up into a great chasm, the forested bluffs of its far side soft and blue in the distance—the Root River Valley. The Root, the mother stream of Trout Creek and scores of other rivers and rills in bluff country, wends its way through a deep glacial trench that grows ever wider as it approaches the Mississippi (see Drive 2). MN 250 coils down the heavily wooded bluff to the valley floor and across the main channel of the Root on an old steel-truss bridge. Lined with cottonwoods, willows, and oaks, the river divides cornfields hemmed in by 150-foot, nearly vertical walls of sandstone and dolomite. Trees clinging to the bluff droop across the road on the approach to Lanesboro. On the left, bikers slip in and out of the trees on the Root River State Trail, a converted railbed running for 40 miles between Fountain and Money Creek Woods east of Rushford.

Lanesboro has been discovered by the tourist industry; so many bicyclists, antique hounds, and bratwurst lovers descend on the village on summer weekends that you can barely find a parking space. But Lanesboro (see Drive 2 for a full description of the town) is still too charming a place to pass by without stretching your legs and taking some refreshment on Parkway Avenue.

Leave town on Minnesota Highway 16 West (follow Parkway past Sylvan Park) and turn left on Fillmore County Road 21 in about 0.75 mile. Deep S-curves sliced through bedrock the color of aged cheddar rise into a narrow valley that gradually widens to accommodate cropland. Then you're riding high on a ridge, with views of neatly demarcated cornfields, farmsteads, and wooded ravines falling away to right and left. CR 21 veers to the right in about 5 miles, sidles down the ridge, and heads straight south, bucking and dipping over swells of pasture and woods.

Turn right on Fillmore County Road 115. There's a ramshackle building on the corner with "Henrytown Country Store" still faintly visible on the weathered wood. This gravel road, which turns into asphalt in about 1.5 miles, winds down into a wooded valley and out onto rolling farmland, passing several Amish farms. Since the 1970s, about one hundred Old Order families have moved to the Harmony area from Ohio, Michigan, and New York State, drawn by relatively cheap farmland and plentiful hardwoods for furniture making. Shunning modern technology, the Amish milk their cows by hand, till their fields with horse-drawn plows, and rely on windmills to pump water. Children learn the three R's in one-room, clapboard schoolhouses without electricity. Black buggies pulled by retired race horses whisk the Amish to market in Harmony, Lanesboro, or Preston. Please— don't drive up to the farmhouses and take photographs! Intensely private, the Amish do open their homes to "the English," but only if you're on an official tour, organized by two firms in Harmony.

CR 115 meets U.S. Highway 52/Minnesota Highway 44 in 6 miles; turn right towards Harmony, a town of about 1,100 that revels in its Amishness. Shops selling Amish furniture, quilts, baskets, candles and baked goods abound on Main Street, and in summer and fall a steady stream of cars and mini-buses leaves the premises of Michel's Amish Tours and Amish Country Tours, bound for the farms. Reservations are recommended; ask at the tourism office on Main Street. Next door, in a century-old building with a crumbling brick facade, Harmony's toy museum displays more than four thousand playthings from the past, including toy tractors, trains, cars, dolls, and animals. Rivaling Lanesboro in tourist draw, the town boasts three bed and breakfasts and a recently expanded motel. In 1997 a new 16-mile paved bike trail connected Harmony with Preston and the Root River Trail, bringing even more visitors in search of Old World charm.

Head south on Minnesota Highway 139 to reach Niagara Cave, one of the finest limestone caverns in the Midwest. Formed over millions of years by water seeping through fractures in the rock, the cave was discovered in 1926 by a farmer whose pigs kept mysteriously disappearing in an open field. Hearing their faint squeals emanating from a hole in the earth, the farmer ventured below and discovered subterranean canyons and gorges with ceilings more than 100 feet high. The cave features a 60-foot waterfall, ancient fossils, stalactites and stalagmites galore, and even a "crystal wedding chapel" where you can tie the knot by candlelight. It's 4 miles on CR 139 to the cave turnoff on Fillmore County Road 30; turn right and follow the signs.

The drive turns east towards Mabel and Spring Grove at this point; you can either return to Harmony and turn right on US 52/MN 44, passing through the village of Canton (more Amish crafts and antiques), or go straight on CR 30, over steeply rolling hills with views of corn and dairy farms. The gravel road joins MN 44 in 6 miles.

The highway dips down to within a mile of the Iowa border, passing through undulating, lightly wooded cropland en route to Mabel, a small town where "Lucky Lindy" lived for a time in his barnstorming days. At least that's the story behind the Charles A. Lindbergh room at the Mabel House Hotel on Main Street. There's also a Steam Engine Museum, chockablock with old machines that come to life during Steam Engine Days, held on the weekend after Labor Day. Thousands converge on the town to watch the engines thresh wheat, saw logs, haul immense loads, and parade down Main Street, chaperoning the Steam Engine Queen and princesses.

"Velkommen til Spring Grove," says a roadside sign in this town of 1,200, settled by Norwegians in the 1850s. The annual Syttende Mai (May 17) Fest celebrates Spring Grove's roots with Norwegian food, arts and crafts, and a parade featuring a 30-foot replica of a Viking longship. The Norse theme continues in Ballard House, an 1893 hotel on Main Street that has been converted into a combination antique store and ice cream parlor. In the summer a local troupe stages a musical in a barn just outside town; before each show playgoers are invited to a picnic with food in keeping with the play's theme.

You passed Houston County Road 4 just before the "Velkommen" sign. Backtrack and turn right at a cemetery on the corner. CR 4 quickly spirals down into a pretty, wooded valley with several dairy farms, then rises again into rolling fields of corn and soybeans. Much of the route ahead is on gravel roads that can coat your car with a fine slurry in the spring and throw up clouds of fine, white dust in the summer. Your reward? Exceptional pastoral beauty in one of southeast Minnesota's most delightful river valleys.

In about 2 miles, turn right at a brick church with a tall white steeple. This gravel road crosses more steeply rolling cropland, then descends through a thickly wooded draw to a T-junction. Turn right and curve down into Beaver Creek Valley, passing a quarry where half the hillside has been gouged away, exposing layers of limestone and dolomite laid down in warm seas hundreds of millions of year ago. Pin oak, black walnut, sugar maple, and other hardwoods cling to the almost sheer bluff; to the right a dense tangle of trees entwined in riverbank grape conceals the valley floor, 250 feet below.

Turn left at a three-way crossroads. Soon the road emerges from the forest and winds along the edge of the bluffs, darkened in spots by stands of spruce and juniper. A sea of corn fills the valley, flowing around the graceful contours of the land—high where a headland thrusts out from the valley wall, low where a coulee splits the hills, providing a storybook setting for the odd farmstead with its inevitable corn silo and wooden barn. Finally, the valley opens out into a timeless vista of rich cropland and pasture cradled by wooded hills, and the road joins the blacktop on Houston County Road 10. Look to the right and you'll see Schech's Mill, a working grist mill built in 1876. For a nominal fee the current owners, direct descendants of a Schech who bought the mill in the late 1880s, will show visitors around the massive limestone building and give the water-powered millstones a spin. You can also buy whole-wheat and corn flour ground at the mill, reached by a dirt road along the banks of Beaver Creek.

Schech's Mill in Beaver Creek Valley near Caledonia.

CR 10 crosses a narrow truss bridge—a popular hangout for trout anglers—and begins a long, sinuous climb out of the valley, passing fractured outcrops of limestone. Before you reach the top, turn right on a township road that mounts a rise and crosses another bucolic valley, intersecting with Houston County Road 1 in 1.5 miles. Turn right on blacktop to reach Beaver Creek Valley State Park, a beautiful little park with miles of hiking trails through virgin hardwood forest and a campground right on the creek, one of the finest brown-trout streams in the state.

Head the other way on CR 1 to reach MN 44 and Caledonia, the seat of Houston County. Despite its name, bequeathed by an itinerant engineer of Scottish descent, the town's early settlers were mostly Norwegians, Swedes, and Germans who labored mightily to clear the fields and erect handsome limestone buildings such as the Houston County Courthouse at Marshall and Washington Streets. A museum complex at the county fairgrounds (Main and Fifth Streets) features three wooden buildings—a church, log house, and country school—that have been moved from elsewhere in the county and fully furnished in pioneer style. A small supermarket, a hardware store, a cafe, and a few shops occupy nineteenth century storefronts along Kingston Street, Caledonia's main drag.

MN 44 heads north across open, rolling farmland, then drops into a deep, wooded valley, coiling past sheer limestone walls and stands of pin oak, maple, elm, hickory, and black walnut. For the next 6 miles the road hugs the foot of the bluffs; cornfields spread to the opposite side of the valley, interrupted only by a line of trees marking the twisting course of Spring and Thompson creeks. The bluffs grow ever higher as you approach Hokah and the end of this drive. A bustling lumbering and milling center 100 years ago, the present village consists of a modest commercial strip strung out along the highway. It's just 7 miles across the Root River Valley to La Crescent, the starting point for Drive 2, and the terminus for Drive 1.

4

Colleges, Cows, and Corn
Northfield to St. Peter via Faribault

General description: A 72-mile ramble through lush, rolling farmland, the historic towns of Northfield and Faribault, and remnants of the Big Woods, the dense hardwood forest that once covered large areas of southern Minnesota.

Special attractions: Green, rolling countryside studded with lakes; Carleton and St. Olaf colleges in Northfield; Nerstrand Big Woods State Park, the largest remaining tract of virgin hardwood forest in southern Minnesota; Alexander Faribault House in Faribault; 1870s steam-powered sawmill near St. Peter.

Drive route numbers: Minnesota Highways 246, 60; Rice County Roads 40, 29, 20, 12, 13, 99; LeSueur County Roads 131, 12, 11, 18, 21, 102.

Location: South-central Minnesota, 50 miles south of the Twin Cities. The drive begins in Northfield and ends in St. Peter.

Travel season: Year-round with fall best for leaf color, and spring for wildflowers at Nerstrand Big Woods State Park. Northfield observes "Defeat of Jesse James Days" on the first weekend after Labor Day.

Camping: Nerstrand Big Woods State Park near Northfield; Roberds Lake Resort and Campground northwest of Faribault; Camp Maiden Rock in Morristown; Camp Dels on Sakatah Lake.

Services: Food, lodging, and gas in Northfield, Faribault, and St. Peter.

Nearby attractions: Twin Cities of Minneapolis and St. Paul; Minnesota Valley National Wildlife Refuge between St. Paul and Belle Plaine; double waterfall and stone windmill at Minneopa State Park near Mankato; historic river towns of Hastings and Red Wing; Cannon Valley Trail, an off-road bike path from Cannon Falls to Red Wing; German-American city of New Ulm northwest of Mankato on U.S. Highway 14.

The drive

White settlers pushing into southern Minnesota in the 1850s encountered what early French explorers dubbed *le Bois Grand* or the Big Woods: a deep forest of sugar maple, basswood, and elm rolling onward to the edge of the prairie, broken only by glades of oak savannah and umpteen lakes and streams. By the 1930s, 90 percent of the Big Woods had been cleared for

Drive 4: Colleges, Cows, and Corn
Northfield to St. Peter via Faribault

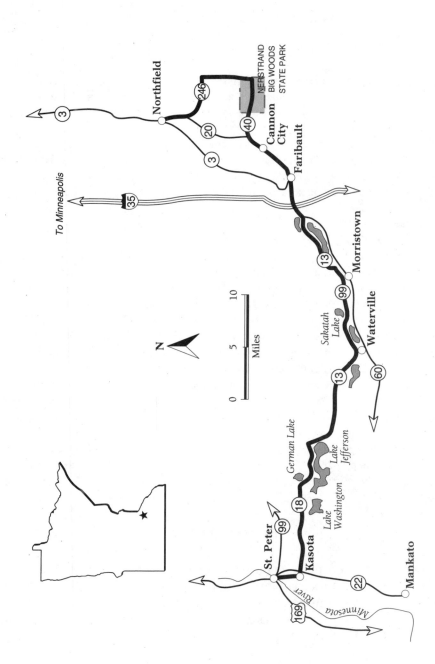

dairy farms and cornfields. Still, strips and pockets of woodland remain, adding variety and color (especially in the fall) to a lush, pastoral landscape worthy of a Grant Wood painting. This 75-mile drive on lightly traveled backroads traverses some of the richest farmland on earth, offering a glimpse of the lost glory of the Big Woods. The historic towns of Northfield, Faribault, and St. Peter provide ample opportunity for refreshment, antique shopping, and strolling in the footsteps of French fur traders, missionaries, and an outlaw named Jesse James.

The sign on Minnesota Highway 3 coming into Northfield says it all: "colleges, cows, and contentment." Founded in the 1850s by edified Yankees who harnessed the power of the Cannon River to mill flour, the town boasts two fine liberal arts colleges, Carleton and St. Olaf. Carleton, the alma mater of economist and philosopher Thorstein Veblen, occupies 800 impeccably landscaped acres atop a hill overlooking downtown. St. Olaf, a bastion of Norwegian culture that has gained worldwide fame for its Christmas concerts, dominates wooded Manitou Heights a mile west of town. Dairying and wheat generated the wealth that built Division Street, an eight-block stretch of ornate nineteenth century facades listed almost in its entirety on the National Register of Historic Places. The 120-year-old Archer Hotel, resplendent in French Second Empire style, anchors a cluster of small eateries frequented by students and faculty from both schools.

The most famous building in town, however, is the former First National Bank, site of an ill-fated raid by the James gang on September 7, 1876. Jesse James, his brother Frank, and six other members of the James-Younger gang found themselves in a deadly gunfight with local merchants when they tried to rob the bank, shooting the head cashier and wounding a teller in the process. Four bandits were killed, and Jesse and Frank led the survivors on a desperate chase into western Minnesota, hotly pursued by a 1,000-man posse. The seven-minute encounter is reenacted by duster-clad gunmen in "Defeat of Jesse James Days," observed on the first weekend after Labor Day. The interior of the old bank building, now a museum, has been reconstructed to look just as it did on the day of the raid. You'll also find guns, photos, contemporary press accounts, and an ear that once belonged to gang member Charlie Pitts.

To begin the drive, go south on Division Street and follow the signs for Minnesota Highway 246. Within minutes you're in open countryside, a pleasing medley of cornfields, cow pasture, and, where the land is dissected by streams, stands of sugar maple, basswood, oak, and green ash. More trees crowd around classic farmsteads with red wooden barns, corn silos, and herds of Holsteins, Minnesota's standard dairy cow. Road cuts reveal multiple layers of the Platteville limestone that underlies much of southern Minnesota. MN 246 bears left after 3 miles, then turns south again for Nerstrand Big Woods State Park.

Nineteenth-century facades on Central Avenue in downtown Faribault.

The entrance is on Rice County Road 40; turn right at the brown state park sign and continue to the park, the largest tract of Big Woods in the state. Twin branches of Prairie Creek have carved deep, secluded clefts through its 1,300 acres, creating picturesque waterfalls and a shady haven for white-tailed deer, grouse, songbirds, and rare plants such as sharp-lobed hepatica and dwarf trout lily, a species unique to southeast Minnesota. Miles of hiking, skiing, and snowmobile trails thread ridgelines and stream banks that explode with color in the spring and fall. CR 40 turns to gravel just past the park gate, but the bumpy ride is worth it, taking you through thick stands of maple, basswood, green ash, and ironwood and up a hill into wooded farmland. Thousands of seedlings planted by school and civic groups reach for the sun near the park boundary—an attempt to reclaim territory for the forest.

Stay on the gravel for another 4 miles, then bear left at a four-way stop onto Rice County Road 29. The blacktop returns on Rice County Road 20, the road to Faribault. Follow it to the end, then turn left on Shumway Avenue and right on First Street Northeast. Downtown lies down the hill, on the other side of the Straight River.

The city owes its name to Alexander Faribault, a French-Canadian who established a fur-trading post here in 1826. His wood-frame home by the river, recently spruced up and furnished in period style, is open for tours by appointment during the warm months. But, like Northfield, the town bears the stamp of settlers from New England in its neat street plan and history as a center of Episcopalian ministry to the Dakota Indians. Central Avenue is lined with classic nineteenth century buildings, including the present home of Dusek's Bakery, highly recommended for its wide selection of pastries. On Second Avenue NW, across from the Rice County Fairgrounds, the Faribault Woolen Mill Co. offers tours of its factory and sweet deals on "Faribo" wool blankets, made in the town since 1865.

A broad swath of lakes and wetlands—well-known to fishermen, waterfowl hunters, and birdwatchers—stretches from Faribault to the Minnesota River at St. Peter. Virtually every lake has a public access where you can slip a canoe or larger craft into the water and set off in pursuit of walleye, or just a suntan. Leave town on Division Street (Minnesota Highway 60), then turn right on Rice County Road 12, crossing the causeway that separates Cannon and Wells lakes. The route follows Rice County Road 13 along the wooded shore of Cannon Lake, passing lake homes and expanses of cattail marsh that teem with nesting redwing blackbirds in the spring. After 4 miles you're back on MN 60, following the leisurely Cannon through low-lying fields and marsh.

Just past the hamlet of Morristown, turn right onto 245th Street West (Rice County Road 99) and into heavily wooded farm country. Glimpses of Lower Sakatah Lake appear through breaks in the trees, then the road crosses a narrow isthmus and swings around the northern shore of Sakatah Lake. The bluffs of this beautiful lake are high and covered with mature maple, elm, and ironwood trees. Near the Le Sueur County line, CR 99 becomes Le Sueur County Road 131. Keep an eye open for white pelicans, Canada geese, coots, mallard ducks, and mergansers. At the end of the lake, turn right onto Minnesota Highway 13, hugging the shore of Lake Tetonka, then strike out on Le Sueur County Roads 12 and 11 through well-watered corn and dairy country.

Geldner Sawmill, a reminder of the days when farmers cleared the Big Woods with hand axes and teams of horses, hunkers beside a catfish pond on CR 13, between German and Jefferson lakes. Turn left at Beaver Dam Resort and drive past cabins and fishhouses to reach the mill, a modest structure of weatherbeaten wood punctuated by a tall, rusty smokestack. Built in 1870, and restored in the early 1980s by Le Sueur County, the steam-driven mill still slices into maple, oak, and ironwood logs the second Sunday of every month from May through September.

Head back to the resort, and follow the road to the left around Lake Jefferson. Le Sueur County Road 18 takes you over a narrow spit of land between lakes (look for more white pelicans) and into fairly flat farmland

The force that leveled the Big Woods: Geldner's Sawmill on Le Sueur County Road 13.

with more corn and soybeans than trees—a sign that you've reached the edge of the historical Big Woods. After about 7 miles, the dark, forested bluffs of the Minnesota River appear in the distance. Turn left on Le Sueur County Road 21 and drop into the valley. In the hamlet of Kasota, once an important quarrying center (the Minnesota and Wisconsin state capitols were built of pinkish Kasota limestone), there's a fine old town hall of red brick, a few houses, and a public boat access.

CR 21 intersects Le Sueur County Road 102 back up the hill, before you enter the village. Follow it through dense bottomland forest and past some rather scruffy riverside businesses to Minnesota Highway 99. A steel-truss bridge spans the river into St. Peter, where the drive ends, conveniently, by the Chamber of Commerce. For a description of the town, see Drive 5, which links this drive with the Twin Cities.

5

Minnesota River Run

Chaska to Mankato along the lower Minnesota River Valley

General description: A 70-mile roller coaster ride shadowing the Minnesota River from Chaska to Mankato. Lightly traveled county roads repeatedly scale and descend the river's heavily wooded bluffs, passing through fertile farmland, pioneer hamlets, and dense bottomland forest. Pit stops in the historic towns of Le Sueur (home of the Jolly Green Giant) and St. Peter.

Special attractions: Lush, rolling countryside with panoramic views of Minnesota River Valley; home of W. W. Mayo, founder of the Mayo Clinic in Rochester; Gustavus Adolphus College and the site of a landmark treaty with Dakota Indians in St. Peter; spectacular double waterfall, 1860s-vintage windmill, and prairie wildflowers at Minneopa State Park near Mankato.

Drive route numbers: U.S. Highway 169; LeSueur County Road 40; Sibley County Road 6; Nicollet County Roads 36, 23; Blue Earth County Road 68.

Location: South-central Minnesota. The drive begins in the Twin Cities suburb of Chaska and ends just south of Mankato.

Travel season: Year-round with early summer ideal for prairie flowers and mid-October best for leaf color. Some riverside roads may be flooded in exceptionally wet springs.

Camping: Carver Park Reserve near Chaska; Peaceful Valley Campsites on US 169 south of Le Sueur; Riverside Park in St. Peter; Minneopa State Park and Land of Memories municipal campground in Mankato.

Services: Gas, food, and hotel/motel accommodations in Chaska, LeSueur, St. Peter, and Mankato.

Nearby attractions: Valleyfair amusement park and Canterbury Park horse racing near Shakopee; Minnesota Vikings training camp in Mankato; Minnesota Valley National Wildlife Refuge between St. Paul and Belle Plaine; German-American city of New Ulm northwest of Mankato on U.S. Highway 14.

The drive

The broad, fertile Minnesota River Valley was formed by a vast torrent of meltwater streaming down from the north at the end of the last Ice Age.

Drive 5: Minnesota River Run

Chaska to Mankato along the lower Minnesota River Valley

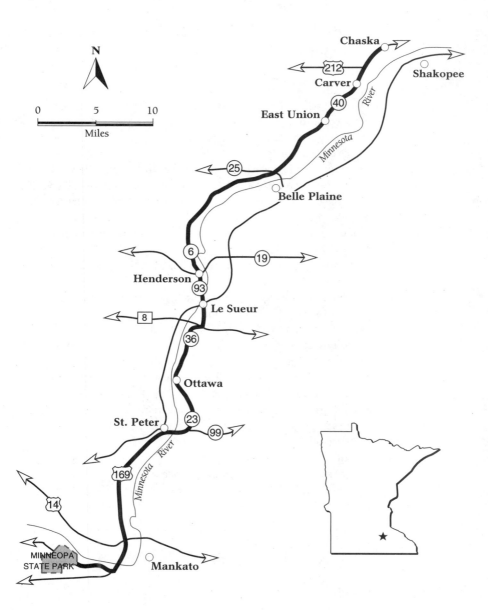

The glacial river Warren ripped down through layers of sandstone and limestone bedrock, forming bluffs that rise 250 feet above the turbid surface of the present river. Lured by rich alluvial soils, thousands of immigrant farmers—Swedes, Norwegians, Germans, Poles—moved to the valley in the years before and after the Civil War. They stayed on after the war to endure brutal prairie winters and founded towns such as Chaska, Carver, Le Sueur, St. Peter, and Mankato. This 70-mile drive, never straying far from the Minnesota River as it loops lazily across the land, visits these places and others that became virtual ghost towns after the railroad passed them by.

The route begins in Chaska, a Minneapolis suburb (head west on U.S. Highway 212) that retains its nineteenth century business district and central square, notable for its classic wooden bandstand and Indian burial mounds. Keep going on US 212, then follow Carver County Road 40 south as it descends the densely wooded bluffs into the village of Carver, named after the eighteenth century English explorer Jonathan Carver. In its heyday 130 years ago the town was a busy grain port and agricultural center served by daily stage service from St. Paul. But the coming of the railroad slowed steamboat traffic in the 1870s, and today Carver consists of a few Victorian houses, a couple of bars, and—hey, this is the 1990s—an espresso deli.

The road winds through thick bottomland forest of elm, cottonwood, black willow, and swamp white oak, then rises into open cropland dotted with horse farms, dairy operations, wetlands, and the occasional U-pick strawberry stand. A ribbon of green, much darker than the soybean and cornfields beside the road, rims the horizon to the left—the forested bluffs of the Minnesota's east bank. Just outside the village of East Union, one of Minnesota's earliest Swedish settlements, a Lutheran church of soft yellow brick testifies to the faith and staying power of the farmers who built it in 1866. Generations of Lunds, Borgs, Carlsons, and Ericksons are laid to rest in the churchyard, shaded by mature elm and cedar trees.

After 7 miles CR 40 spirals down from the bluff top to the valley floor, curving past a wide, muddy elbow of the river fringed by willows and cottonwoods. Cross Minnesota Highway 25 and go straight on Sibley County Road 6, along a broad, island-studded stretch of river bordered by dairy farms and spacious fields of corn, soybeans, and alfalfa. In 1993 tens of thousands of acres along the Minnesota flooded, ruining crops and transforming fields into lakes.

The road quickly clambers into uplands that are safe from floodwaters, passing some unsightly gravel mining pits and the beautiful Church of St. Thomas Jessenland, the nucleus of an early Irish settlement that has long since faded away. Minnesota Highway 93 takes over from CR 6 in the one-horse town of Henderson; follow it through a shady tunnel of trees to US 169, then take the next exit and cross the river into Le Sueur.

Lutheran church in East Union, one of Minnesota's earliest Swedish settlements.

Home of W. W. Mayo, founder of the Mayo Clinic, in Le Sueur.

Welcome to the home of the Jolly Green Giant! The big fellow beams from a hilltop billboard just north of town on US 169. Originally the personification of the Minnesota Valley Canning Company, which began processing corn, green beans, peas, and other local produce in 1903, the Giant now works for Minneapolis-based Pillsbury. A couple of blocks down Main Street, the restored home of one of America's medical pioneers stands in the shadow of a grain elevator. Dr. William W. Mayo, who, with his sons William and Charles, founded the Mayo Clinic in Rochester, lived and practiced in this simple wood-frame house from 1859 to 1863. The country doctor's original desk and some of his medical instruments are preserved in his second-story examining room.

Main Street turns into Nicollet County Road 36 south of town; take it past more gravel pits into open, sunny farmland, holding your nose as you encounter several well-lubricated feedlots on the left of the road. Eight miles over the bluff tops brings you to the tiny hamlet of Ottawa, with its limestone Methodist church and town hall, built in 1859 and 1860 respectively. It was all downhill from there; more buildings of stone and brick sit in ruin, half-hidden by scrub and tall grass. Pick up Nicollet County Road 23 and keep going south along the foot of bluffs cloaked in elm, basswood, sugar and silver maple, butternut, and black ash.

The valley flaunts its immensity here; the eye ranges for miles over a vast expanse of prairie grass, scrub, marsh, and sinuous, slow-moving river—a refuge for wildlife such as red-winged blackbirds, red-tailed hawks, muskrats, and turtles. A right turn on Minnesota Highway 99 takes you over a steel-truss bridge into St. Peter.

This tidy, sedate college town almost became the state capital in 1857, when territorial Governor Willis A. Gorman and several legislators who had bought land in the area introduced a bill authorizing the transfer of the seat of power from St. Paul. Alas, St. Peter's aspirations were thwarted by Joe Rolette, a flamboyant lawmaker who made off with the bill and holed up in a St. Paul hotel playing cards until the session was over. Instead, the town won the dubious honor of hosting the state's first insane asylum in 1866. Still in operation, the St. Peter Regional Treatment Center (on US 169 just south of Minnesota Highway 22) houses a museum chronicling the history of the treatment of mental disorders.

Ready for lunch? The Linnaeus Arboretum at Gustavus Adolphus College, up the hill from US 169 on College Avenue, offers shady picnic spots with sweeping views of the valley. Sculptures by Paul T. Grandlund ring modernistic Christ Chapel with its dramatic curtain wall and rapier-thin spire.

If time permits, drive half a mile north of town on US 169 to Traverse des Sioux Park, site of the signing of a landmark 1851 treaty between the Dakota Nation and U.S. government. The Dakota relinquished control over 24 million acres of land, unleashing a flood of white settlement into Minnesota Territory. In return they received a reservation along the Minnesota River and an annual annuity of about 12.5 cents an acre. The Treaty Site History Center contains exhibits about the treaty, the people involved, and life at this ancient river crossing before and after the signing. Rough trails wind through the prairie grass to the site of a mission and fur trading post that flourished in the 1850s, only to disappear after the clerics and merchants moved to St. Peter.

Mankato, another old fur trading post that survived to support a quarrying industry, a state university, and the Minnesota Vikings's summer training camp, is best appreciated from US 169 as it sweeps through town on an extended overpass. Enjoy the 12-mile drive down from St. Peter—trees cling grimly to sheer limestone walls to your right, while the river and great reaches of wetlands and floodplain forest sprawl grandly to the left—then keep on going. Your destination is Minneopa State Park, a wonderful patch of wildness three miles south of Mankato. Turn right on Blue Earth County Road 69; it's a little less than a mile to the park entrance and the falls of Minneopa Creek.

The Dakota people called the falls *Minnienneopa,* or "water falling twice," and the reason is plain: this is a double waterfall, cascading 50 feet

"Water falling twice": Minneopa Falls at Minneopa State Park near Mankato.

in two steps into a deep, mossy gorge. A stone arch spans the creek between the upper and lower falls, offering a vertiginous view of the cataract as it thunders over a ledge of hard sandstone. The trail continues around to another spectacular overlook, then drops into the gorge below the falls where the Minneopa suddenly runs quiet and clear.

The bulk of the park lies on the other side of Minnesota Highway 68 (follow Blue Earth County Road 117 down the hill and follow the signs to the campground). A gravel road crosses tallgrass prairie in the process of being reclaimed from invading woodland en route to the Seppman Windmill. An elegant cone of limestone built by a German stone mason in 1862, the mill ground wheat from surrounding farms until a lightning storm stilled its sails in 1890. A half-mile trail gives you the option of hoofing it through boulder-strewn meadows ablaze with bergamot, false indigo, goldenrod, and other prairie flowers in the summer.

The drive ends here; you can return to the Twin Cities on US 169, or drive 30 miles to New Ulm, the starting point for Drive 7.

6

Luverne–Lake Shetek–Walnut Grove

General description: A 115-mile circuit over the high, gently rolling farm country of southwest Minnesota. U.S. Highway 75, Minnesota Highway 30, and county roads almost devoid of traffic cross windswept ridges and fertile valleys thick with corn, soybeans, and remnants of the tallgrass prairie that greeted the pioneers. Towns on the route include stone-built Luverne and Pipestone, the "End-O-Line" village of Currie, and Walnut Grove of *Little House on the Prairie* fame.

Special attractions: Unique quartzite architecture in Luverne and Pipestone; Minnesota's largest bison herd and virgin prairie at Blue Mounds State Park; Pipestone National Monument; Laura Ingalls Wilder Museum and dugout site in Walnut Grove; End-O-Line Railroad Museum in Currie; biking, hiking, and boating at Lake Shetek State Park.

Drive route numbers: U.S. Highways 75, 59; Minnesota Highways 30, 267; Pipestone County Road 16; Murray County Roads 4, 38, 22; Redwood County Roads 78, 5.

Location: Southwest Minnesota. The drive begins in Luverne and loops to the north and east, ending in Walnut Grove.

Travel season: Spring and late summer are ideal for prairie flowers. Walnut Grove stages its Laura Ingalls Wilder Pageant on the first three weekends in July. Drive with caution in the winter, when sudden blizzards can create high drifts and white-out conditions.

Camping: Blue Mounds State Park near Luverne; Lake Shetek State Park near Currie; Plum Creek Park outside Walnut Grove.

Services: Gas, food, and lodging in Luverne, Pipestone and towns along U.S. Highway 14.

Nearby attractions: Jeffers Petroglyphs, Minnesota's largest concentration of Native American rock art; wind farms on Buffalo Ridge near Marshall; the McCone Sod House near Sanborn, a replica of an 1870s "soddie" constructed from strips of virgin prairie.

The drive

Before white settlement the state's southwest corner was an ocean of tallgrass prairie dotted with islands of marsh, the domain of Dakota Indians who ranged across the wavetops of big bluestem and switchgrass on horseback, hunting waterfowl, antelope, and bison. With the arrival of white set-

Drive 6: Luverne–Lake Shetek–Walnut Grove

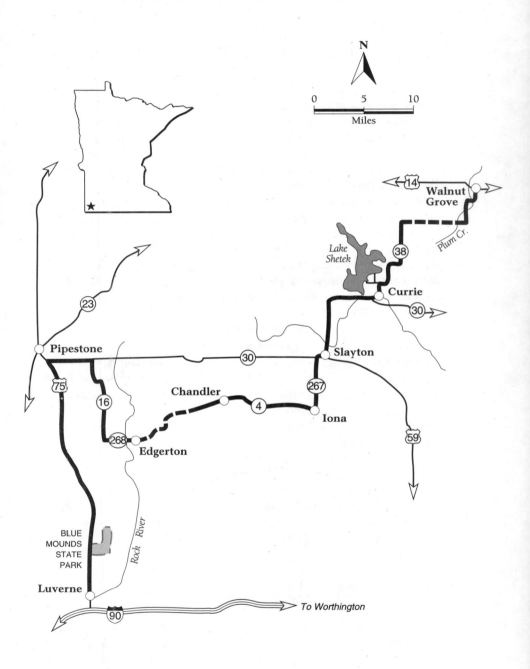

tlers in the 1870s, the tangled profusion of native grasses and wildflowers gave way to homesteads and neat rows of cultivated crops. The Minnesota prairie is one of the nation's leading producers of corn, soybeans, sunflower seeds, wheat, and hogs.

Although the prairie is no more, you still feel the solitude and sense of infinite space that the pioneers experienced on this drive over the high, rolling plains and on to the "Great Oasis" around Lake Shetek. The area is rich in both Native American and pioneer heritage. Minnesota's largest bison herd grazes at Blue Mounds State Park, the source of the beautiful stone used in many nineteenth-century buildings; Indian artisans still fashion peace pipes from a hard native mineral at Pipestone National Monument; and the spirit of Laura Ingalls Wilder endures in Walnut Grove, the town where her Pa built a "little house on the prairie" in 1874.

The drive begins in Luverne, a farm town of 4,400 just off Interstate 90. Many downtown buildings are constructed from Sioux quartzite, a hard Precambrian sandstone that ranges in hue from pink to magenta. Nineteenth-century stonemasons displayed considerable skill in using stone of different hues to create decorative patterns around doorways and windows and along rooflines. Outstanding examples of this lost art include the Rock County Courthouse at North Cedar and East Luverne Streets, with its bands of limestone and round tower topped by a wooden cupola, and the Hinkly House at 217 North Freeman, a mansion built in 1892 that now houses a county historical museum. The Chamber of Commerce is at 102 East Main, next door to the Palace Theatre, a restored vaudeville house.

U.S. Highway 75 bisects the town and heads due north into a vast, largely treeless plain. Look to your left and you can almost see South Dakota, just beyond a horizon that seems to stretch forever over expanses of corn and pasture. Within a couple of miles the Blue Mound rears up, a massive dome of Sioux quartzite that has been scoured free of the ancient glacial till that covers most of the region. Boulders and fractured chunks of pinkish rock poke out of the thin soil. Soon, flowing prairie grass appears to the right—the western flank of Blue Mounds State Park, a 1,500-acre tract that was never broken by the plow. To get to the park, turn right on Rock County Road 20 and continue for about 1.5 miles to the entrance.

The Blue Mound—so named because it looked blue from a distance to pioneers traveling west—terminates abruptly in a spectacular cliff line on its eastern side. As much as 90 feet high in places, this escarpment offers a breathtaking view of the surrounding countryside. Miles of hiking, snowmobile, and ski trails take you along the cliffs, through oak woods at its base, and onto the prairie, aflame with flowering cacti and wildflowers such as blazing star, coneflower, black-eyed susan, and bottle gentian. Big bluestem, the king of the prairie grasses, grows 7 feet tall by the end of

Bison at Blue Mounds State Park.

summer. If you're lucky, you'll get within snorting distance of a small bison herd—the descendants of three animals transplanted from Nebraska in the 1960s. Local legend (unsubstantiated by the archaeological record) has it that prehistoric Indians stampeded bison off the edge of the Blue Mound.

US 75 takes a safer path, dropping through rock-strewn hills to gently rolling farmland. Fields of corn and soybeans alternate with pasture that on some farms sprouts more quartzite than turf. Receiving only an average of 24 inches of rain annually, the grass here isn't lush enough to feed dairy cattle; the chief breeds are Black Angus and Hereford, sustained over the winter by ample supplies of hay and corn. Farmsteads ringed by groves of trees—all planted by settlers—float like islands in a wide sea of cropland and pasture.

The thoroughly broken prairie rolls on for 21 miles to Pipestone, like Luverne, a showcase of stone masonry. Follow the signs to downtown, almost all of which is on the National Register of Historic Places. The town's most striking buildings are the Calumet Hotel, built in 1888 of two-tone quartzite and restored in 1980 to its full Victorian glory; the Moore Block, with its whimsical, intricately carved gargoyles; and the august Pipestone County Courthouse, topped by a domed clocktower and figure of Justice. The staff of the Pipestone County Museum at 113 South Hiawatha Avenue conduct free walking tours year-round.

Pipestone's Calumet Hotel, built in 1888 of two-tone quartzite.

Pipestone was an important cultural center long before these monuments to western civilization rose on the prairie. For centuries, Indians from tribes all over the Midwest made sacred pilgrimages to a wooded valley north of town. Henry Wadsworth Longfellow's *The Song of Hiawatha* recounts the myth of the Great Spirit Gitche Manitou, who called all the Indian nations together on the rocky crags above Pipestone Creek. Warning them that they would perish if they could not live in harmony, he showed them how to quarry the valley's soft red stone and fashion it into peace pipes.

Today, Native American artisans still quarry the stone and carve it into pipes, jewelry, and other objects at Pipestone National Monument, half a mile north of town off Hiawatha Avenue. A 0.75-mile walking path passes the quarries and threads the creek gorge with its precipitous walls and waterfall. A quartzite spire called Leaping Rock bears the scratched signature of cartographer Joseph Nicollet, who camped here during an expedition to the area in 1838. The Three Maidens, a trio of gigantic glacial boulders, form the backdrop for The Song of Hiawatha Pageant, a nighttime dramatization of the poem held in late July and early August.

Leave town on Minnesota Highway 30, heading east through seemingly limitless fields of soybeans and corn. After 5 miles, turn right on Pipestone County Road 16 and ride the crest of a modest ridge 8 miles south to Minnesota Highway 268. Turn left into Edgerton, a hamlet with a couple of gas stations, and follow MN 268 as it curves to the left. Turn right on the first township road that you come to; there's a farmstead with a gray pole barn on the corner.

The gravel road descends into the Chanarambie Valley, a narrow bluff-lined passageway formed by glacial meltwater 11,000 years ago. Chanarambie Creek, surprisingly puny in comparison with the width and depth of its valley, winds through lush cattle pasture at the bottom. Crossing the stream, the road climbs the other side and terminates at a T-junction in 2 miles. From this ridge, straddling Pipestone and Murray Counties, you can see for miles over the valley with its rich folds of corn and pasture. Turn left and again drop down to the creek, spanned by a one-lane wooden bridge. In another 2 miles you'll turn right on Pipestone County Road 4 and follow the meandering Chanarambie east, passing corn, dairy, and sheep farms nestled against low, grassy bluffs.

It's 6 miles to tiny Chandler, dominated by a couple of "prairie castles"— grain elevators with huge metal feed bins. Cross Minnesota Highway 91 on CR 4 and continue through flat farmland to Iona, an even smaller place that nonetheless has its own prairie castle. Turn left on Minnesota Highway 267, then right on MN 30 after about 5 miles. The route passes Slayton airport, skims the town limits and swings north on U.S. Highway 59 towards what early settlers called the Great Oasis—a region of woods, lakes, and streams that stood out in stark contrast to the treeless prairie surrounding it. At the center of this area sits Lake Shetek, a magnet for homesteaders 130 years ago and for boaters, fishermen, and bicyclists today.

MN 30 branches off to the right and crosses Beaver Creek on the way to Currie, a village of 300 people that benefits mightily from its proximity to Lake Shetek State Park. Turn left on Murray County Road 38 to reach Currie's heart, anchored by Mill Street Mercantile, an old clapboard general store. The End-O-Line Railroad Park and Museum, just across the cottonwood-shaded Des Moines River, recalls an era when the Iron Horse was Currie's only link to the outside world. A wooden turntable used to rotate locomotives for the return trip down a spur line still operates outside the old depot and engine house, now repositories for a fascinating array of antique railroad equipment. Kids will love the HO-scale model train display, and a somewhat larger train that picks up riders for an "around the world" tour of the grounds.

You can rent bikes at Mill Street Mercantile and ride to Lake Shetek on a 3-mile bike trail that loops back to town along the Des Moines River. Or you can drive, turning left on Murray County Road 37 and following the signs to the park entrance. The park, reclaimed from pioneer farms and woodlots, is truly an oasis, thick with burr oak, hackberry, basswood, ironwood, elm, and other hardwood trees. The forest shelters foxes, mink, beavers,

*Pioneer cabin at Lake Shetek State Park, survivor of
an Indian attack during the Dakota Conflict.*

and coyotes, while several small lakes, marshes, and ponds provide food and nesting cover for white pelicans, coots, grebes, night herons, and other waterfowl. CR 37 continues through the park to a boat access and picnic area with a view of the big lake and two heavily wooded islands.

Look for a cabin of rough-hewn logs by the roadside: on August 20, 1862 a Dakota war band attacked the cabin, killing farmer Andreas Koch and forcing his wife to flee with other settlers to a marshy area that became known as Slaughter Slough. A century later the cabin was moved to the park and restored to its pre-raid appearance with typical furniture, kitchen utensils, and farm tools of the day.

Retrace CR 37 out of the park and continue straight on CR 38 over gently rolling cropland. The road jogs north, then east and north again, crossing Robbins Slough—a watering hole for Canada geese and white pelicans—and drawing ever closer to the imperceptible crest of the Coteau des Prairie ("highlands of the prairie"), a huge glacial moraine that covers parts of six Minnesota counties and extends into Iowa and South Dakota. Turn right on Murray County Road 22, then after 5 miles, left on Murray County Road 92. At the Redwood County line turn right; within 2 miles a line of trees marks the twisting course of Plum Creek. Turn left on Redwood County Road 78 and follow the ribbon of green through a county park to Redwood County Road 20. Turn right and cross the creek into Walnut Grove, the setting for the TV series *Little House on the Prairie*.

The Ingalls family really did live here, initially in a sod dugout on the banks of Plum Creek north of town. CR 20 ends directly opposite the Laura Ingalls Wilder Museum; exhibits include the original altar from the Ingalls's church, scale models of their real-life and TV series homes, and a quilt made by Wilder and her daughter. To get to the old homestead, take Redwood County Road 5 (Eighth Street) 1 mile north and turn right at the sign. At the end of the road a wooden footbridge crosses the swift-flowing creek to the dugout site, a shallow depression shaded by cottonwoods and willows. "Fragments of a Dream," a pageant staged in Walnut Grove on the first three weekends in July, reenacts the trials and joys of Laura's pioneer childhood.

The drive ends here, on U.S. Highway 14, the "Laura Ingalls Historic Highway." The Ingalls family took this road west to DeSmet, South Dakota, in 1879; you can take it east through small farming communities to New Ulm, the starting point for Drive 7. Jeffers Petroglyphs, the state's largest known concentration of Indian rock art, is well worth a sidetrip. More than 2,000 figures of turtles, bison, horned humanoids, thunderbirds, and other motifs have been chipped into slabs of quartzite erupting out of the prairie. To get there, turn right on U.S. Highway 71, left on Cottonwood County Road 10 and follow the signs to the site just off Cottonwood County Road 2.

7

The Sioux Trail
The Minnesota River from New Ulm to Lac Qui Parle

General description: A 120-mile trek along the broad, lush valley of the Minnesota from New Ulm to Laq Qui Parle, a rest stop for hundreds of thousands of geese, mallard ducks, and other waterfowl in the spring and fall. A federal scenic byway, the route passes through rich farmland and small river towns, digressing briefly to visit historic sites that were flash points in an Indian war 130 years ago.

Special attractions: Authentic German crafts, music, and food in New Ulm; historic sites such as Fort Ridgely, a frontier outpost that withstood two Indian attacks in the Dakota Conflict of 1862, and the restored Harkin general store; Chippewa Pioneer Village in Montevideo; Canada geese, white pelicans, herons, and other birdlife along the Minnesota River; superb fishing and birdwatching on Laq Qui Parle; Arv Hus Museum in Milan.

Drive route numbers: U.S. Highways 212, 59; Minnesota Highways 67, 7, 40; Nicollet County Road 21; Renville County Roads 5, 15, 81; Laq Qui Parle County Road 33.

Location: South-central to western Minnesota. The drive begins in New Ulm and ends in the town of Milan near Laq Qui Parle.

Travel season: Year-round with midsummer ideal for prairie flowers, late September to early October best for leaf color. Some gravel roads may be too muddy for travel after the spring thaw.

Camping: Flandrau State Park in New Ulm; Fort Ridgely State Park south of Fairfax; Upper Sioux Agency State Park and Memorial Park near Granite Falls; Lagoon Park in Montevideo; Laq Qui Parle State Park near Watson.

Services: Gas, food, and hotel/motel accommodations in New Ulm, Redwood Falls, Granite Falls, and Montevideo.

Nearby attractions: Lower Sioux Agency near Redwood Falls, site of first battle of Dakota Conflict; canoeing, hunting, fishing, and birdwatching in Laq Qui Parle Wildlife Management Area south of Milan and Big Stone National Wildlife Refuge near Ortonville; Minneopa State Park near Mankato (see Drive 5); historic Gilfillan Farm and Estate, on Minnesota Highway 67 southeast of Redwood Falls; Laura Ingalls Wilder Museum and dugout site in Walnut Grove (see Drive 6).

Drive 7: The Sioux Trail
The Minnesota River from New Ulm to Lac Qui Parle

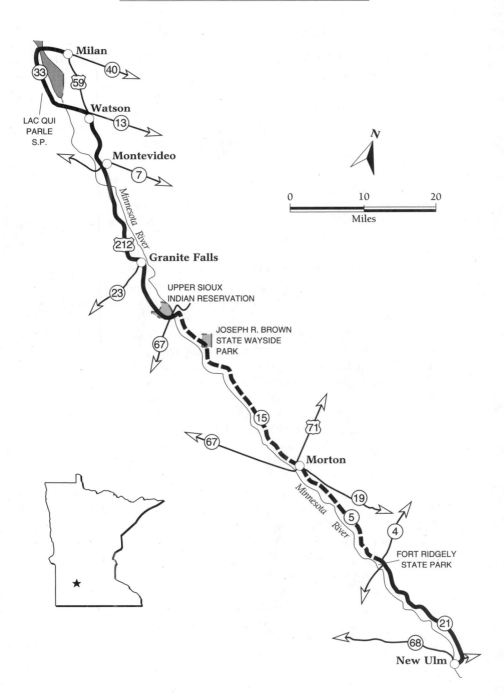

The drive

Minnesota is a Dakota word meaning "clouded water," referring to the light-colored clay the Minnesota River carries in suspension as it snakes across a broad valley hemmed in by wooded bluffs. Much of the drive passes through what was once the last stronghold of the Dakota; in the summer of 1862 thousands of warriors under Chief Little Crow battled the U.S. Army and local militia at New Ulm, Fort Ridgely, and Birch Coulee near Morton. The Dakota were defeated and exiled to South Dakota, and settlers from Germany, Scandinavia, and Eastern Europe flooded into the "Suland" to break the prairie sod. Agricultural centers such as New Ulm, Granite Falls, and Milan still bear the imprint of their European roots.

Intensive corn, soybean, hog, and dairy farming has caused serious water pollution; along much of the river's length it's not advisable to swim, or eat the big catfish that lurk on the bottom. But the uncultivated backwaters, sloughs, and wooded banks of the Minnesota teem with wildlife, especially in the spring and fall, when tens of thousands of birds migrate along the river. Laq Qui Parle, a broadening of the river north of Montevideo, is renowned for its hordes of migratory waterfowl. Much of the 120-mile route, a National Scenic Byway, is on gravel roads—prepare for a few bumps and dust clouds from passing tractors and pickups. Your perseverance will be rewarded by vistas of the Minnesota coiling through rich bottomlands, frequent wildlife sightings, and close encounters with the ghosts of Indians and pioneers on the historic Sioux Trail.

New Ulm, a lively city of 13,000 at the junction of the Minnesota and Cottonwood Rivers, wears its Teutonic heart on its sleeve. Brick buildings embellished in Bavarian style line its shady, precisely laid-out streets. A Glockenspiel with animated, gyrating figures chimes the hours on Minnesota Street. Smoked sausage, apple strudel, and locally brewed Schell's beer top the menus of local restaurants. Festivals celebrating Germanic culture and food include the Minnesota Festival of Music at the end of April, Heritagefest in late July, and Octoberfest in mid October.

On August 19 and 23, 1862, hundreds of Dakota warriors laid siege to the town, killing 26 residents and burning 190 buildings. William H. Mayo, founder of the Mayo Clinic in Rochester (see Drive 5), was one of the doctors who tended the wounded after the attacks. Schell's Brewery, in continuous operation since 1860, was one of the few buildings that escaped destruction. A half-mile drive along the steep, wooded banks of the Cottonwood (look for the Schell's sign on Broadway) leads to the ivy-covered brewhouse and Schell family mansion, surrounded by a formal flower garden and deer park.

Nineteenth-century Teutonic facades on Minnesota Street in New Ulm.

Leave town on Broadway (Minnesota Highway 15). The road crosses the muddy Minnesota and meets Nicollet County Road 21, a National Preservation Route, in about 2 miles. Turn left; before you spreads a broad valley flanked by 250-foot-high bluffs cloaked in oak, sugar maple, basswood, and other hardwoods. Shimmering waves of corn and soybeans cascade down to the river from the road, which hugs the shady lee of the bluff above. Hundreds of dead, ghostly-white trees line the riverbank, the legacy of 1993 floodwaters that inundated millions of dollars worth of crops in the valley.

The village of West Newton, 9 miles upstream from New Ulm, was an important port of call for steamboats in the 1870s, before the railroad killed the river trade and a grasshopper plague devastated local farmers. Today the only building left standing in West Newton is Alexander and Janet Harkin's General Merchandise Store, tucked into the wooded bluff on the right. In its cool interior, fully restored by the Minnesota Historical Society, it's still the 1870s; about 40 percent of the merchandise on the shelves is original, left when the store closed in 1901. Costumed guides display their wares—bolts of dress fabric, milk churns, shaving razors, patent medicines for man and beast—and tell the story of the Harkins and the town's demise.

Broad vistas of the valley open up as CR 21 crosses Little Rock Creek and rises higher up the bluff. Rolling expanses of corn, soybeans, and pasture surround handsome farmsteads with uniformly white outbuildings and neatly mown lawns. Beyond, great egrets and night herons stalk the shallows of sloughs and ponds fringed with cattails and reeds. Keep a sharp lookout and you're also likely to spot Canada geese, mallards, coots, and red-tailed hawks. After about 8 miles, CR 21 crosses Nicollet County Road 4 and turns into gravel. Turn right on Nicollet County 30 to reach Fort Ridgely State Park, the site of a pivotal battle in the Dakota Conflict. The fort, most of which was demolished for building material after the war, occupies an open blufftop about a mile past the park entrance.

On August 20, 1862, and again two days later, 180 soldiers fought off repeated attacks by hundreds of Dakota warriors with musket fire and with cannons loaded with canister shot. The restored commissary, constructed of native granite, contains exhibits describing the battles, the Dakota grievances that led to the attacks, and the life of soldiers and officers at an isolated frontier post. Outside, you can take a self-guided tour of what remains of the fort's barracks, officer's quarters, bakehouse, and other buildings. The surrounding state park features a nine-hole golf course and miles of hiking, horseback, and snowmobile trails that wind through wooded ravines and prairie meadows.

Return to the riverbank on CR 30 and turn right; after a couple of miles CR 21 becomes Renville County Road 5. Trees crowd the narrow gravel road on both sides, parting every few hundred yards to offer views of the river bottom, a tangle of cattails, prairie flowers, willows, and cottonwoods. Small wood-frame homesteads nestle at the foot of oak-wooded bluffs to the right. After 8 miles, outside the village of Franklin, CR 5 turns into Renville County Road 51. It's another 3 miles of gravel to Minnesota Highway 19, designated the Sioux Trail. Turn left into Morton, a hamlet of 430 people that most visitors associate with Jackpot Casino.

The casino is operated by Mdewakanton Dakota living on the Lower Sioux Indian Reservation across the river, site of the ill-fated Lower Sioux Agency. An interpretive center tells the story of the Agency and the U.S. government's attempt to transform the nomadic Dakota into farmers. Near starvation after a crop failure in 1861, and denied food until the tribe's annuity arrived from Washington—"Let them eat grass," a resident trader said—the Dakota sacked and burned the Agency on August 18, 1862. To reach the interpretive center, cross the river on MN 19/U.S. Highway 71 and turn left on Redwood County Road 2.

The drive continues on Renville County Road 15, a left turn off US 71 west of Morton. The valley here is narrower, confined in a gorge cut by glacial meltwater through some of the oldest rocks on the continent. Morton gneiss, a coarse-grained, pinkish-gray rock prized in building, was formed 3.6 billion years ago by tremendous forces deep within the Earth's crust. Outcrops of gneiss and granite appear on the opposite bank as CR 15 drives northwest, skirting fields of corn and wheat and crossing small streams percolating out of the woods.

After about 25 miles CR 15 turns to asphalt and scales the wooded bluffs, passing a large white barn with what appears to be a grain elevator sticking out of its roof. Turn left on Renville County Road 81 and wind back down the bluff. About 1.5 miles farther on, the ruins of a large stone house overlook a beautiful vista of cornfields and bottomland forest. Joseph R. Brown, a frontier fur trader and Indian agent, lived here for less than a year with his Dakota wife and 12 children before the outbreak of war forced the family to flee. The house, built of native granite, was looted and burned; only low, fractured walls remain, overgrown with grass and prairie flowers.

The Sioux Trail continues for another 4 miles, riding the edge of the bluff. Then CR 81 scrambles out of the valley and runs straight across gently undulating corn and soybean fields to a T-junction. Turn left; within half a mile the gravel ends at a main road that descends into the valley. Follow it across the narrow, mud-banked Minnesota and turn right onto Minnesota Highway 67 at the top of the wooded bluff. The entrance to Upper Sioux Agency State Park is on the right, a mile beyond the green corridor of the Yellow Medicine River. Like its sister installation downstream, the Upper Agency was set upon by marauding Dakota in the summer of 1862. Most of the buildings were destroyed, but one brick duplex has been restored to its pre-war appearance. There's also an interpretive center with a great view, and more than 16 miles of hiking, horseback, and snowmobile trails that wander along the banks of the Yellow Medicine and over prairie knolls and bluffs.

MN 67 passes through wooded farmland and the Upper Sioux Indian Reservation en route to Granite Falls, a farming and quarrying center with a notorious favorite son—Andrew J. Volstead, the author of Prohibition. His simple wood-frame house at 163 South Ninth Avenue has been preserved as a museum with exhibits on the Volstead Act and another piece of legislation that had a more lasting impact—a 1922 law that allowed farmers to form cooperatives in order to bargain for price. There's a riverside park just off Prentice Street where you can watch mallards and white pelicans diving for fish below the dam. A steel suspension bridge spans the water to more parkland and picnic areas on the opposite bank.

Follow Prentice and Granite Streets through a quiet, leafy neighborhood to reach U.S. Highway 212. The route climbs the bluff and parallels the river for about 9 miles, offering expansive views of the river valley below. Outcrops of granite and gneiss, stripped bare by the vast glacial river that passed this way ten thousand years ago, litter roadside pastures. Then US 212 swings close to the river, visible through a screen of cottonwood and ash, before crossing into Chippewa County south of Montevideo.

That's Mon-tuh-*vid*-ee-oh, not Mon-tuh-vuh-*day*-oh, by the way. The name, probably inspired by the vantage point offered from the bluffs at the confluence of the Minnesota and Chippewa rivers, means "to view from a mountain" in Spanish. The farm town of 5,500 has a sister-city relationship with its namesake, the capital of Uruguay. A bronze statue of Jose Artigas, hero of Uruguayan independence, graces a six-block pedestrian mall downtown, and the whole town goes south of the border during Fiesta Days on the third weekend in June. Chippewa City Pioneer Village, located at the corner of US 212 and 59, recreates a nearby town that briefly flourished in the 1860s before the prairie reclaimed it. The museum features more than 20 original and replica buildings, including a schoolhouse, church, post office, general store, and log cabin.

From downtown, follow Canton Avenue (Chippewa County Road 15) over the Chippewa River and turn right on US 59/Minnesota Highway 7. Crossing the corn- and soybean-rich plateau between the Minnesota and Chippewa River Valleys, the route passes through the village of Watson and turns westward on Chippewa County Road 13. It's 3 miles to the Minnesota River, flowing sluggishly out of an expanse of reeds, still water, and drowned trees that would have made an ideal setting for the movie *Swamp Thing*. Laq Qui Parle, a bulge in the river stretching for 12 miles upstream, owes its existence to this natural dam of silt and decaying vegetation at the mouth of the Laq Qui Parle River.

Laq Qui Parle Mission, site of Minnesota's first church.

Missionaries chose this place for the state's first church in 1835; turn right at the bridge to reach a wooden chapel, a reconstruction of the original Laq Qui Parle Mission. At this remote outpost, the domain of colorful fur trader Joseph Renville, missionaries compiled the first Bible, dictionary, and grammar books in the Dakota language. The church contains displays on Renville, the Wahpeton Dakota, and the mission, which was abandoned in 1854.

On the other side of the bridge CR 13 turns into Laq Qui Parle County Road 33, a pretty drive through the lush floodplains of the Minnesota and Laq Qui Parle rivers. This road may be impassable in the spring, when melt-water surges out of the lake into the backwaters and sloughs. Skirting Laq Qui Parle State Park, CR 33 crosses another bridge and curves around to the park entrance. A tree-lined park road runs along the shore of the lake to a boat access with a swimming beach and picnic area. *Lac Qui Parle* is the French translation of a Dakota word meaning "lake that talks;" during cold winters the ice on the lake creaks and groans, echoing off the surrounding bluffs. The full expanse of the lake reveals itself as CR 33 continues north; cottonwood, maple, and ash trees rim the shore, giving way to open pasture and prairie dotted with granite outcrops on the bluffs.

The Laq Qui Parle Wildlife Management Area encompasses virtually the entire lakeshore. White pelicans nest on islands in the lake, and in the fall hundreds of thousands of Canada geese, whistling swans, and ducks descend to feed on the lake's abundant fish and aquatic vegetation. The route passes another boat landing—an excellent place to watch flocks of gulls and pelicans on rocky islets near shore—then crosses the lake on Minnesota Highway 40.

Milan, a village of 350 that is as staunchly Norwegian as New Ulm is German, lies 6 miles away through rolling farmland speckled with ponds and cattail marshes. Turn left on Chippewa County Road 21 to enter the two-block business district. The Arv Hus Museum on the left, housed in a brick building that was a harness shop in the 1880s, sports a colorful facade with Norwegian rosemalling by resident Karen Johnson, a nationally recognized master of the art. Inside, there's a shop selling traditional crafts and a small museum with hundreds of photos of Milan in its heyday at the turn of the century.

The drive ends here. US 59/MN 7 leads back to Montevideo; MN 40 will take you east to Willmar and connections with U.S. Highways 12 and 71.

8

St. Cloud–Little Falls–Sauk Centre

General description: An 80-mile drive along the Mississippi River from St. Cloud to Little Falls, the boyhood home of aviator Charles Lindbergh. The trip continues southwest through undulating, wooded farmland to Sauk Centre, the birthplace of novelist Sinclair Lewis and the inspiration for *Main Street*. Lightly traveled state and county roads pass through small farming communities and skirt numerous lakes, streams, and wetlands.

Special attractions: The Lindbergh farmhouse and interpretive center at Charles A. Lindbergh State Park; a rare tract of virgin white pine outside Little Falls; Sinclair Lewis's home and the restored Palmer House Hotel in Sauk Centre; canoeing, fishing, and birdwatching on the slow-moving Mississippi and area lakes.

Drive route numbers: Stearns County Road 1 (The Great River Road); Morrison County Roads 21, 224, 12; Minnesota Highways 27, 28.

Location: Central Minnesota, north and west of St. Cloud.

Travel season: Year-round with early October best for leaf color. Sauk Centre celebrates Sinclair Lewis Days during the third week in July.

Camping: St. Cloud Campground & RV Park on Stearns County Road 8; A-J Acres Campgrounds near Clearwater; Charles A. Lindbergh State Park; public campground in Sauk Centre and nearby at Birch Lake State Forest.

Services: Gas, food, and lodging in St. Cloud, Little Falls, and Sauk Centre.

Nearby attractions: St. John's University Abbey and Church in Collegeville, west of St. Cloud on I-94; Minnesota Military Museum at Camp Ripley, north of Little Falls; Runestone Museum in Alexandria, and the lake country of Otter Tail County; sandhill cranes, great blue herons, wood ducks, and other waterfowl at Sherburne National Wildlife Refuge, east of St. Cloud.

The drive

Central Minnesota is a land of lakes and languid streams, gently rolling and blessed with deep, fertile soil left behind by the glaciers. An abundance of farm produce—milk, cheese, pork, corn, soybeans, alfalfa—springs from this rich soil. And occasionally, so has greatness. Charles Lindbergh, the "lone eagle" who flew across the Atlantic to glory in 1927, grew up on a farm on the banks of the Mississippi just outside Little Falls. Less than 50 miles to the southwest lies Sauk Centre, the town that nurtured Nobel Prize-

Drive 8: St. Cloud–Little Falls–Sauk Centre

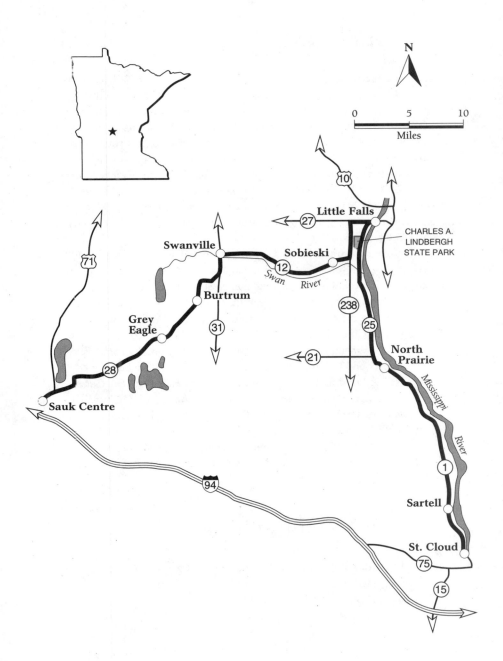

winning author Sinclair Lewis. This 80-mile drive traverses a pastoral landscape that hasn't changed much since Lindbergh and Lewis were in short pants. The Mississippi riverfront north of St. Cloud is still largely undeveloped; red wooden barns out of the 1890 Sears catalog nestle among groves of bur oak, maple, and ash. And small towns like Little Falls and Swanville, with their stolid brick facades and quiet, shaded streets, look a lot like Gopher Prairie, the setting for Lewis's novel *Main Street*.

St. Cloud is named for the city in France that Napoleon built for Empress Josephine. Too bad this city of 38,000 on the Mississippi doesn't live up to its romantic, mellifluous name. Downtown, built of brick and native, fine-grained granite that was also used in the construction of the Minnesota State Capitol and St. Paul Cathedral, has been swallowed by ever-widening circles of highways, parking lots, and subdivisions. But two city amenities, the Stearns County Heritage Center and Munsinger Botanical Gardens, are definitely worth a visit. The Heritage Center, on 33rd Avenue South off Stearns County Road 75, features Ojibwe and Dakota artifacts and lodges, a log barn with antique farm equipment, and a replica of a granite quarry. A lily pond, a wishing well, and more than 50,000 types of flowers and shrubs grace Munsinger Gardens, on the east bank of the river across from St. Cloud State University.

Head north on Minnesota Highway 15 (9th Avenue North) through a residential area; Stearns County Road 1, the Great River Road, splits off to the left in about 2 miles. The road through the satellite community of Sartell sticks close to the riverbank, lined with well-kept gardens, roadside plantings, and tall spruce trees. The river, relatively narrow and content to flow calmly between low banks, glistens through a belt of cottonwoods and aspen that ensures the river dwellers's privacy. North of Sartell the route, marked by green "Great River Road" signs, becomes distinctly rural. Roadside stands of pine and spruce protect fields of corn and oats from the winds that come from the west, over low ridges dotted with groves of evergreens and hardwoods.

As CR 1 approaches the Morrison County line the ridges become more heavily wooded, and the farms bigger and more spread out, marked by clusters of corn silos poking above living stockades of mature shade trees. The Great River Road continues on Morrison County Road 21 to the hamlet of North Prairie with its 120-year-old brick church, then follows Morrison County Roads 25 and 52 to the dam at Zebulon Pike Lake. A bulge in the river named for the U.S. Army lieutenant who explored the area in 1805, the lake teems with muskie, bass, northern pike, trout, crappie, and bluegill. Turn left after a couple of miles, then right on 130th Avenue (Morrison County Road 224). The 4-mile drive to Charles A. Lindbergh State Park winds through a patchwork of woodlands and fields, hugging the riverbank for most of the way. At Pike Creek Landing, another boat access, there's a lovely view of the Mississippi flowing sedately between low banks over-

The Mississippi River near Charles A. Lindbergh State Park.

hung with maple, cottonwood, and willow trees.

The entrance to the park, a 330-acre oasis of pine, oak, and grassland along the banks of Pike Creek, is on the left. Over 100 acres once constituted the Lindbergh family farm; the land was donated to the state in 1931 in memory of the aviator's father, a progressive Republican congressman. The wooden farmhouse where "Lucky Lindy" spent his boyhood summers sits across the road on the banks of the Mississippi, in a grove of oak, maple, and pine trees. The house, built in 1906, contains family mementos and the 1916 Saxon auto in which Charles chauffeured the elder Lindbergh during his unsuccessful gubernatorial campaign. A footpath leads to the Lindbergh House History Center, a low-slung, modernistic structure built into the river bluffs. Exhibits include parts of Lindbergh's first airplane, a World War I-vintage Jenny, and letters in which he reminisces about his youth on the farm. A trail loops along a stretch of wooded riverbank where Lindbergh swam, fished, flushed rabbits, and dreamed of flight.

It's 2 miles to Little Falls, across the river on Minnesota Highway 27. Big Muddy gushes over a spillway to the right—all that remains of a natural feature that the Ojibwe called *Kakabikansing*, or "little falls with the square cut-off rock." The falls were harnessed in the 1890s to drive lumber, flour, and paper mills that attracted thousands of white settlers. Broadway East, the town's main drag, retains a frontier look with its three-story brick buildings arrayed along a wide street. On the second weekend in June the town celebrates Little Falls River Fest with parades, craft shows, and fireworks.

Head back across the river and straight on for about a mile on Broadway West (MN 27) to reach a tract of virgin white pine that the lumber companies somehow missed in their otherwise clean sweep of central Minnesota. The entrance to Pine Grove Park and Zoo is on the right. The trees, some 2 feet in diameter and 110 feet tall, cast deep shadows in a picnic area and along the road to a small zoo with deer, bears, wolves, bison, and other animals. Admission is free to both the zoo and the Dewey-Radke House, a restored 1893 mansion.

MN 27 intersects with Minnesota Highway 238 a couple of miles outside town, amid flat cornfields and pasture relieved by isolated stands of pines and spruce. After 3 miles turn right on Morrison County Road 12, another river road that follows the unassuming Swan through rolling pasture and fields of corn and sweet clover. To the left, the Swan flows unseen through a tangle of bottomland forest and wetland. Hay bales trussed up like Swiss rolls dot the fields during the summer and early fall—feed that will sustain the dairy herds through the long winter ahead. The pastures, woods, and big farmsteads roll on through minuscule Sobieski, anchored by an impressive Catholic church of yellow brick, and Swanville, a slightly larger place sporting an old-fashioned, red-capped water tower. The two-block Main Street features an imposing bank with massive limestone pillars and a barbershop that could have sprung from a Norman Rockwell painting.

The highway swings around the shore of Pepin Lake and becomes Minnesota Highway 28 on the west side of town. The lake, dotted with Alumacraft trolling for walleye and panfish on summer days, is the first of many on the way to Sauk Centre. Particularly scenic, rimmed with verdant hardwoods, are Moose Lake, about 5 miles south of Swanville, and Bass Lake near Grey Eagle. Both lakes have wayside parking and ramps for launching boats or canoes.

South of Burtrum, a speck on the map that somehow manages to sustain a saloon and grocery, the terrain is rolling and seemingly uninhabited, a pastiche of meadows, woods, and cattail marsh. But the farmsteads and waving seas of corn soon return, and continue for 10 miles through Grey Eagle and Ward Springs. Where the glaciers planed the earth flat, the cornfields and dairy pastures form a continuous carpet of green; where the ice paused or retreated, leaving behind mounds of till too steep to plow, cultivated fields wrap around the base of low hills draped in oak, aspen, and ash.

MN 28 joins U.S. Highway 71 about a mile outside Sauk Centre, *aka* Gopher Prairie. Sinclair Lewis described it as "a town of a few thousand in a region of wheat and corn and dairies and little groves" in the prologue to *Main Street*. The dairy center on the southern tip of Big Sauk Lake hasn't changed much since the 1920s, except that the inhabitants hold Lewis in

The Original Main Street in Sauk Centre.

much higher esteem today than when his scathing portrayal of small-town pettiness and hypocrisy was first published in 1920. Main Street (US 71) is now dubbed The Original Main Street, and Third Avenue has been renamed Sinclair Lewis Avenue.

The Eastlake cottage where Lewis grew up, the youngest son of a stern, regimented country doctor, is a couple of blocks west on Sinclair Lewis Avenue. The turn-of-the-century decor includes some of the writer's personal effects: a tiny wooden bed, a chess set, a pewter vase he bought as a gift in Stockholm when he received the Nobel Prize in 1930. The Sinclair Lewis Interpretive Center, on Main Street near the Interstate 94 exit, features exhibits on the Lewis family, Sinclair's career, and the methods he used to weave fact and fiction in 23 novels. The Palmer House Hotel—suspiciously reminiscent of Minniemashie House in *Main Street* with its tin ceiling and wood paneling—is an appropriate place to toast literary genius. According to local legend, Lewis worked as a night clerk at the hotel—until he was fired for reading and daydreaming on the job. After a lifetime of wandering, Lewis returned to Sauk Centre for good in 1951; his ashes are buried in Greenwood Cemetery, east of town on Sinclair Lewis Avenue.

The drive ends here. It's 40 miles west on I-94 to Alexandria, the starting point for Drive 9. Or you can head in the opposite direction to St. Cloud and the Twin Cities.

9

Otter Tail Loop
Alexandria–Pelican Rapids–Fergus Falls

General description: A 150-mile, zig-zagging tour of lake-studded farm-land, woods, and prairie between Alexandria and Fergus Falls. The route, part of which follows a state scenic byway, scales the modest heights of the Leaf Hills and hugs the shore of innumerable lakes dotted with fishing re-sorts and cabins. The towns of Battle Lake and Pelican Rapids provide an opportunity to stock up on refreshments and nightcrawlers, while two state parks and Inspiration Peak offer wilderness solitude.

Special attractions: Kensington Runestone Museum in Alexandria; pan-oramic views of Leaf Hills and surrounding countryside from Inspiration Peak; 1880s-vintage grist mill and riverside park in Phelps; Otter Tail County Historical Museum in Fergus Falls; hiking, cross-country skiing, and bird watching in Lake Carlos, Glendalough, and Maplewood State Parks; fishing, boating, and swimming in Otter Tail, Lida, and dozens of other lakes in the region.

Drive route numbers: Minnesota Highways 78, 108; Douglas County Roads 11, 5, 6; Otter Tail County Roads 1, 3, 14, 24, 44, 45.

Location: West-central Minnesota. The drive begins in Alexandria on Interstate 94 and ends in Fergus Falls.

Travel season: All year. The area's hardwood forests explode with color in early October. Seasonal events include the Phelps Mill Summer Festival in mid-July, and Alexandria's Festival of Lakes in mid August.

Camping: Lake Carlos State Park and Eden Acres Campground & Resort near Alexandria; Sunset Beach Resort and Campground, Battle Lake; Maplewood State Park near Pelican Rapids; Swan Lake Resort south of Fergus Falls.

Services: Gas, food, and hotel/motel accommodation in Alexandria, Battle Lake, Pelican Rapids, and Fergus Falls.

Nearby attractions: Resort center of Detroit Lakes; Tamarac National Wildlife Refuge, 43,000 acres of wilderness northeast of Detroit Lakes; musical, theatrical, and literary events in New York Mills, an artists colony on U.S. Highway 10; native prairie and glacial landforms such as kettle lakes, drumlins, and eskers at Glacial Lakes State Park, south of Alexandria near Starbuck.

Drive 9: Otter Lake Trail
Alexandria–Pelican Rapids–Fergus Falls

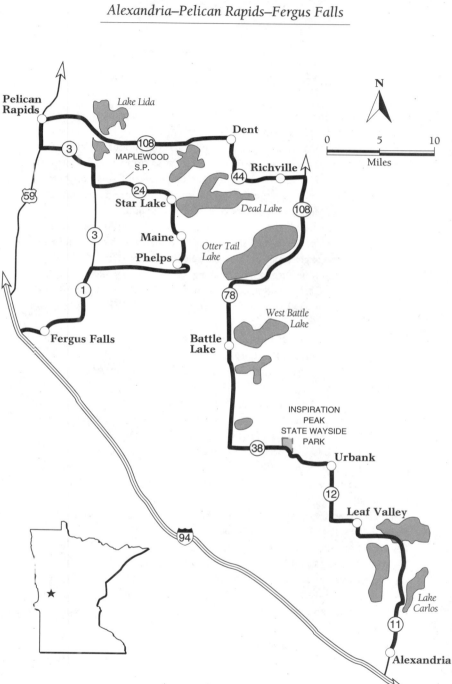

The drive

Literally hundreds of lakes, formed by retreating glaciers, bejewel the rolling prairies and woodlands northwest of Alexandria. Brimming with game fish and fringed by hardwoods, the lakes draw anglers by the boatload during the summer, and cross-country skiers and snowmobilers in the winter, when a thick mantle of snow covers the area. The same ice sheets that carved out the lakes and countless prairie potholes also created the Leaf Hills, a chain of wooded uplands north of Alexandria, and the rumpled terrain near Pelican Rapids.

Where there aren't lakes or hills, there's farmland—mile after mile of corn, wheat, soybeans, and dairy pasture stretching to the horizon under a big sky. Once home to both Dakota and Ojibwe tribes, the region attracted white settlers in the 1860s who broke the prairie sod and cut down the trees that mark the western extreme of the hardwood forests. Alexandria, Pelican Rapids, and Fergus Falls are former wheat-milling centers that now do a roaring trade as gateways to the lake country.

The route snakes through this variegated landscape, following a state scenic byway for much of the way, and—if the runes scrawled on a controversial artifact in Alexandria can be believed—the trail of Vikings who wandered into western Minnesota more than six hundred years ago.

Alexandria, a town of 8,000 ringed on three sides by lakes, milks its connection to Norsemen of yore for all its worth. "Alexandria, birthplace of America" proclaim signs at the city limits. Shops along Broadway (Douglas County Road 29), a bustling thoroughfare with an antique mall and several restaurants and cafes, peddle Viking mugs, T-shirts, and toy helmets. "Big Ole," a 28-foot statue of a Viking warrior, stands guard outside the Runestone Museum Cultural Center at the north end of Broadway.

A glass case inside the museum—also the Chamber of Commerce— holds the source of all the hoopla: a large, flat stone inscribed with Nordic runes. In 1898 Swedish farmer Olaf Ohman claimed to have found the stone entwined in the roots of a tree on his farm near Kensington. The chiseled inscription describes the travels of a band of Vikings who wandered westward from the East Coast in 1362 and were attacked by Indians. Although scholars have declared the stone a hoax, it still has supporters. There's also an exhibit on Ojibwe and Dakota culture, and next door several nineteenth century buildings, including a log cabin, general store, single-room schoolhouse, and chapel, have been preserved in Fort Alexandria Pioneer Village.

Minnesota Highway 29 (The Viking Trail, of course) splits off from Third Avenue seven blocks east of the museum; follow it north and turn left on Douglas County Road 42. The route skirts the shore of Lake L'Homme Dieu, passing Three Havens County Park on the right, then after 2 miles swings left on Douglas County Road 11, crossing an isthmus between Lake Darling and Lake Carlos. CR 11 continues along the heavily wooded shore of Lake Carlos, offering glimpses of grand lake homes down long gravel drives. After a mile or two the houses fade away, to be replaced by expanses of hardwoods, pasture, and farmsteads with large red barns, the boundaries of their fields marked by glacial boulders rooted from the earth.

The road turns to gravel about a mile before the turnoff on Douglas County Road 62 to Lake Carlos State Park, a 1,200-acre preserve of deciduous forest, grassy meadows, and wetlands at the northern tip of the lake. Miles of hiking, horseback, cross-country ski, and snowmobile trails wind along the shore, around tamarack bogs and through low hills thick with maple, basswood, aspen, and oak. Deep and clean, Carlos harbors an abundance of walleye, northern pike, bass, and crappie.

CR 11 continues over the knobby, pitted back of the Alexandria moraine, through vast meadows of tall grass and cattails fringed by hardwoods. At a T-junction turn left and follow Douglas County Road 5 on a roller coaster through the Leaf Valley, past neatly demarcated fields of corn, hay, alfalfa, and wood-frame homesteads ringed by stockades of mature maples, elms, and oaks. When you come to Ebenezer Lutheran Church—a vision of Midwestern Gothic with its tall white steeple erupting out of a field of corn—bear right on Douglas County Road 6, then pick up CR 5 again opposite the Leaf Valley Store and Mercantile Co., a one-story wood and brick structure that sells everything from minnows to mushrooms. After 3 miles turn right on Douglas County Road 12, which turns into Otter Tail County Road 59.

In Urbank, a village with a feed co-op and a pretty, steepled church, turn left on Otter Tail County Road 38. Suddenly the terrain becomes hillier; the road rises and dips through cornfields and marsh along the shore of Lake George, drawing ever closer to a line of heavily wooded ridges—the Leaf Hills. Formed by immense quantities of soil and gravel deposited at the leading edge of the Wisconsin ice sheet ten thousand years ago, the hills extend for some 20 miles to the northeast.

One of the highest points in the chain is Inspiration Peak, accessible from a side road off CR 38. Called "rustling-leaf mountain" by the Ojibwe, the hill owes its present name to novelist Sinclair Lewis (see Drive 8), who waxed poetic about the view from the summit, 400 feet above Spitzer Lake: "… a glorious 20-mile circle of some fifty lakes scattered among fields and pastures, like sequins fallen on an old Paisley shawl." The vista from an observation platform at the top still inspires. A walking path from the parking lot ascends the hill's wooded slopes for 0.25 mile, emerging in a meadow painted with sumac and prairie wildflowers.

CR 38 stays in the hills for another 7 miles, riding the crests and troughs of the moraine past Spritzer Lake and neatly kept dairy farms. Turn right on

Lutheran Church and corn in the Leaf Valley.

Minnesota Highway 78 and descend gradually to flatter terrain, threading the marshy passageway between two lakes. It's another 8 miles to Battle Lake, a lively resort village named for a skirmish between Dakota and Ojibwe warriors in 1795. The two-block main street sports a candy store selling homemade fudge, a tea room, and an art gallery. If you're here on a summer weekend, check out the flea market by the wide, sandy shores of West Battle Lake.

MN 78 skirts the lakeshore, slips past First Silver Lake to the west, and heads due north through flat farmland towards Otter Tail Lake, the largest body of water in the county. A 2.5-mile detour on Otter Tail County Road 16 leads to Glendalough State Park, one of the last large tracts of undeveloped lakeshore in western Minnesota. Once a game farm hunted by U.S. presidents, this new park contains six lakes and hiking and cross-country ski trails that are still under development. Otter Tail is immense in popularity as well as surface area; lake homes and cabins line the shore, masked by a dense screen of aspen, oak, and maples. Side roads lead to cabins and resorts on more than a dozen other lakes just to the east. Keep an eye out for the boat access at Pelican Bay; shaded picnic tables let you enjoy the lake breeze and gaze across the 4-mile breadth of the lake. On a sunny day the water is turquoise in the shallows, a deep indigo farther out.

An historic marker a mile up the road tells the sad tale of Otter Tail City, once the county seat and an important stop for Red River oxcarts on the "woods trail" from St. Paul to Pembina in present-day North Dakota. When the seat of government was moved to Fergus Falls in 1872, the town was abandoned; not a single building remains standing.

North of Otter Tail Lake the route jogs across sparsely populated farmland and woods dotted with small lakes and marshes. About 3.5 miles past Rush Lake, connected to Otter Tail by the winding umbilical of the Otter Tail River, turn left on Otter Tail County Road 14 and follow it through Richville to the junction with Otter Tail County Road 44. After 6 miles this road joins Otter Tail County Road 35 at pretty, cattail-fringed Bolton Lake; turn right and continue to Dent, a village of a few hundred anchored by a Conoco station. Minnesota Highway 108 leads the way west across Rice Lake and into sharply rolling countryside studded with more lakes: Pine, Pickerel, McDonald, Round, and Star. Some are ringed by small cabins; others are completely undeveloped, home only to white-tailed deer, beavers, muskrats, and shorebirds.

Soon the terrain becomes even hillier; the uplands of the Alexandria Moraine have returned, covered with a rich tapestry of hardwoods, open grassland, and wetlands. The entrance to Maplewood State Park is on the left. Occupying a series of hills rising up to 300 feet above the valley floors, the park features more than thirty lakes, the state's biggest ironwood tree, a

Bolton Lake on Otter Tail County Road 35 near Dent.

large beaver dam, and fine views of Lake Lida and the surrounding forest from Hallaway Hill Overlook. MN 108 rolls on past Moore Lake, down a steep slope and across a narrow neck of land that separates the south arm of Lake Lida from the main body of water to the north. The lake ranks among the most beautiful in the state, with hills cloaked in aspen, birch, and maple crowding to the shore and "islands" of bulrushes and cattails. The road clings to the shore for a couple of miles, then turns west toward Pelican Rapids.

This bustling resort town of 1,900 boasts the "world's largest pelican," a cast-concrete statue of *Pelecanus erythrorhynchos* in E. L. Peterson Memorial Park. The Pelican River gushes noisily over a dam at the big bird's feet, and a cable suspension bridge leads to walking paths shaded by mature maple, oak, and ash trees.

U.S. Highway 59 (Broadway) runs south for a couple of miles to Otter Tail County Road 3, a scenic dogleg back into the hill country. Turn left and follow it along the southern edge of Maplewood State Park, past dairy farms, cornfields, and small ponds nestled among wooded uplands. CR 3 and Otter Tail County Road 1 will take you all the way to Fergus Falls, through wooded farmland and past several lakes. But a more roundabout route goes through Phelps, a magical spot hidden amongst the cornfields to the west of Otter Tail Lake. To get there, turn left on Otter Tail County Road 24, then

Phelps Mill and dam on the Otter Tail River.

right on Otter Tail County Road 41 at the sign for Phelps Mill. Follow the road through the hamlet of Star Lake and along the reedy shore of Dead Lake (it's prettier than it sounds), bearing left on Otter Tail County Road 115. After 3 miles turn left on Otter Tail County Road 74, which curves around onto Otter Tail County Road 45. There's a picturesquely dilapidated antique store on the corner—all that's left of the community of Maine. Three more miles bring you to Phelps, a village that time has treated somewhat more kindly.

Phelps Mill, an imposing structure of white clapboard and brick, sits on the banks of the Otter Tail River by a dam and narrow steel-truss bridge. Built in 1889, the mill operated for 40 years, buying wheat from area farmers and turning it into flour for sale to general stores in towns like Battle Lake and Dent. Inside, interpretive displays explain how the arcane machinery—still faintly redolent of flour—was used in the milling process. Across the road, the 1891-vintage Phelps Mill Store invites visitors to sit a spell on the veranda and bask in a bygone era. The mill, dam, and a nearby log cabin (complete with log outhouse) are now part of a county park with swimming, picnicking, and limited camping facilities. On the second weekend in July, artists, artisans, and ethnic food vendors gather at the park for the Phelps Mill Summer Festival.

Turn left at the store and continue for a couple of miles along the shores of two lakes to Otter Tail County Road 1, the main road to Fergus Falls. Twenty miles of undulating farmland and woods brings you to the county seat, a city of 12,300 straddling the Otter Tail River. CR 1 runs right into West Lincoln, a pleasant commercial thoroughfare lined with ash trees and turn-of-the-century buildings. A 0.25-mile brick walkway along the river leads to Veteran's Memorial Park, passing by an old flour mill, City Hall (modeled after Independence Hall in Philadelphia), and a dam with a small hydroelectric plant. The Otter Tail County Historical Museum, on West Lincoln at Fourth Avenue, is one of the best county museums in the state; exhibits include a painstakingly detailed replica of a nineteenth-century "Main Street," an Indian birch dwelling in a winter setting, and miniature and life-sized farmyard models.

The drive ends here. Interstate 94 will take you back to your starting point in Alexandria, or beyond to Sauk Centre, the terminus for Drive 8.

10

Crosby to Mora via Mille Lacs

General description: Passing out of the North Woods into farming country, this 80-mile route traces the scenic western shore of huge Mille Lacs and threads innumerable smaller lakes and wetlands. The towns of Crosby and Mora showcase the area's cultural and historic diversity.

Special attractions: Grand views of Mille Lacs, Minnesota's second largest lake; Croft Mine Historical Park and Cuyuna Range Historical Museum in Crosby; an outstanding museum with exhibits on the Mille Lacs Band of Ojibwe; hiking, boating, bird watching, and cross-country skiing at Mille Lacs Kathio and Father Hennepin State Parks; Swedish ambience and jumbo-sized Dala Horse in Mora; superb walleye fishing on Mille Lacs.

Drive route numbers: U.S. Highway 169; Minnesota Highways 210, 18, 27, 47; Crow Wing County Road 6; Mille Lacs County Roads 26, 35.

Location: East-central Minnesota. The drive begins in Crosby on the Cuyuna Iron Range and ends in the Swedish farming community of Mora, south of Mille Lacs.

Travel season: Year-round with early October best for leaf color, January and February ideal for cross-country skiing, snowmobiling, and ice fishing. The Mille Lacs Band holds a pow-wow on the third weekend in August, and Mora hosts the Vasaloppet cross-country ski race on the second Sunday in February.

Camping: Mille Lacs Kathio and Father Hennepin state parks on Mille Lacs; city campgrounds on Serpent and Yawkey lakes outside Crosby; Hilltop Family Campground on Ann Lake near Mora; Camperville Campground north of Mora.

Services: Gas, food, and lodging in Crosby, Garrison, Mora, and at major resorts on Mille Lacs.

Nearby attractions: Fishing and scuba diving in Cuyuna Range mine pits; golfing, boating, and fishing on the White Fish chain of lakes north of Brainerd; Rice Lake National Wildlife Refuge east of Aitkin; whitewater canoeing and kayaking at Banning State Park near Sandstone; museum chronicling the disastrous forest fire of 1894 in Hinkley on Interstate 35.

Drive 10: Crosby to Mora via Mille Lacs

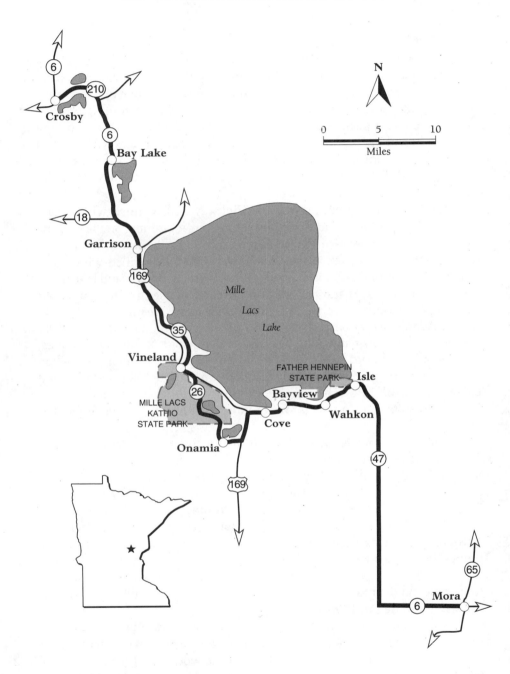

The drive

Befitting its name, Mille Lacs ("a thousand lakes") is gigantic, sprawl-ing amoeba-like over the map of central Minnesota. Cherished by walleye fishermen—in winter as well as summer—and the home of the thriving Mille Lacs Band of Ojibwe, the lake traditionally marks the boundary be-tween the North Woods and the agricultural south. The town of Crosby, the starting point for the drive, is an old iron mining town, surrounded by for-est and ore pits transformed by nature into deep, cold lakes; Mora, on the opposite side of the big lake, was founded by Swedish farmers who still feel a strong affinity for their ancestral homeland. This 80-mile route explores the shore of Mille Lacs and the surrounding countryside, a medley of smaller lakes, marshes, forest, and cropland.

Crosby's Main Street (Minnesota Highway 210) is lined with ornate brick buildings dating to the 1920s, the boom years for mining on the Cuyuna Iron Range (see Drive 15). Two museums chronicle the days when miners toiled in the nearby Portsmouth and Yawkey pits, now filled with water from natural springs and stocked with rainbow, brook, brown, and lake trout. The Cuyuna Range Historical Society Museum, housed in the town's old train depot at Hallett Avenue and First Street North, features displays on Cuyler Adams, who discovered iron on the range (and named the area by combining his own name with that of his dog, Una), mining techniques, and the 1924 Milford Mine disaster, in which forty-one men died when water from a nearby lake rushed into the mine through an underground passage. At Croft Mine Historical Park, north of town off Second Avenue East, you can take a simulated tour of mine workings hundreds of feet be-low the surface.

On the way out of town, MN 210 slices between two natural lakes—Serpent, with its multitude of bays rimmed by rich woodland, and Agate, low-lying and bound by bulrushes and cattails. In Deerwood, host of an arts and craft festival during the second weekend in August, Crow Wing County Road 6 splits off and heads south through rolling woods, marshland, and hayfields to Bay Lake, one of the larger satellites of Mille Lacs. Walleye, muskie, northern pike, and other game fish lurk in the weeds along its many points and coves, making Bay Lake a prime destination for both anglers and those who prefer to watch the action from shore. Ruttger's Resort, nestled in thick pine, birch, and oak woods to the left, is the oldest multi-use resort in the state, founded in 1898.

CR 6 continues along the lake's western shore, offering views of large stands of mature pine, lakes that segue into bogs sparsely covered with dwarf spruce, and the odd hayfield carved out of the woods. In Katrine, 3 miles beyond Ruttger's, a gas station enjoys a gorgeous vista of an arm of Bay Lake stretching toward a richly wooded peninsula. On the other side of the road

Giant fiberglass walleye in Garrison on Mille Lacs.

a verdant carpet of bulrushes and cattails rolls toward Maple Lake, intensely blue on sunny days.

Another 3 miles brings you to Minnesota Highway 18, a main artery linking Mille Lacs with Brainerd. Turn left, passing two more lakes and extensive swaths of marshland on the way to Garrison, your first port of call on Mille Lacs. When early explorers first encountered Mille Lacs—called Spirit Lake by the Dakota—they thought they had reached the Pacific Ocean. The wooded bluffs along the shore drop lower and lower as the eye ranges out over the water, disappearing entirely in the center of the lake. Seagulls and heavy swells that pound the shore on windy days reinforce the illusion of an ocean at Garrison's door. A lakeside park off U.S. Highway 169—look for a giant walleye rendered in fiberglass—is a great place to feel the lake breeze and watch fishing boats in pursuit of walleye, northern pike, and muskie.

A starkly different scene greets the visitor in winter; fish houses—tiny shacks equipped with gas heaters, toilets, and sometimes TVs—dot the frozen surface of the lake. Truly a hardy breed, ice anglers dip their lines in holes cut through the ice and wait patiently, often with something cold in one hand. "Streets" worn by the passage of cars and pickups (the ice grows up to a foot thick by January) neatly divide the ranks of fish houses. Besides the view, there's not much to see in Garrison; the rebuilt Blue Goose Inn, a McDonalds, and a couple of gas stations cater to fishermen staying at lakeside resorts and travelers on US 169.

The highway hugs the coast for the next 4 miles, passing Pike Point and old-time fishing resorts on St. Albans Bay. Their docks extend for 30 feet or more into shallows bristling with bulrushes. Headlands draped in hardwood forest offer some protection from the vicious storms that sweep across the lake in winter, piling shattered ice on the roadway. The road turns inland for a couple of miles, then skims the surface of Wigwam Bay with its small, picturesque marina. The lake disappears behind a screen of woods south of the bay, but you can stay close to the water on North Shore Scenic Drive (Mille Lacs County Road 35), which veers to the left in about a mile.

A handsome vista of bulrushes, rocky islets—a favorite perch for seagulls—and distant Sha-Bosh-Kung Point opens up, framed by roadside oaks and maples. The point is the setting for the Mille Lac Band's annual pow-wow on the third weekend in August; band members and American Indians from all over the country gather for three days of traditional dancing, drumming, singing, crafts, and games. There's always plenty of fried bread and sweet corn on hand, and the general public is invited.

North Shore Drive continues along the low shore into the Mille Lacs Indian Reservation, a small tract of woods and cattail marsh reluctantly deeded to the Ojibwe by the U.S. government in 1926. For years the Mille Lacs Band had been pressured to move to the White Earth Reservation in northwestern Minnesota; in 1911 a sheriff's posse set fire to the village. But Chief Wadena—called "the most obstinate Indian in the whole Mille Lacs

View of Sha-Bosh-Kung Point on Mille Lacs County Road 35.

Band" by a contemporary federal official—refused to budge. Today the reservation is still impoverished, but money for new housing and a community school and clinic flows from the blackjack tables and one-armed bandits at Grand Casino Mille Lacs on US 169.

The road passes a public boat access, clusters of modest homes sequestered in the woods, and a water tower emblazoned with the Band's emblem: a peace pipe superimposed over an outline of the state. The casino and a high-rise hotel loom on the other side of highway. The Mille Lacs Indian Museum, one of the finest of its kind in the country, lies just ahead. The architecture of the low-rise building, opened in 1996, is striking: a long window wall curves along the shoreline, catching reflections of aspen trees and the lake, and a colorful frieze suggestive of traditional beadwork girdles the roofline.

Inside, exhibits tell the story of the Mille Lacs Band, past and present. The "Four Seasons Room," a 360-degree diorama with life-size figures modeled on actual band members, depicts the hunting and gathering lifestyle of Ojibwe three hundred years ago. Elsewhere in the museum, storyboards outline Ojibwe history (originally from the eastern Great Lakes, the tribe was forced west by the Iroquois in the late 1600s), pow-wow contestants perform on video, and local artisans demonstrate maple syrup processing, wild ricing, and crafts such as beadwork and birchbark basketry. Next door, a couple of 1930s-vintage gas pumps stand outside the reservation's restored trading post, now a gift shop selling books and craftwork made by various American Indian tribes.

Return to US 169 and continue along the shore, bound by bulrushes and waving cattails. In about a mile a historical plaque at the mouth of the Rum River marks the site of Izatys, once the capital of the Mdewakanton Dakota. The French explorer Sieur Du Luth spent the winter of 1679 at the village, and liked it so much that he claimed the entire region for France. Armed with French muskets, the Ojibwe won a decisive battle over the Mdewakantons in 1750, driving them out of the northern forests and onto the prairie.

You can stay on the highway, slipping in and out of woodland and marsh bordering the lake, or strike inland through Mille Lacs Kathio State Park, one of the largest nature preserves in the state. To take the latter route, turn right on Mille Lacs County Road 26. The entrance to the park is on the right. Miles of trails support every conceivable mode of alternative transportation: pedestrian, horseback, cross-country ski, and snowmobile. If you have time to explore, you'll be rewarded with glorious views of sharply rolling hills cloaked in maple, aspen, ash, and oak. A 100-foot observation tower affords a hawk's-eye-view of the forest canopy, lowlands speckled with tamarack bogs and beaver ponds, and to the north, Mille Lacs's infinite horizon.

Canoes are available for a paddle on the Rum River—the escape route for those defeated Dakota warriors 250 years ago.

Back on CR 26, the route passes through woods and marshland and crosses the Rum, winding lazily through thickets of bulrushes where it enters Shakopee Lake. In the summer swallows flit over the tall reeds, catching insects on the fly. Warren Lake comes next, its boggy shore spiked with dwarf spruce, then Lake Onamia, half-choked with scrub and bulrushes. Crossing the Rum once again, take Minnesota Highway 27 into Onamia, a nondescript town with a grocery store, a gas station, and a couple of cafes. The Soo Line Trail, a converted railbed for bikes, links Onamia with Isle, 11 miles away on Mille Lacs. Turn left on US 169/27 to return to the big lake. MN 27 splits off to the right and curves through the resort village of Cove, then heads east through woodland and cattail marsh to Wahkon, another cluster of houses and shops on the bay of the same name. Approaching Isle, fields of corn and soybeans appear; to the south woods and wetlands increasingly yield ground to pasture and cropland.

Father Hennepin State Park, occupying a forested headland to the west of Isle, has 4 miles of hiking trails and a long, sandy swimming beach. A picnic area and two campgrounds offer splendid views of Isle Harbor and a series of wooded points and bays stretching up the eastern shore of Mille Lacs. To get to the park, named for a French Jesuit priest who was captured by the Dakota and held prisoner at Izatys in 1680, turn left on Mille Lacs County Road 29. The road skirts the lakeshore, bound by tall cattails and bulrushes, then enters the park through a lush corridor of hardwoods underlain by ferns.

Isle's tidy, three-block Main Street boasts a pizza joint, a couple of antique stores, and the Mille Lacs Lake Museum, housed in a 1901 schoolhouse. Old photographs, costumes, ship manifests, logging implements, and other exhibits preserve the legacy of Swedish immigrants who settled the area in the 1880s, working in the logging camps and draining the swamps for cropland. The village hosts the Mille Lacs History Festival and Rendezvous on the last weekend in June. Activities include old-time music, crafts demonstrations, children's games, blackpowder shooting, and tomahawk throwing.

The route turns away from the lake at this point and heads south through gently rolling woods, marshland, and farm fields. Turn right on Minnesota Highway 27/47, then veer right on MN 47 in 2 miles. A long avenue of pines—bulwarks against the winds that blow unimpeded across mile after mile of wetlands to the west—leads through spruce, aspen, and oak forest interspersed with hay pasture and cornfields. The road dips down to the Knife River, then rises again through stands of hardwoods bordering the Mille Lacs State Wildlife Management Area, 39,000 acres of forest and wetland inhabited by deer, black bears, coyotes, red foxes, and dozens of species of waterfowl, including trumpeter swans.

Another wildlife management area envelopes a good portion of beautiful Ann Lake, 7 miles farther on. MN 47 sweeps by its southernmost tip, serving up a vista of limpid water and forested bluffs. Turn left on Kanabec County Road 6. You're finally out of the woods now; the last 7 miles of the drive cross a rolling, park-like landscape of hay pastures and cornfields at the forest edge.

The drive ends in Mora, a farm town of 3,000 that isn't shy about trumpeting its Swedish heritage to the world. Mora's namesake and sister city is famous for its Dala Horses—gaily painted, miniature figures carved out of wood. That explains the 22-foot-tall orange horse standing in a city park off Union Street, billed as the largest Dala Horse in North America. And the toy-horse images adorning lamp posts and storefronts downtown. Other reminders of the Old Country include the Moraklocka, a jumbo-sized replica of a traditional Swedish clock, and the Gothic clocktower and rosemalled eaves of the People's National Bank. The second Sunday in February is the biggest day of the year for Mora; thousands of cross-country skiers and spectators descend on the town for the Vasaloppet, a 58-kilometer race through the woods and meadows of Kanabec County.

Several major highways converge in Mora. Take Minnesota Highway 23 east to Interstate 35, or west to St. Cloud, the starting point for Drive 8. Minnesota Highway 65 is the scenic route south to the Twin Cities.

11

Brainerd–Nisswa–Cross Lake–Crosby

General description: An 85-mile circle route from Brainerd into the popular, rolling lake country of central Minnesota. The drive, mostly on quiet county roads, includes a loop around prestigious Gull Lake, stops in resort communities such as Nisswa, Pequot Lakes, and Cross Lake, and a foray into the Cuyuna Iron Range, where the deepest lakes are man-made.

Special attractions: Animated, talking Paul Bunyan at Paul Bunyan Amusement Center in Brainerd; Lumbertown USA, a replica of a nineteenth century logging village on Gull Lake; Paul Bunyan Trail between Brainerd and Hackensack; hiking, cross-country skiing, and horseback riding in Pillsbury State Forest; Croft Mine Historical Park in Crosby; picturesque resort villages of Nisswa, Pequot Lakes, and Cross Lake; fishing, canoeing, waterskiing, biking, golf, tennis.

Drive route numbers: Minnesota Highways 371, 210, 6; Crow Wing County Roads 77, 1, 3, 11 (The Great River Road), 145, 15, 6.

Location: Lake country of central Minnesota. The drive begins in the resort hub of Brainerd and ends in Crosby, an old mining town on the Cuyuna Iron Range.

Travel season: Year-round with early October best for leaf color, January and February ideal for cross-country skiing and snowmobiling.

Camping: Sullivan's Resort & Campground on North Long Lake near Brainerd; Rock Lake Campground in Pillsbury State Forest; Upper Cullen Campground, Nisswa; Highview Campground & RV Park, Breezy Point; Serpent and Yawkey lake, campgrounds in Crosby.

Services: Gas, food and lodging in Brainerd, Crosby, and at resorts on major lakes such as Gull, Hubert, and Pelican.

Nearby attractions: Hot rod and motorcycle racing at Brainerd International Raceway; fishing and scuba diving in Cuyuna Range mine pits; Mille Lacs, the second largest lake wholly within the state; Crow Wing State Park and Minnesota Military Museum at Camp Ripley, south of Brainerd on US 371; Deep Portage Conservation Reserve, an environmental education center near Hackensack with hiking and cross-country ski trails.

Brainerd–Nisswa–Cross Lake–Crosby

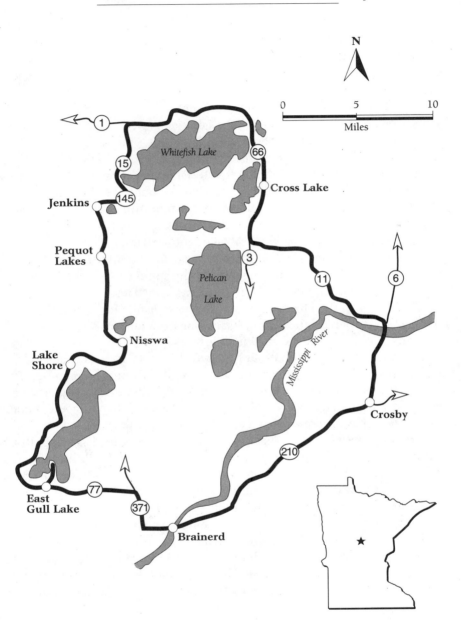

The drive

Generations of Minnesotans and Iowans have come north to play in the rolling lake country north of Brainerd. The attractions are obvious: pristine waters brimming with walleye, muskie, trout, and other game fish; sandy beaches ideal for swimming and sunning; thick forests of pine, birch, aspen, and maple laced with cross-country skiing and snowmobile trails. Almost completely logged off in the nineteenth century, the area had developed a thriving resort industry by the 1920s; families journeyed by rail or car to small communities such as Nisswa, Breezy Point, and Pequot Lakes, still home to some of the swankiest fishing and golf resorts in the Upper Midwest. North Woods beauty combines with recreational opportunity on this 85-mile circuit around prestigious Gull Lake, through the Whitefish chain, and east to Crosby on the long-dormant Cuyuna Iron Range. A short segment of the route follows the youthful Mississippi as it winds through a heavily glaciated landscape of kettle lakes and wetlands.

Belying its Neanderthal, iniquitous image in the movie *Fargo*, Brainerd is lively and pleasant, if a bit congested in the summer. A logging and railroad boom town in the late 1800s (the city was named for Ann Eliza Brainerd Smith, the wife of the president of the Northern Pacific Railroad), the "City of Pines" today derives the bulk of its income from tourists streaming north to resorts, boat accesses, and snowmobile trails. Brainerd International Raceway, north of town on Minnesota Highway 371, also attracts thousands of hot rod, drag racing, and Superbike fans from May through September. The Chamber of Commerce and tourist information center is located at the corner of Minnesota Highways 210 and 371, near a 1920s-vintage concrete water tower shaped like an ice cream cone.

Follow MN 210 west to get out of town, crossing the Mississippi River and passing Northland Arboretum, a 500-acre plant and wildlife preserve with 12 miles of hiking and cross-country ski trails. Turn right on MN 371, stopping at the corner if the kids insist on chatting with Paul Bunyan. A 27-foot animated statue of the mighty lumberjack greets visitors by name and spins tall tales inside the Paul Bunyan Center, which also features a bunkhouse with snoring loggers, a miniature golf course, kiddie rides, and helicopter excursions. The newly developed Paul Bunyan Trail, a converted railbed for bicyclists, in-line skaters, and snowmobilers stretching 46 miles north to Hackensack, begins directly behind the nearby Super One grocery store.

MN 371, naturally, is called the Paul Bunyan Expressway. Press on for about 4 miles along this commercial strip, then turn left on Crow Wing County Road 77 (Pine Beach Road). Suddenly you're in the North Woods, winding through dense aspen, spruce, and pine woods. A lake gleams through the trees to the right, and then another just over the Cass County line. Gull Lake, the playground of Minnesota's elite for 70 years, lies just ahead. Deep and clear, with numerous points and bays that shelter game fish and lure cool breezes, the lake is ringed by full-service resorts and lavish summer homes. Former Minnesota governors Floyd Olson, Luther Youngdahl, and C. Elmer Anderson owned cabins on Gull.

Now Cass County Road 77, the route descends a hill, slips between two lakes and arrives at the entrance to Cragun's Lodge & Resort, a famous establishment with on-premise tennis courts, boat and ice house rental, and miles of hiking, cross-country ski, and snowmobile trails. The East Gull Lake airport is just across the road for the convenience of executives who like to fly up from the Twin Cities or Chicago for the weekend. It's another mile to another prestigious address on Gull, Madden's Resort. An impeccably groomed golf course fringed with pine, spruce, and birch rolls toward unseen Steamboat Bay on the right.

To get a taste of the resort lifestyle, and a sense of what life was like on Gull before the big pines fell, turn right at the Madden's sign. Cass County Road 18 winds through the resort and out onto a scenic peninsula, ending at Lumbertown USA, a replica of an 1870s village built on the site of a former lumber camp. You can tour thirty period buildings, take a riverboat ride, and go eyeball-to-eyeball with wax likenesses of Buffalo Bill Cody, Sitting Bull, Lillian Russell, and other turn-of-the-century celebrities.

CR 77 continues around the lake, skirting Pillsbury State Forest, Minnesota's oldest state forest. Cutover land donated by lumber baron John S. Pillsbury became the nucleus of a forest of 14,750 acres, home to black bears, ospreys (look for their nests in a grove of drowned, long-dead pines to the left of the road), and coyotes. Side roads provide access to picnic areas, boat ramps, and hiking and horseback trails. The terrain on CR 77 is hilly, rumpled by moraines and sand ridges left by the same glaciers that gouged out the lakes. Near the village of Lake Shore, on a spit of land thrusting into the lake, the road bucks and dips over ancient sand dunes shaded by birch, maple, and oak trees. Long driveways offer glimpses of forested bluffs across the water.

In a couple of miles the road slips across the northern arm of the lake, rimmed by private boat docks, and passes 80-year-old Grand View Lodge on the way back to MN 371. Nisswa, once the headquarters of the Upper Mississippi band of the Ojibwe (the name means "three lakes"), is 2 miles up the road. After the railroad reached the area in the early 1900s, tourists would board steam-powered launches on nearby Nisswa Lake to reach resorts on Gull Lake and the Cullen chain. Nisswa is still very much on the beaten path, with cutesy shops, a German-style restaurant, and a 1920s-era hotel remodeled into an espresso bar. The town's old railroad depot, next to the Chamber of Commerce on Main Street, contains exhibits on local rail-roading.

Follow Main Street down to Lower Cullen Lake and around its wooded shore; the route rejoins MN 371, splits two lakes lined with tall spruces and pines, and heads north through woodland and hay fields to Pequot Lakes. This village of 840 people has two claims to fame: its water tower, painted to look like a giant red and white fishing bobber dangling above the highway; and Beanhole Days, a festival with live music, arts and crafts, and a flea market. If you happen to be in town on the second Wednesday in July, you can line up for a free plate of beans, cooked in the ground in cast iron pots.

For more sophisticated pleasures, you'll have to make a sidetrip to Breezy Point, a year-round recreational mecca 4.5 miles east on Crow Wing County Road 11. Established in 1921 by the flamboyant Captain Billy Fawcett (publisher of *Captain Billy's Whiz Bang*, a Jazz-Age version of *Esquire*) the resort features condominiums, a convention center, a marina, two golf courses, two restaurants, and hiking and cross-country ski trails.

Continue on MN 371 to tiny Jenkins and turn right on Crow Wing County Road 145 at the sign to Silver Sands Resort. The road winds through woodlands of pine, spruce, aspen, birch, and oak, passing the occasional bog and minor roads leading to lake cabins. After 3 miles, the road to Silver Sands splits off to the left; take it over sandy hills and through woods and

Up on the lake: canoes at Driftwood Resort.

Crow Wing County Road 66, along the shore of Big Trout Lake in the Whitefish chain.

meadows along the shore of Lower Hay Lake, lined with a row of mailboxes and neatly tended flower beds—evidence of more cabins hidden in the trees. The road meets Crow Wing County Road 15 at a T junction in 2 more miles; turn right. The entrance to the Driftwood Resort, a classic family resort with wooden cabins nestled in a grove of mature pines, is a mile farther on. The 1.5-mile-long drive to the main lodge, along a narrow road encased in cool foliage, is justification enough for a visit; but there's also the Minnesota Resort Museum, with displays on area logging, fishing, winter sports, and life "up on the lake" in the 1920s.

CR 15 continues through woods, corn fields, and green meadows to Crow Wing County Road 1. For the next 9 miles the route traverses a flat outwash plain amply watered by streams and patches of marsh. Large fields of hay—about the only crop that will grow in this region of short summers and sandy soil—break up the expanses of jackpine, aspen, birch, and oak.

Turn right on Crow Wing County Road 66, and head south into the Whitefish chain of lakes, an immensely popular resort area. The lakes—Upper Whitefish, Lower Whitefish, Big Trout, Cross Lake, and several smaller bodies of water—are the handiwork of humans, not glacial ice; at the turn of the century the U.S. Corps of Engineers built a number of dams on the Mississippi, turning thousands of acres of lowlands into prime walleye and muskie habitat. Within a mile Big Trout Lake appears on the right, rimmed with tall stands of pine and spruce. As with virtually all the lakes, there's a public access for canoes and boats. Vistas of sparkling water and piney shores abound for the next 3 miles as CR 66 splits Island Lake and Ox Lake, sweeps around Moonlit Bay on Rush Lake, and crosses a boat channel between Cross Lake and Daggett Lake.

A cluster of shops to the left signifies your arrival in "downtown" Cross Lake, population 1,100. Like Nisswa, this old logging village wouldn't exist if not for the hordes of summer visitors (and increasingly, year-round residents) who must leave their lakeside hideaways occasionally to buy groceries or a treat at Dairy Queen. On the right, parkland along the shore of Cross Lake where it empties into the Pine River invites strolling beneath big pines and oaks. A wooden fishing platform extends along the river below the Pine River Dam, built of concrete and steel in 1888.

Leave Cross Lake on Crow Wing County Road 3; after about 7 miles you'll turn left on Crow Wing County Road 11 and enter Crow Wing State Forest, a patchwork of dense woodland, hay fields, and isolated homesteads. It's another 7 miles to the Great River Road, a national scenic route that closely parallels the Mississippi River. Bearing left, cross the Pine River on a narrow steel-truss bridge and continue on CR 11 through almost unbroken pine, aspen, and oak forest. Gaps in the trees to the right reveal glimpses of the river, a far cry from the Big Muddy of more southern climes; the Mississippi meanders discreetly across the land, confined within low banks only 100 yards apart.

Turn right on Crow Wing County Road 6, crossing the river and passing Rabbit and Clinker lakes on the left. Lush wetlands fringed with trees and laced with languid streams line the 5-mile route to Crosby, the heart of the Cuyuna Iron Range (for a description of Crosby, including Croft Mine Historical Park, see Drive 10). Underground mines and open pits on the Cuyuna Range produced millions of tons of iron and manganese from 1911 until the 1960s, when the mines became uneconomical to operate. Then Crosby and other nearby mining towns such as Ironton, Cuyuna, and Trommald shrunk drastically in size, and nature reclaimed the mines. Several "lakes" in the area, including Mahnomen and Portsmouth west of Crosby, are actually disused ore pits that have filled with groundwater. The mine lakes are stocked with several species of trout, and scuba divers come from all over the state to explore a waterworld of submerged forests and abandoned mining buildings.

The drive continues on MN 210; follow CR 6 south to Serpent Lake (this one, shrouded in woodland, is natural) and bear right through Ironton. It's about 12 miles back to Brainerd, through mostly flat, wooded terrain dotted with bogs and cattail marsh. Alternatively, you can stay in Crosby, the starting point for Drive 10.

12

Headwaters Loop
Park Rapids–Itasca State Park–Bemidji–Walker

General description: A 130-mile circuit between Park Rapids and Walker, traversing quintessential Paul Bunyan country—rolling expanses of aspen, birch, spruce, and pine dotted with myriad lakes, including gigantic Cass and Leech lakes. Portions of the route follow the Great River Road from Lake Itasca, the source of the Mississippi, eastward through state forest lands into the Chippewa National Forest.

Special attractions: The source of the Mississippi River, large stands of virgin pine, and historic log buildings at Itasca State Park; interpretive Bog Walk in Bemidji State Park; photogenic, giant statues of Paul Bunyan and Babe the Blue Ox in Bemidji; biking on the Heartland State Trail between Walker and Park Rapids; hiking, horseback riding, skiing, and snowmobiling in Chippewa National Forest and Paul Bunyan State Forest; spring wildflowers, fall colors, and bird watching.

Drive route numbers: U.S. Highways 71, 2, 197, 371; Minnesota Highway 200; Clearwater County Roads 2, 40; Hubbard County Roads 9, 29, 35; Beltrami County Roads 21, 17, 20, 19, 12, 39; Chippewa National Forest Road 2171.

Location: North-central Minnesota. The drive begins in the resort town of Park Rapids and ends in Walker on the shores of Leech Lake.

Travel season: Year-round, with early October best for leaf color. Winter views can be vivid, with pines, spruce, and other evergreens standing out boldly against a snowy backdrop. Keep in mind that heavy snowfalls can temporarily close some county and forest roads, and it's a good idea to carry emergency food and extra blankets in case of a breakdown.

Camping: Itasca and Lake Bemidji state parks; Chippewa National Forest campgrounds at Knutson Dam, Nushka, and Norway Beach near Cass Lake; Horseshoe Bay Campgrounds near Walker; dozens of resorts near Park Rapids, Bemidji, Cass Lake, and Walker also have camping facilities.

Services: Plentiful gas, food, and lodging in Park Rapids, Bemidji, Cass Lake, and Walker. Itasca State Park has two restaurants, a small motel, rental cabins, and a youth hostel.

Nearby attractions: Smoky Hills Artisan Community near Park Rapids; Camp Rabideau, a restored Civilian Conservation Corps camp on Beltrami County Road 39 south of Blackduck; walking and biking on the Heartland State Trail between Walker and Park Rapids; Dorset, a tiny hamlet with three restaurants; Tamarac National Wildlife Refuge, a 43,000-acre sanctuary for bald eagles and migratory waterfowl west of Park Rapids.

The drive

Pristine lakes that stretch forth like little seas; pine trees as tall as a six-story building; bald eagles, loons, black bears, and other wild animals. The state and national forest lands northeast of Park Rapids capture the essence of northern Minnesota. They're the mythical stomping grounds of Paul Bunyan and his Blue Ox, Babe, whose hoofprints supposedly made all those lakes. And they're the source of the continent's mightiest river. The Mississippi begins its 2,348-mile long journey to the Gulf of Mexico at Lake Itasca, in the shade of old-growth white and red pines that survived the logging era. This 130-mile circular drive from Park Rapids to Walker cuts through the heart of the North Woods, visiting Itasca and following the youthful Mississippi as it makes its way though pine forest, wetlands, and large, wind-swept lakes.

Park Rapids, founded in 1880 as a logging center, has made the transition to North Country gateway quite nicely. An art deco movie theater, antique stores, gift shops, and several restaurants line Park Avenue (U.S. Highway 71) downtown. The town has a historical museum, an art museum, and three bed and breakfasts, two of them on the broad, piney Fish Hook River. During the summer a flotilla of fishing boats congregates below the dam, trolling for walleye, bass, northern pike, trout, and muskie. There's a tourism information kiosk on US 71, just south of town.

The Smoky Hills Artisan Community, 6 miles west on Minnesota Highway 34 near Osage, is worth a side trip if you're interested in traditional crafts. Blacksmiths, wood carvers, candle makers, glassblowers, potters, and tie-dyers demonstrate their skills in 18 wooden buildings arrayed along covered boardwalks in the midst of the Smoky Hills State Forest.

Leave town on US 71, shadowing the Fish Hook River as it flows through park-like groves of pine and spruce to Fish Hook Lake. You'll pass Deer Town on the left, a frontier-style theme park with stagecoach rides, a children's farm, a trout pond, and five species of tame deer. Then the highway swings west, passing Portage Lake on the left, and heads north through gently rolling woodland interspersed with conifer bogs, cattail marsh, meadows, and dairy pasture. Side roads lead to resorts and cabins on Island, Two Inlets, and other lakes that, like Fish Hook, have a reputation for fine game fishing. Evergreens such as white spruce, balsam fir, and red pine—"climax" species in the boreal forest—stand out boldly against a backdrop of aspen, birch, green ash, and other deciduous trees.

The trees draw closer to the road and rear ever higher as you approach Itasca State Park, Minnesota's largest and oldest state preserve. Legendary logger Paul Bunyan could fell whole forests with a single swipe of his double-bladed ax, and he kept at it for 80 years, until virtually all the towering

Drive 12: Headwaters Loop

Park Rapids–Itasca State Park–Bemidji–Walker

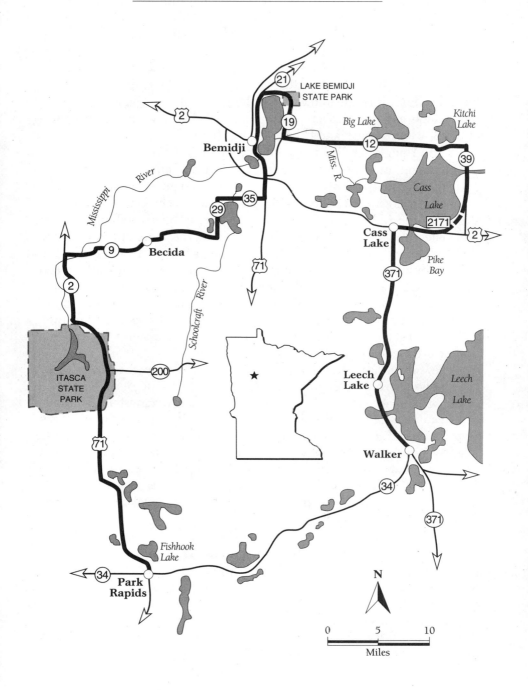

white and red pines that covered Minnesota were gone. But Paul and the logging companies didn't kill all the giants of the forest. Itasca, established in 1891, contains one of the state's largest concentrations of old-growth pines. Some, more than 100 feet tall and bearing the scars of wildfires, are three hundred years old. They survived the axe and the crosscut saw because Lake Itasca, one of 157 lakes within the park, isn't just any lake; it's the source of the Mississippi River.

Turn left on Minnesota Highway 200; the park's east entrance is 0.3 mile ahead, on the left. Immediately, the forest envelops you: huge pines, their trunks as straight as temple columns, rise through a dense understory of birch, white spruce, and balsam fir. It's about a mile to the information office and Douglas Lodge, a magnificent log building overlooking the East Arm of Lake Itasca. Built in 1906, the lodge has original wicker furniture, two dining rooms, and restored historic suites and guest rooms.

From here a network of hiking, biking, horseback, and cross-country ski trails branch throughout Itasca's 32,000 acres. You can explore the park quite effectively by car; a 14-mile circuit follows the shore of Lake Itasca to the Mississippi headwaters, then loops back on a narrow, twisting, one-way track through the forest. You'll find yourself pulling over frequently to take in views of Lake Itasca and Elk Lake, visit historic sites such as a pioneer cabin and five-hundred-year-old Indian mound group, and simply marvel at the majestic trees. A breathtaking view of the forest canopy and three lakes awaits at the top of Aiton Heights Fire Tower, accessible via a half-mile trail near the end of Wilderness Drive.

Few people leave Itasca without succumbing to the urge to tiptoe across the Mississippi, only a few yards across where it flows out of a marsh at the north end of Lake Itasca. The river's source remained a mystery for almost three centuries after Hernando de Soto stumbled upon the lower Mississippi in 1541. Finally, in 1832, Henry Rowe Schoolcraft was guided to the headwaters by an Ojibwe chief named Ozawindib, or Yellow Head. Schoolcraft, a geologist and Indian agent, derived the name Itasca from the Latin phrase *veritas caput*, meaning "true head." An interpretive center tells the story of the search for the river's source, and the Dakota and Ojibwe people who knew where it was all along.

Leave the park by the north entrance, marked by a green-and-white Great River Road sign. You'll see more of these as the route zig-zags along the course of the Mississippi, which arcs north and east before turning towards New Orleans. Clearwater County Road 2 crosses MN 200 and heads north through mixed stands of aspen, birch, and jack pine—second-growth forest that naturally regenerated on cutover pine lands. Many trees are snapped off 10 feet above the ground—victims of a powerful windstorm that also toppled hundreds of Itasca's pines in 1995.

Stepping stones over the Mississippi River at Lake Itasca.

After about 6 miles CR 2 descends into a shallow valley framed by jack pine and balsam fir. At the bottom, percolating lazily through scrub and tall reeds, is the Mississippi, narrow enough to span in one leap. Turn right on Clearwater County Road 40; the road dips down once again into the Mississippi River Valley, hardly worthy of the name. The sluggish stream, half choked by tall reeds and cattails, winds past a caved-in cabin—a relic of some settler's dashed dreams. CR 40 turns to gravel in a couple of miles, continuing on Hubbard County Road 9 through mature balsam fir, black spruce, and aspen forest. On the right a stream filters out of a lake rimmed with evergreens, bound for the Mississippi. The La Salle River is just one of dozens of rivers, creeks, and rills that find their way to the Father of Waters, draining a vast expanse of low-lying woodland and conifer bog.

CR 9 continues on asphalt past the log-built Becida Store, roller coasting over a series of ridges piled up by bulldozing glaciers. Hay pastures and isolated stands of spruce, fir, and jack pine break up the swells of aspen, birch, and maple, which blaze gold and scarlet in the fall. Turn left on Hubbard County Road 29 (Plantagenet Drive). A boulevard of jack pine and spruce twists and dips past driveways leading to cabins and homes on Plantagenet Lake. After about 4 miles bear right on Hubbard County Road 35, which intersects with US 71 south of Bemidji. Turn left, then keep straight on Minnesota Highway 197 (The Paul Bunyan Trail) as it curves around the shore of Lake Bemidji into town. *Bemidji* means "lake with water flowing through" in Ojibwe; the river you cross at the railroad tracks is the Mississippi, which flows eastward from another, much wider outlet on the lake's far shore.

Like Park Rapids, Bemidji makes its living off tourists instead of lumber these days. First-time visitors—especially those with kids—make a beeline for one of the most photographed landmarks in Minnesota: Brobdingnagian statues of Paul Bunyan and his Blue Ox, Babe. Crafted out of concrete and steel in 1937, the dynamic duo gaze out over serene Lake Bemidji from a lakeside park. In the nearby tourism office, also built in the 1930s, a massive fireplace incorporates stones from every state in the country. Bemidji's compact, walkable downtown features a number of historic buildings, including the Chief Theatre (home to the Paul Bunyan Playhouse, a summer stock company), a neoclassical courthouse topped by a golden figure of Justice, and a 1909 Carnegie library.

Beltrami County Road 21 (Paul Bunyan Drive) parallels the lakeshore as it heads north, passing a commercial strip and the wooded, lakeside campus of Bemidji State University. In about 3 miles turn right on Beltrami County Road 52, then immediately left on Beltrami County Road 17. The road skims the wooded lakeshore, passing small resorts and homes with big, leafy yards. A little farther on there's a public boat access where you can park and look out across the lake, almost completely encircled by forest and bound by bulrushes close to shore. Shaped like a right foot, the lake was formed from two huge blocks of ice left imbedded in the earth by a retreating glacier; eventually the ice cubes melted, filling the lake basin.

Paul Bunyan and his bovine sidekick on the shore of Lake Bemidji.

The route rejoins CR 21 briefly, then swings east on Beltrami County Road 20, offering splendid views of the lake stretching 5.5 miles to the south. Lavish homes occupy choice lakeside lots, shaded by mature red pines. Lake Bemidji State Park, just ahead on the right, was logged off 90 years ago along with the rest of the lakeshore. Aspen, maple, birch, black spruce, and a few stands of remnant pine now cover its 6,000-odd acres. But 8 miles of hiking, mountain biking, and cross-country ski trails offer marvelous views of the lake, frequented by loons, black terns, gulls, and ospreys, and the park's "knob and kettle" topography. A 0.25-mile boardwalk takes you into the soggy depths of a spruce-tamarack bog, home to rarely seen, uniquely adapted plants such as orchids, pitcher plants, and insect-devouring sundews.

Turn right on Beltrami County Road 19 about 0.75 mile beyond the park entrance. The road passes a conifer bog, its soft green surface dotted with dwarf black spruce, then plunges into pine and hardwood forest along the lakeshore. Weekend cabins—private enclaves within the park—hunker under tall red pines on the right. CR 19 continues through the woods, crossing the Mississippi River near the point where it emerges from the lake. Another half mile brings you to Beltrami County Road 12, part of the federally designated Great River Road. Turn left; the road crosses woodland, hay pasture, and the Mississippi—much wider now and flowing rapidly through a rock-strewn gorge—en route to the Chippewa National Forest.

Roughly half the forest's 650,000 acres (see Drive 14) is covered with water in the form of marshes, conifer bogs, and lakes. You can believe it as CR 12 bores eastward past the northern tip of Lake Andrusia—another melted ice block—and other lakes and ponds rimmed with cattails and reeds. A bridge spans a narrow channel between Kitchi and Pug Hole Lakes, part of the feeder system for massive Cass Lake. To the right, beyond a Sargasso Sea of reeds and bulrushes, the big lake glistens through a notch in Pug Hole's wooded shore. The road runs into Beltrami County Road 39, a National Forest Scenic Byway, in about 2 miles. Turn right, heading south through wetlands and thick stands of white spruce and balsam fir. For the last time on the drive, you cross the reed-bound Mississippi River, flowing out of Cass Lake towards Lake Winnibigoshish, an even bigger puddle of water to the east.

Gravel roads lead to national forest campgrounds at Knutson Dam and Nushka. Just over the Cass County line, turn right on another gravel road, National Forest Road 2171. Paralleling the lakeshore, this tight, leafy passageway tunnels through a park-like stand of mature red pine. Planted in 1904, the 80- to 90-foot trees have been regularly thinned since the 1930s; they're scheduled to be clear-cut in 2014. The road, lined with woodland wildflowers in the spring and summer, winds on through dense, natural

Ninety-foot red pines along National Forest Road 2171 in the Chippewa National Forest.

stands of aspen, spruce, oak, and remnant red and white pine, emerging onto blacktop in 3 miles. Turn right, and right again on U.S. Highway 2, passing the entrance to Norway Beach, another national forest campground.

Pike Bay, a globular arm of Cass Lake, suddenly emerges from behind the trees on the left. Then the road spans a narrow strait, opening up a broad vista of water and verdant shoreline. A rest area on the right has interpretive displays on the lake the Ojibwe called "place of the red cedars." Star Island, the home of Ozawindib, the chief who guided Schoolcraft to the source of the Mississippi, has an unusual distinction: its own lake, completely cut off from the main body of Cass Lake.

The village of Cass Lake, headquarters of the Chippewa National Forest and the 27,000-acre Leech Lake Indian Reservation, consists of a two-block Main Street and a modest cluster of goods and services at the junction of U.S. Highways 2 and 371. An old train depot, on the left as you approach 371, serves as both a tourism information center and historical museum. Turn left on US 371; the National Forest headquarters, a three-story structure built entirely of virgin red pine in 1935, is on your right. A 50-foot-tall fireplace made of glacial boulders dominates the lobby, which has exhibits on the forest, lake ecology, and Ojibwe culture.

Continue on US 371 through thick evergreen and hardwood forest dotted with ponds, marshes, and bogs. After several miles, the highway bursts onto the shore of Leech Lake at Kabekona Narrows. The view from the bridge, encompassing a cattail marsh, lushly wooded headlands, and a 2-mile reach of open water, is impressive; but Walker Bay represents only a fraction of the surface area of Leech Lake, the third largest body of water in the state. The lake is 40 miles wide, with 154 miles of shoreline wrapped round a myriad of capes, points, bays, and coves. Renowned for its muskellunge, or "muskie," Leech also yields bumper catches of walleye, northern pike, and bass—even in the winter, when fishermen forsake their boats for heated shacks set over holes in the ice.

Walker, 3.5 miles ahead, is named for Thomas B. Walker, a lumber baron and art collector who surveyed it for the St. Paul & Duluth Railroad in the 1890s. His Red River Lumber Company used a mustachioed Paul Bunyan as its trademark in the 1920s; Paul's tall tales, told and retold in the area's lumber camps, first appeared in print as promotional literature. On Walker's lively main street, a couple of cafes, an ice cream shop, a bookstore, and clothing stores cater to 1,000 residents and the summertime influx of "lake people." Chase on the Lake on Cleveland Avenue, billed as one of the finest hotels in the northwest when it opened in 1922, still draws guests and diners to the shore of Walker Bay. The town also has two excellent museums on the area's history and wildlife, across the highway from a city park with a boat access and picnic facilities.

The drive ends here. Minnesota Highway 34 will take you back to

Park Rapids, paralleling the Heartland State Trail, an abandoned railbed that has been converted into a trail for biking, hiking, horseback riding, and snowmobiling. The 27-mile segment between Walker and Park Rapids passes through Akely, home to another Paul Bunyan statue, and Dorset, a hamlet with a two-digit population and three restaurants. Bikes can be rented in Walker, Akely, Dorset, and Park Rapids. The Heartland Trail also connects with the North Country National Scenic Trail, a long-distance hiking trail traversing the Chippewa National Forest, and a number of multi-use trails in the Paul Bunyan State Forest.

Scenic US 371 continues south from Walker to Brainerd, the starting point for Drive 11.

13

Up on the Border
The Rainy River from
Voyageurs National Park to Lake of the Woods

General description: Water is omnipresent on this two-part drive along Minnesota's wild, sparsely populated border with Canada. Choose either a quick trip to island-studded Voyageurs National Park, or a 100-mile route along the wooded banks of the Rainy River to Lake of the Woods, one of the largest lakes on the continent and home to trophy-size walleye and sturgeon. Both routes leave from International Falls, a town that relishes its bone-chilling winters.

Special attractions: Boise Cascade mill tours and Ice Box Days (only for the truly hardy) in International Falls; Grand Mound, the largest prehistoric burial mound in the Upper Midwest; guided boat tours, wilderness hiking, and snowmobiling in Voyageurs National Park; boating and fishing on Rainy River and Lake of the Woods; hiking, fishing, and bird watching at Zippel Bay State Park; opportunity to see deer, moose, bears, bald eagles, loons, and other wildlife.

Drive route numbers: Minnesota Highways 11, 172; Lake of the Woods County Road 8.

Location: Extreme north-central Minnesota, along the Canadian border. The main route begins in International Falls and ends at Zippel Bay State Park on Lake of the Woods. A shorter, secondary leg runs east to Voyageurs National Park.

Travel season: All year, but beware of temperatures in the single or minus digits and hazardous driving conditions in the winter. Also, tourist attractions and many resorts either close or keep short hours during the cold months.

Camping: International Voyageur RV Park, International Falls; Borderland's Rocky Pine Campground, near Island View; Zippel Bay and Franz Jevne state parks; Lake of the Woods Campground, 10 miles north of Baudette off MN 172. Many resorts on Rainy Lake and along the Rainy River also have camping facilities.

Services: Hotel accommodations, food, and gas in International Falls and Baudette. Gas and food may be also be available at resorts.

Nearby attractions: Abandoned gold mines on Little American Island and Kettle Falls Hotel in Voyageurs National Park; Lake of the Woods Casino in Warroad; hunting and bird watching in Red Lake Wildlife Management Area; Fort St. Charles, a restored French outpost in the Northwest Angle; Fort Frances Museum and Cultural Center and a replica of a French fur trading post in Fort Frances, Ontario; Lake of the Woods Provincial Park on the Canadian side of the lake.

The drive

Minnesota's entire northern border consists of water; try to walk into Canada and you'll get your feet wet, either in a lake, river, marsh, or bog. More than two hundred years ago these boundary waters served as a highway for French-Canadian *voyageurs* who paddled birchbark canoes deep into the continent in search of beaver pelts. Today you still need a canoe, motorboat, snowmobile, or floatplane to get to most places "up on the border." But one long stretch of boundary water is accessible from blacktop—the Rainy River. The Rainy flows placidly for more than 100 miles between two massive bodies of water—Rainy Lake and Lake of the Woods.

This two-part drive follows the river for its entire length, passing through forest and pasture lands on the edge of semi-wilderness. Voyageurs National Park, two state parks, and public boat accesses let you get close to the water, the domain of moose, beaver, white pelicans, bald eagles, and dozens of species of waterfowl. International Falls is the starting point for both segments of the drive: a 22-mile jaunt east to Voyageurs and back along Minnesota Highway 11; and a 100-mile journey in the opposite direction, ending at Zippel Bay State Park on Lake of the Woods. You can drive either route, or both.

International Falls, the model for the hometown of cartoon characters Rocky and Bullwinkle, revels in its frigid weather. The "ice box of the nation" regularly posts the lowest winter temperatures in the Continental U.S., and cold-weather product testing contributes half a million dollars annually to the local economy. A 22-foot thermometer in Smokey Bear Park, on the way into town on MN 11, says it all: the mercury bottoms out at -60 degrees F. If you want to experience the Big Chill for yourself, come to town for Ice Box Days on the last two weekends in January. Events include the Freeze Yer Gizzard Fun Run, Voyageur Loppet Ski Race, and ice fishing contests on Rainy Lake.

The city is an important port of entry to Canada (Fort Frances, Ontario lies just across International Bridge), and the site of a Boise Cascade paper mill that makes its presence known in the nostrils. The mill offers free guided

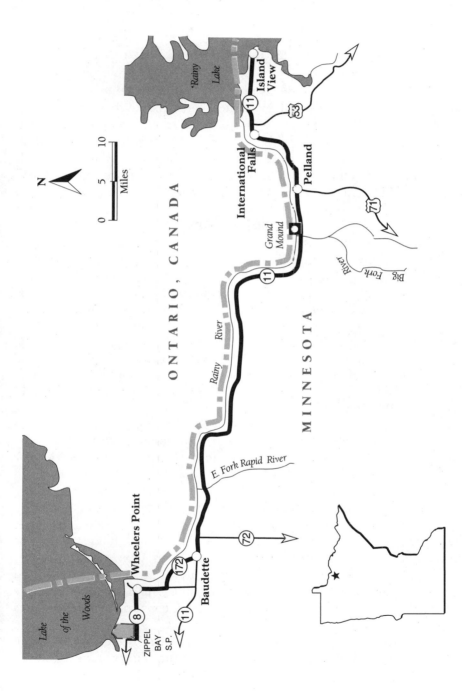

tours in the summer that demonstrate each step in the paper making process, from logging to bleaching to packaging. The town's Travel Information Center is located at the junction of MN 11 and Minnesota Highway 53, near U.S. Customs.

International Falls to Voyageurs National Park

This segment of the drive is ideal for a half-day outing to the edge of the park, where all roads stop and visitors must take to the water or air to explore farther. From the Travel Information Center, head east on MN 11, crossing the railroad tracks that serve Boise Cascade's shipping yard. Aspen, jack pine, and spruce logs piled as high as a four-story building sit beside the road, awaiting transport to the mill. More log mountains line the Canadian side of the Rainy River just 2 miles from its birth in Rainy Lake. Soon you're out in the country, moving through aspen, spruce, pine, and maple forest that grows progressively thicker and taller towards Jackfish Bay. Side roads lead to lakeside resorts, homes, and a seaplane base, the jumping-off point for fishing and sightseeing excursions in Voyageurs and Canadian waters.

A vast expanse of cattail marsh encircles Tilson Bay, where a creek flows to the lake through a rock-bound inlet. Here the 2.7 billion-year-old, glacier-scoured rocks of the Canadian Shield erupt to the surface, a foreshadowing of the rugged, island-studded terrain of Voyageurs. Hiking, cross-country ski, and snowmobile trails weave around lichen-painted outcroppings of granite and basalt along the inlet and south of the road.

A little farther on, Koochiching County Road 96 splits off to the right and winds through the forest for 1.5 miles to the Rainy Lake Visitors Center at Voyageurs. Huge slabs and knobs of granite thrust out of the thin soil. An airy, modern structure of wood and granite with stunning views of the lake, the visitors center contains exhibits on the area's history, from the *voyageur* era through to the late 1800s, when the great pine forests were leveled and gold fever briefly gripped the region.

Outside, you can stroll down to the dock and gaze out into Black Bay, rimmed with evergreen forest and dotted with rocky islets—havens for bald eagles, osprey, mergansers, loons, and other birds. This is home port for the *Pride of Rainy Lake*, a 49-passenger cruiser; from May through October daytrips and overnight cruises range out into the lake's pristine bays and coves, visiting abandoned gold mines on Little American Island and the historic Kettle Falls Hotel, built in 1913 to house construction workers on a nearby dam.

Return to MN 11 and turn right to reach Island View, a little slice of vacation paradise. Bucking and dipping down the spine of a rocky penin-

The Rainy Lake dock in Voyageurs National Park, departure point for cruises to the lake's remote bays and islands.

sula, the road passes a fire tower and glorious views of the lake on the way to one of the remotest and most desirable addresses in northern Minnesota. Large summer homes occupy rocky crags and groves of mature pine and spruce at the end of long, sinuous driveways. Crossing a bridge over a bay dotted with evergreen-clad islands, the drive ends at Sha-sha Resort, where you can eat lunch surrounded on three sides by water.

International Falls to Lake of the Woods

Traffic jams won't be a problem on this drive; the route traverses one of the most sparsely populated regions of the state, an immense swath of woodland and swamp that swallows all roads a few miles inland from the Rainy River. A farmer's nearest neighbor may live 30 miles away, and places such as Manitou, Birchdale, and Frontier are virtual ghost towns, abandoned in the 1930s when the logging industry collapsed. It's a good idea to fill the gas tank before setting out for Baudette, 75 miles away.

Follow MN 11 west past the domed Koochiching County Courthouse and International Mall (a big draw for Canadian shoppers) into flat, open woodland and pasture well away from the river. This is a major truck route for trans-border haulers; you're likely to see a lot of Ontario and Manitoba

The Rainy River at Franz Jevne State Park.

license plates. Most of those trucks head south on U.S. Highway 71, 11 miles west of International Falls. You bear right on MN 11, crossing the birch-lined Little Fork River into a patchwork of woods, meadows, and hayfields sloping gradually down to the Rainy. Beef and dairy cattle—the growing season here is too short for arable farming—graze in pastures as flat and even as a bowling green. Soon the road swings close to the Rainy River, offering glimpses of gently flowing water, wooded banks, and farm-steads on the Canadian side, so close that you can see paint peeling on the barns.

Grand Mound, the largest Indian burial mound in the Upper Midwest, is just ahead on the right. Over 2,000 years ago, a culture known as the Laurel Group interred their dead in the 40-foot-high earthen dome and four smaller mounds located at the mouth of the Big Fork River. A low-slung, modern building contains exhibits on the Laurel Indians and other native peoples who lived here as long ago as 3,000 B.C. From the history center, a short trail cuts through moist bottomland forest to the mounds, draped with ferns and impaled by huge trees. This ancient burial ground still breathes mystery. Pot hunters tunneled into the Grand Mound at the turn of the century, but it has never been fully excavated, and probably never will be; state law prohibits disturbance of Indian cemeteries.

If you want to see modern forestry management at work, turn left on Koochiching County Road 1 and right on a narrow forest road. The self-guided Boise Cascade Woodlands Tour (pick up a brochure at the TIC in International Falls) passes stands of Norway pine, aspen, and white spruce in various stages of cultivation, and a black spruce bog. A boardwalk keeps you high and dry while you search for Labrador tea, bog cranberry, and sphagnum moss. The road, which loops back to MN 11 in about 2 miles, is part of the Loman Line, a railroad spur built in the teens to haul lumber out of the virgin forests along the Big Fork, Little Fork, and Black rivers. Today there's not much left of Loman, the old logging town at the end of the line; just a few decaying storefronts and a simple clapboard church.

The Rainy River turns 90 degrees to the north at this point, and the highway follows, keeping its distance for a few miles, then sweeping in close to mirror the river's every crook and bend. Hayfields—dotted with neatly trussed hay bales in the late summer and fall—alternate with rich stands of birch, aspen, spruce, and balsam fir. The land seems deserted; only isolated farmsteads, set far back from the road, and an occasional wood-frame house indicate that anybody lives in this Empty Quarter of the state. Ontario, visible for long stretches as the Rainy curves west again, seems equally devoid of human life.

But folks from other parts of Minnesota don't come to the border country for companionship; they come to fish. At Franz Jevne State Park (turn right on Koochiching County Road 85) I met four guys from International Falls setting up camp on the riverbank. They were after walleye, the king of Minnesota game fish; for the chance of a tasty "shore lunch" (fresh battered fish fried over an open fire with potatoes, baked beans, and onions), they were willing to forego showers and flush toilets.

Franz Jevne makes up for its lack of creature comforts with some pleasing views of the river, both from a public boat access and the riverbank near a rare stretch of rapids. To reach the rapids overlook, turn left through a gate and follow a steep and narrow dirt road through the forest. A foot trail leads down to the water from a small parking lot on the right.

West of the park the Rainy is noticeably wider, swollen by the multitude of streams flowing out of the swamplands on both sides of the border. Breaks in the trees and open stretches of shoreline offer broad vistas of the river, curving grandly through hayfields and tracts of mixed evergreen and hardwood forest. The mouth of the Rapid River, just over the Lake of the Woods County line, is a popular fishing spot. Here the glacial till that covers so much of northwest Minnesota has been stripped away; the river dashes into the Rainy through a narrow, granite gorge crowned by mature pines.

MN 11 stays close to the river the rest of the way into Baudette, crossing several streams and Minnesota Highway 72, another main artery for Canadian truckers. Baudette, with 1,100 frostbite-inured residents, is the only town in Lake of the Woods County. Two gas stations, a grocery store, and four motels cater to fishermen and boaters heading up to the big lake, just 21 miles downstream. Cultural attractions are scarce in Baudette, unless you count "Willie Walleye," a piece of piscine sculpture overlooking the wide, reedy mouth of the Baudette River. For some insight into the area's history, stop in at the Lake of the Woods County Museum, on the left as you come into town. In 1910, after an extremely dry summer, peat fires swept in from the south, leveling the town and killing thirty-four people. Tourist information is located on MN 11 just west of town.

Head west on MN 11, then turn right on Minnesota Highway 172 towards Lake of the Woods. Beyond the airport and the Winter Road River— so named because its frozen surface provided a pathway for log drives— woodlands give way to expansive, table-top fields of wheat, alfalfa, and corn. Secondary roads lead to a string of small fishing resorts on the Rainy River, growing ever wider as it approaches the lake.

Finally, the road heels to the left at Wheelers Point, and the Rainy reveals its gaping mouth, over half a mile wide. Forested bluffs on the Canadian side set off the lighter green of bulrushes along the shore. As at Island View, a resort occupies the choice real estate at the end of the line. In this case it's Wigwam Lodge, a full-service resort with a restaurant and bar overlooking a small marina. There's usually a stiff breeze blowing in from Fourmile Bay, directly to the north. The line of trees on the horizon is Currys Island, a sliver of sand that protects Wigwam and other resorts from the full brunt of storms rolling off the lake.

To experience the big lake in its full splendor, backtrack on MN 172 to Lake of the Woods County Road 8 and turn right; the road crosses woodland, cow pasture, and a marsh-bound inlet on the way to Zippel State Park, 3,000 acres of prime waterfront. The entrance is on Lake of the Woods County Road 34, at the end of a verdant tunnel of jack pine, birch, and aspen forest. Continue straight ahead on a dirt road (beware of white-tailed deer popping out of the woods, especially at dusk) to the park's swimming beach. Suddenly you're standing on the shore of the ocean, or what could pass for the ocean, if not for the lack of saltwater tang in the air. Surf foams on a sandy beach littered with clam shells, driftwood, and smooth pebbles; herring gulls and mergansers wheel along the shore; and there's nothing but water on the northern horizon.

It's 80 miles to the northern tip of the lake, deep into Ontario, and 22 miles to the Northwest Angle, the northernmost point in the Lower 48. An eighteenth-century surveying error gave the U.S. jurisdiction over the Angle, a vast tract of forest and bog that can be reached only by boat, or a long drive through Manitoba. A replica of Fort St. Charles, a palisaded enclosure built by French explorer Sieur de La Verendrye in 1732, is located at Angle Inlet on the north shore.

A trail behind the beach leads to a rock jetty overlooking Zippel Bay, a calm reach of water, wooded shoreline, and wetlands. Sandhill cranes and endangered piping plovers nest in a large marsh across from the sheltered boat access and fishing pier, the site of a fishing village earlier in the century. You can also reach the bay by car; return to the park office and turn right.

The drive ends here. MN 11 will take you to Warroad, an ideal departure point for Fort St. Charles and resorts in the Northwest Angle. The best route south, towards the Mississippi headwaters region and Drives 12 and 14, is MN 72 out of Baudette.

14

Edge of the Wilderness Loop
Grand Rapids–Bigfork via Minnesota Highway 38

General description: A 70- to 85-mile loop through the dramatically glaciated terrain of the Chippewa National Forest between Grand Rapids and Bigfork. Scaling richly wooded moraine hills and skirting numerous lakes, marshes, and bogs, the route passes semi-primitive recreation areas and a state park with virgin stands of pine. Choose between two alternate returns to Grand Rapids: through the woods or through the man-made canyons of the Mesabi Iron Range.

Special attractions: Forest History Center and Judy Garland Museum in Grand Rapids; wonderful views of lakes and hills in Chippewa National Forest; virgin pine and spectacular glacial topography at Scenic State Park near Bigfork; Trout Lake Recreation Area, a wilderness tract developed from a grand summer estate; the Big Fork River, one of the Upper Midwest's premier canoe routes; Wabana Trails and Wildflower Sanctuary; hiking, mountain biking, horseback riding, cross-country skiing, snowmobiling, bald-eagle watching.

Drive route numbers: Minnesota Highway 38; Itasca County Roads 7, 60, 335. Either US 169 or Itasca County Roads 49 and 59 to return to Grand Rapids.

Location: North-central Minnesota. The drive begins and ends in the paper milling and resort town of Grand Rapids.

Travel season: Year-round, with early October best for leaf color, and January through early March ideal for skiing and snowmobiling. Grand Rapids's Tall Timber Days, held on the first weekend in August, features wood-chopping and log rolling contests, chainsaw carving demonstrations, and an arts and crafts festival. Judy Garland fans shouldn't miss a city-wide festival in her honor on the last weekend in June.

Camping: Primitive camping at Trout Lake Recreation Area, Suomi Hills, and Chippewa National Forest campgrounds such as North Star Lake and Moose Lake (west of MN 38 on CR 19); full service camping at Scenic State Park, Prairie Lake Campground on CR 49, and many lake resorts.

Services: Gas, food, and lodging in Grand Rapids. More limited services in Marcell and Bigfork.

Nearby attractions: Iron mine tours at Hill Annex State Park near Marble; giant red and white pines at Schoolcraft State Park near Deer River; Leech Lake and Lake Winnibigoshish, two of the largest lakes in the state (and prime walleye waters); Hafeman Boat Works on Itasca County Road 6 west of Bigfork, where traditional Ojibwe canoes are hand-crafted from birch bark and spruce roots.

The drive

North of Grand Rapids the mostly flat terrain of the Chippewa National Forest becomes sharply rolling, the legacy of a glacier that momentarily halted its advance, dumping vast amounts of sand, gravel, and boulders on the land. Minnesota Highway 38, *aka* the Edge of the Wilderness Scenic Byway, runs along the knobby backbone of the Marcell Moraine, winding through wooded hills that cradle dozens of deep, clear lakes. From Grand Rapids, Judy Garland's home town, this 70- to 85-mile drive snakes over the Laurentian Divide to the village of Bigfork and Scenic State Park, a preserve of virgin pine. Two alternate routes loop back to Grand Rapids. You'll want to take this one slow, stopping frequently to drink in a lakeside vista or stretch your legs on a forest trail.

Grand Rapids has been a lumber town since the 1870s, when huge rafts of pine logs began floating down the Mississippi River to the town's sawmills. Today, logging trucks deliver loads of aspen, jack pine, and spruce to Blandin Paper, a sprawling facility on the river bank. The plant belches steam and an occasional objectionable odor, but doesn't mar the charm of Grand Rapids, the seat of Itasca County and the center of a burgeoning tourist trade.

The Central School, a beautifully restored example of Richardsonian Romanesque architecture, anchors the historic business district. A Yellow Brick Road laid out on the grounds leads to a museum on the third floor that pays homage to native daughter Frances Ethel Gumm, better known as Judy Garland. The star of *The Wizard of Oz* lived in Grand Rapids (her simple wood-frame house is located on U.S. Highway 169 south of town) as a young girl. The school also contains a county historical museum, shops, and restaurants. You'll find tourist information in the town's refurbished railroad depot, a block south on NW Third Street.

For a taste of what it was like to be a lumberjack, visit the Forest History Center (from downtown, turn right on Golf Course Road), a meticulous recreation of a turn-of-the-century logging camp. As new "recruits," visitors receive an orientation tour of the mess hall, smithy, bunkhouse—where seventy men slept two to a straw mattress during the winter logging

Drive 14: Edge of the Wilderness Loop
Grand Rapids–Bigfork via Minnesota Highway 38

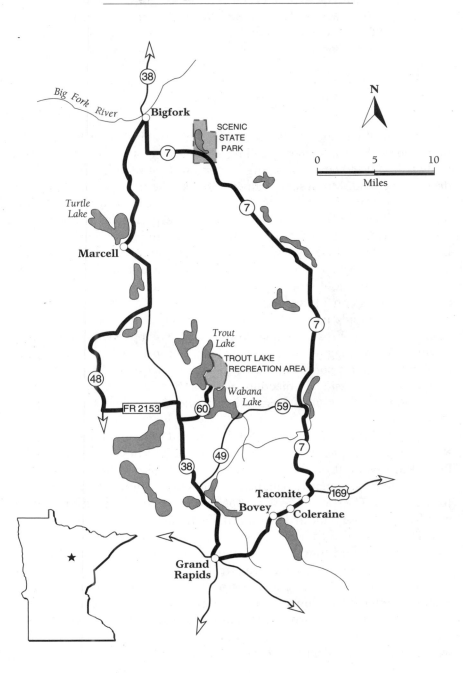

season—from costumed guides. At a nearby Forest Service ranger cabin, restored to its 1930s appearance, another suitably attired raconteur tells stories about the lonely, sometimes dangerous, life of a forest service patrolman.

Go west on U.S. Highway 2 (Fourth Street) to pick up MN 38; the road passes through a residential district and swings around an oval lake rimmed with homes on the way north. It's easy to lead-foot it on the wide, unobstructed S-curves; be aware that you're still in the city, in a 30 mph zone. For the first few miles the terrain is gently rolling, carpeted with mixed deciduous and evergreen forest. Swaths of cattails, ferns, and sumac—a study in scarlet and gold in the fall—line the roadside. Here and there a meadow or hay field breaks up the pastiche of woods and marshland. But before long the road begins to twist and buck as it rises from a broad outwash plain onto the Marcell Moraine, left behind when the Wisconsin ice sheet began to recede ten thousand years ago. Small "kettle" lakes and bogs appear, water-filled depressions in the mountains of soil and gravel deposited at the edge of the glacier.

Hidden away in this freshly sculpted lakescape is a 6,000-acre tract of forest and crystal-clear water that is an outdoor enthusiast's dream. Trout Lake Recreation Area, originally the grand summer retreat of a Chicago lumber baron, encompasses 11 completely undeveloped lakes wrapped in maple, aspen, birch, and scattered pine. Bald eagles, osprey, loons, and herons nest in the area, and the lakes teem with trout, bass, walleye, northern pike, and panfish. Ten miles of disused roads and trails, closed to motorized traffic but accessible to hunters, walkers, cross-country skiers, and mountain bikers, radiate out from the old lodge and cabins on the shore of Trout Lake. The Joyce family called their estate *Nopeming*, meaning "place of rest" in Ojibwe.

To get there, turn right on Itasca County Road 60, then left on Itasca County Road 335 (Bluewater Road) in 1.5 mile. This gravel road winds through dense forest for another 2.5 miles, passing Bluewater Lodge; a U.S. Forest Service sign marks the entrance to a dirt lot where you can leave your car and hike in to the estate.

Back on MN 38, the route continues into the Chippewa National Forest, a 660,000-acre wilderness containing over 600 lakes and countless marshes and conifer bogs. The Chippewa, one of the nation's oldest national forests, provides a refuge for hundreds of species of animals, including beavers, fishers, porcupines, black bears, and timber wolves. The forest also boasts the highest concentration of breeding bald eagles in the Lower 48; over 200 pairs nested in the forest in 1997. Identifiable by their large wingspan and white heads and tail feathers, the birds can often be spotted at dusk or dawn, swooping along lakeshores in pursuit of fish.

Entering the Chippewa National Forest on Minnesota Highway 38.

The lakes come thick and fast now, in all shapes and sizes, like uncut diamonds strewn across green felt. Taking the path of least resistance, the road sweeps close to the shore of each lake before clambering up the next ridge, opening up vistas of forested bluffs, waving cattails, and mirrored sky. At Kremer Lake, a trout water lined with spruce and mature pine, there's just enough room for the asphalt to squeeze between it and a smaller companion, aptly named Surprise Lake. Marshes and conifer bogs—former kettle lakes that have gradually filled in with decaying vegetation—create sunlit openings in an otherwise seamless mosaic of birch, aspen, maple, balsam fir, and pine.

County and forest roads split off from MN 38, bound for more remote lakes such as Orange, Little Horn, and Adele, many with public accesses for fishing or canoeing. To explore this wild, watery hinterland, try Forest Road 2153, a left turn onto gravel just north of Johnson Lake; the road intersects with Itasca County Road 48, which brings you back to the highway via Little Bowstring and Grave lakes. FR 2153 cuts through Suomi Hills, an outstanding area for hiking, mountain biking, cross-country skiing, and primitive camping. Twenty-one miles of trails weave through dense hardwood and evergreen forest and around small lakes frequented by loons, beavers, deer, and bald eagles. Two trailheads with parking and toilets are located on MN 38 near Johnson and Day lakes.

Kremer Lake, one of dozens of pristine "kettle" lakes on Minnesota Highway 38.

The relief grows even more pronounced as you approach the Laurentian Divide, marked by a sign across the road from a wayside rest. Here, at 1,524 feet above sea level, the streams feeding all those lakes part company. North of this point, they flow to Hudson Bay; to the south they pour into the Mississippi River, eventually reaching the Gulf of Mexico. North Star, perhaps the most spectacular lake on MN 38, is just ahead, on the downward slope to Canada. Golden crescents of reed and stands of black spruce—dwarfed by their soggy, acidic environment—share the lake's high, convoluted shore with groves of red pine, birch, and aspen. The lake has a national forest campground and a boat access.

Marcell, little more than a built-up crossroads, has a gas station, a Post Office, a combination cafe and laundromat, and a small lumber mill. Bear right on MN 38, passing the Marcell Ranger Station, where you can pick up maps of the Chippewa National Forest and information on hiking, cross-country skiing, snowmobiling, and fishing. The road wends its way through evergreen and hardwood forest, shrub swamp, and conifer bog, gradually descending from the hills into an outwash plain laced with small, meandering streams. Few lakes on this stretch lie close to the road, but they're accessible from Forest Road 2423 and other secondary forest roads. Four-wheel drive is recommended, especially in the winter and early spring.

The "Big" in Big Fork refers to the river—one of the premier canoeing streams in the Midwest—not to the town, Bigfork, which can muster only 400 year-round residents. An important logging center as recently as the 1940s, Bigfork now serves as a supply stop for canoeists and fishermen. A two-block strip along the highway includes three gas stations, a supermarket, and a small department store. Turn right on Itasca County Road 7, crossing the Big Fork as it flows leisurely between low banks swathed in reeds and cattails. Re-entering the national forest, the road passes through undulating woods and wetlands, part of a broad outwash plain. But the land rises again as you approach Scenic State Park, slipping between two lakes rimmed with marsh and pond weed.

Scenic is one of Minnesota's hidden gems, a cluster of near-pristine lakes surrounded by birch, cedars, and magnificent stands of old-growth timber. Early in the century, when the forests along the Big Fork were falling to the cross-cut saw, a group of residents banded together to save some of the virgin pine. The fruit of their efforts can be seen on the shore of Coon Lake, 2 miles from the park entrance: white and red pines as tall, straight, and stout of trunk as the columns inside a medieval cathedral. You can breathe in their fragrance at picnic tables near a swimming beach and fishing pier.

The nearby lodge, a refurbished log building with a fieldstone fireplace, contains displays on the big pines, wildlife, and the Civilian Conservation Corps, which built the lodge and many of the park's other log and stone buildings in the 1930s. An esker—a sinuous ridge of sand and gravel formed by a river flowing beneath the surface of a glacier—separates Coon from Sandwick Lake. A 0.75-mile hiking/cross-country ski trail runs along the esker's pine-clad backbone to Chase Point, a prime viewing spot for loons, bald eagles, ospreys, and pileated woodpeckers.

CR 7 continues through woodlands of aspen, birch, white spruce, and balsam fir in the national forest and George Washington State Forest, spanning small streams and skirting kettle lakes and expanses of shrub swamp and conifer bog. Gravel roads branch off to resorts and cabins on popular fishing lakes such as Antler and Wasson lakes. Generally fairly flat, the road rears up periodically to negotiate ancient lake beaches and hummocks of glacial debris. Just past the junction with Itasca County Road 50 the route crosses the Taconite Trail, a snowmobile highway between Grand Rapids and Ely.

Leaving the Chippewa National Forest, CR 7 parallels the heavily wooded shore of long, skinny Lawrence Lake for about 3 miles before intersecting Itasca County Road 59. At this point you can pick between two equally scenic but very different return routes to Grand Rapids. Stay on CR 7 for a taste of the Mesabi Iron Range (see Drive 15), the now largely abandoned mining district stretching northeast through Hibbing and Virginia. Crossing the meandering Prairie River, the road descends rapidly past 100-foot piles of ore tailings colonized by aspen, jack pine, and balsam fir to U.S. Highway 169. More artificial, ruddy hills surround the old mining towns of Taconite, Bovey, and Coleraine on this 13-mile stretch of the "Iron Trail." In addition to a large pit lake—an open mine that has filled with groundwater—Coleraine boasts a lovely natural lake with a swimming beach and boat access.

A shorter alternate route follows CR 59 and Itasca County Road 49 through gently rolling woodland and meadows back to MN 38. Wabana Trails and Wildflower Sanctuary, a 480-acre tract of woods, lakes, and wetlands with six miles of hiking and cross-country ski trails, is located on CR 59. Look for a small sign on the left, 0.4 mile before the junction with CR 49. Wildflowers you're likely to encounter along the trails between April and July include lily-of-the-valley, bunchberry, columbine, bellwort, trillium, and hepatica.

15

The Iron Trail
Hibbing–Virginia–Biwabik–Ely

General description: Manmade lakes and hills that are slowly being reclaimed by nature give way to ancient, forested highlands on this 110-mile route through the Mesabi and Vermilion Iron Ranges. A detour off the Iron Trail wanders into the remote (and very cold) community of Embarrass, known for its pioneer-era log houses and barns.

Special attractions: Stunning views of hills, pit lakes, and mini-canyons created by a century of intensive mining; Hull Rust Mahoning, the world's largest open-pit iron mine; Ironworld Discovery Center outside Chisholm; Minnesota's oldest and deepest underground mine at Tower Soudan State Park; mountain biking and downhill and cross-country skiing at Giant's Ridge Recreation Area near Biwabik; distinctive Finnish architecture and handicrafts in Embarrass.

Drive route numbers: U.S. Highways 169, 53; Minnesota Highways 73, 135, 169; St. Louis County Roads 21, 26.

Location: Northeast Minnesota. The drive begins in the iron mining town of Hibbing and ends in Ely, gateway to the Boundary Waters Canoe Area Wilderness.

Travel season: January and February are prime time for skiing at Giants Ridge and the state parks. Late September and early October offer vivid splashes of green and gold against a backdrop of ruddy hills and intensely blue lakes. Embarrass throws a Finnish-American Summer Festival on the second weekend in June.

Camping: Mesaba Co-op Park in Hibbing; West-2-Rivers Campground in Mountain Iron; Sherwood Forest Campground in Gilbert; Vermilion Trail Park near Biwabik; Hoodoo Point Campground outside Tower; Fall Lake and Silver Rapids campgrounds near Ely.

Services: Gas, food, and lodging in all the major Range cities: Hibbing, Chisholm, Virginia, and Ely. More limited services in Biwabik, Mountain Iron, Gilbert, and Tower.

Nearby attractions: Hill Annex Mine State Park near Calumet, a large open-pit mine that can be explored by bus; U.S. Hockey Hall of Fame in Eveleth; hiking, fishing, and cross-country skiing at Bear Head Lake State Park between Tower and Ely; canoeing, fishing, and camping in the Boundary Waters Canoe Area Wilderness.

Drive 15: The Iron Trail

Hibbing–Virginia–Biwabik–Ely

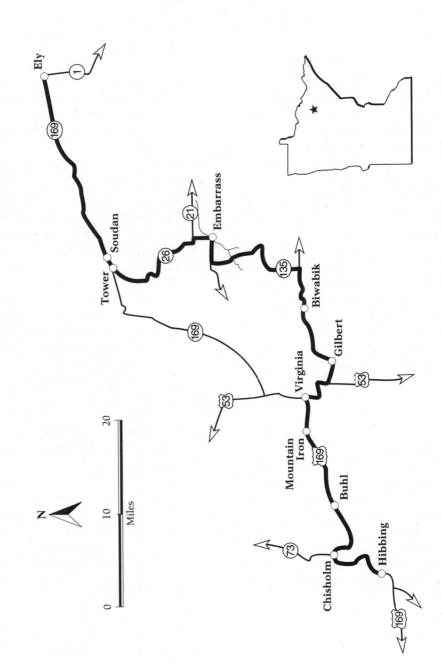

The drive

The Mesabi Iron Range was once one of the ugliest places on earth, a barren landscape of huge open pit mines surrounded by mountains of discarded rubble. For eighty years, billions of tons of iron ore were ripped from the low hills northwest of Duluth, supplying the materiel for two world wars and sustaining steady economic growth in Range cities such as Hibbing, Chisholm, Virginia, and Eveleth. The mining companies did nothing to mitigate the devastation caused by their operations. But hard times and Mother Nature can work wonders; when the top-grade ore was exhausted in the early 1960s, many mines were closed, allowing the pits to fill with groundwater and trees to colonize the man-made hills.

This 110-mile drive slices through the red-rock heart of the Mesabi, still healing after 30 years of mine reclamation by the state. Dozens of ore pits have been transformed into deep, blue lakes popular with fishermen and scuba divers. The route continues over the wholly natural, ancient highlands of the Giant's Range to the old mining town of Ely, today a thriving resort center on the edge of the Boundary Waters Canoe Area Wilderness. On the way you pass the state's deepest underground mine and visit Embarrass, a farming community with an enduring Finnish heritage.

Hibbing is the capital of the Iron Range, a stolid, workmanlike city of dark-red brick buildings and simple wood-frame houses. Bob Dylan grew up in one of those houses and attended Hibbing High School before leaving for the bright lights of Minneapolis in 1959. Devastated by the collapse of the mining industry in the 1970s, Hibbing has a new air of prosperity; shops, restaurants, and cafes line spruced-up Howard Street downtown, and the Paulucci Space Theatre, a multi-media planetarium, rises Phoenix-like from a base of ore tailings on U.S. Highway 169.

Mining still goes on in Hibbing; for a look at modern mining operations—and one of the wonders of the industrial age—follow the "Mine View" signs off Howard Street. The streets of old Hibbing—relocated building by building after World War I to make way for mine expansion—lead to an observation area on the edge of the Hull Rust Mahoning Mine, the largest open-pit iron mine in the world. The chasm that yawns on the other side of a chain-link fence staggers the imagination: since 1895, 1.4 billion tons of earth have been gouged out of Hull Rust, creating a miniature Grand Canyon 3 miles long and 2 miles wide. Sheer, ruddy cliffs drop hundreds of feet to the bluish-green surface of a pit lake dotted with "islands" of unexcavated rock. In the distance, minuscule dump trucks—actually gargantuan machines capable of hauling 170 tons of ore—trundle over fresh lodes of gray, iron-bearing taconite. In an on-site interpretive center retired miners will gladly pepper you with facts about the mine and taconite processing.

Heading north on US 169, it's obvious where much of that 1.4 billion tons ended up: in great flat-top mounds that tower as high as 200 feet above the road. Stands of young aspen, birch, and jack pine—some planted, others sprung from seeds deposited by the wind and birds—cling to steep banks of shattered, reddish-black rock. This mini-alpine landscape reaches a crescendo near Chisholm, 5.5 miles north of Hibbing; the highway crosses a deep canyon, offering a vista of rugged, partially forested slopes extending almost to infinity. A pit lake glistens in the distance—just one of forty-five inactive mines that ring the city.

Turn right on Minnesota Highway 73, at the feet of a monumental figure toting a shovel and pickaxe. The 85-foot statue of a miner, cast in bronze and steel in 1987, guards the entrance to Ironworld Discovery Center, a theme park with hands-on mining exhibits, ethnic food, craft demon-

An 85-foot statue of a miner guards the entrance to Ironworld Discovery Center in Chisholm.

The Wacootah pit lake in Mountain Iron, abandoned in 1964.

strations, and dance performances. A seven-minute trolley ride circumnavigates Glen Godfrey Mine, one of the most beautiful pit lakes on the Range. The food booths alone are worth a visit to Ironworld: immigrants from forty countries worked the mines, bringing with them dishes such as Cornish pasties (a turnover with a beef and vegetable filling), Finnish mojakka (beef or fish soup), and Slovenian potica (a sweet bread made from walnuts, honey, and butter).

MN 73 continues into Chisholm past the Minnesota Museum of Mining, repository for all sorts of climb-and-touch mining equipment, including a 1907 steam locomotive and a dump truck with 9-foot-tall wheels. Main Street, typical of Range cities with its two-story brick facades and imposing, neoclassical city hall, ends at a causeway spanning Longyear Lake, a natural lake fringed with woodland. The highway crosses the lake and curves around the shore to rejoin US 169 in about a mile.

A large pit lake appears on the right, a jagged fjord softened by aspen and jack pine along its rim. Then tailing piles, some anvil-shaped and thickly wooded, others conical and bare like the summits of active volcanoes, loom ahead. For the next 30 miles, the highway winds past more artificial lakes and faux mountains in one of the most intensively mined sections of the Iron Range. Turn off in any of the communities along 169—Buhl, Kinney, Mountain Iron—and you'll find a pit lake, fenced off for the protection of children and the foolhardy. The complex of pits around Mountain Iron, where iron was first discovered by Leonidas Merritt in 1890, is particularly impressive. For a panoramic view of the town and its starkly beautiful surroundings, exit 169 into downtown (graced by a bronze statue of Merritt) and follow the signs to the Wacootah Overlook. To the left, a turquoise lake nestles at the bottom of the Wacootah Mine, abandoned to the encroaching forest in 1964. To the right, naked terraces of taconite rise to a hilltop processing plant operated by USS Minntac, one of seven mining companies on the Range.

Virginia is the second largest town on the Range, and Hibbing's biggest rival for tourist dollars. "The best thing to come out of Hibbing," a Virginia resident told me, "is Highway 169." Certainly the city can claim superiority in the small-town charm department, with two natural lakes and Olcott Park, an oasis of green with a historical museum, rock garden, and 6,000-square-foot tropical greenhouse. The rock garden, greenhouse, and hundreds of mature trees in the park date to the 1930s, when the Work Projects Administration (WPA) came to the rescue of a city with 70 percent unemployment. And Virginia teeters on the edge of a Big Hole almost as spectacular as Hull Rust: the Rouchleau Mine Group, a vast, interconnected complex of open pits and collapsed underground shafts.

A jumbo-sized yellow dump truck sits atop a 200-foot tailings pile at Mineview in the Sky, an observation area on U.S. Highway 53 south (take Second Avenue West from downtown). A gravel road curls up to the summit, also occupied by a tourist information office. Sheer cliffs streaked with red, blue, and yellow—different grades of natural ore—plunge 450 feet to the surface of a lake. The bottom of the Rouchleau Mine lies 190 feet below that.

Just beyond Mineview, veer left on Minnesota Highway 135. Here, in a section of the Range without active mines, old tailings piles covered with aspen, maple, jack pine, fir, and spruce blend in with natural hillocks and swells. The land heaves into denuded, unnatural forms again near Gilbert, a town of 2,000 on the aptly named Lake Ore-Be-Gone, but soon subsides into rolling expanses of woodland and muskeg as you approach Biwabik.

Biwabik (the name is derived from the Ojibwe word for iron) has rejected its grimy mining past to cultivate a sleeker image as an *apres-ski* playground. Giants Ridge Recreation Area, one of the Midwest's premier downhill and cross-country ski complexes, is 4 miles north of town. Community leaders have opted for a Bavarian theme on Main Street: colorful murals of alpine meadows and shepherdesses adorn the facade of the Salznwalz Cafe, and the steeply pitched gables of City Hall echo Old World architecture. In December, Biwabik hosts Weihnachtfest, a city festival with lighting displays, fireworks, ethnic crafts, carriage rides, and polka music.

MN 135 schlusses out of town along the shore of Embarrass Lake, a lovely reach of forested bluffs and islands that hints at the natural beauty that existed on the Range before the steam shovels went to work. Vermilion Trail Park has picnic grounds, lakeside campsites, and hiking trails. The turnoff on Minnesota Highway 38 to Giants Ridge is just ahead. The multi-million-dollar facility has 19 downhill runs and 60 kilometers of cross-country ski trails, rated from easy to well-nigh suicidal.

The slopes that provide all that winter fun are the glacier-scoured flanks of the Giants Range, a granite ridge that rises near Virginia and runs for 50 miles along the North Shore. Also known as the Laurentian Divide, the ridge separates two huge watersheds—rain and snow falling north of this point flows north to the border lakes and Hudson Bay, while precipitation below the divide runs eastward to Lake Superior and on to the Atlantic Ocean via the St. Lawrence River.

In about a mile the highway abruptly heads uphill through heavily wooded tailings piles, then swings to the left for the main assault on the ridge. Overshadowed by huge granite outcrops draped in aspen, spruce, maple, and old-growth white pine, the road rises higher and higher towards the ridgetop—in Indian legend the lair of a giant hero who hunted wild animals with boulders plucked from the earth. The Ojibwe called him *Mesabi*—an appropriate name for a region in which billions of tons of rock have been torn from the ground. The crest, 400 feet above the surrounding plain, offers a spectacular view of waves of lush woodland crashing down the northern slope of the Giants Range. Then you're riding those waves down through the forest and into the broad, low-lying valley of the Embarrass River.

Nobody committed a faux pas on the river; the name comes from the French *embarras*, meaning "obstacle." At the time of the fur trade the river was often low and littered with driftwood, making canoeing difficult. Today, maneuvering a canoe on the narrow, reed-bound stream still looks like a tough assignment. Two miles through rolling woodland brings you to the junction with St. Louis County Road 21 and the community of Embarrass, famous for its rare and distinctively Finnish log buildings. Three-hour tours of the pioneer homesteads, scattered amidst cutover fields and encroaching forest, depart at 10 A.M. and 2 P.M. daily during the summer from the Embarrass Visitors Center, a rough-hewn log structure on the right. Inside, there's a mockup of a sauna—a hallowed ritual for early settlers who endured incredibly cold winters without central heating. Embarrass vies with International Falls for cold-weather bragging rights; the mercury plummeted to -57 degrees F on Jan. 20, 1996.

Turn right on CR 21 to reach "downtown" Embarrass, not much more than a crook in the road near the river. A Finnish fence of slanted, rough-cut poles encloses the Sisu Tori Craft Shop, where local artisans make traditional hand-woven rugs and felt slippers, and several outbuildings, including a 1901 log playhouse and a sauna that's listed on the National Register of Historic Places. Across the road, a community hall constructed of massive pine logs hosts the Finnish-American Summer Festival on the second weekend in June.

St. Louis County Road 26 splits off to the left 2 miles north of Embarrass. Follow it through gently rolling woodland, marsh, and conifer bog back to MN 135, then turn right towards the village of Tower, once the locus of an iron mining district that predates the Mesabi but has now faded into history. Charlemagne Tower opened the first iron mine on the Vermilion Range in 1884, building a railroad to haul the ore to Lake Superior and bringing in Swedish and Cornish miners who helped make Tower a thriving trade center. Today, more than 30 years after the nearby Soudan Mine closed down, Tower's 500 year-round residents make a living selling gas, bait, and burgers to fishermen and boaters heading to Vermilion Lake, one of Minnesota's largest and most beautiful bodies of water. For a view of the lake, called "Lake of the Sunset Glow" by the Ojibwe, turn left on St. Louis County Road 697; the road winds through woods and meadows to Hoodoo Point on Pike Bay, ringed with granite ledges and studded with islands clad in pine and spruce.

The Soudan Mine, now a state park encompassing 1,200 acres of lakeshore, is 2 miles north on Minnesota Highway 169. A park road twists up forested granite slopes to the mine buildings, painted an austere gray and black. Unlike the mines of the Mesabi Range, Soudan was an underground operation; the main shaft, topped by a tall, rusty headframe, plunges 2,400 feet into bedrock, following a vertical vein of high-grade hematite. After a three-minute elevator ride to the lowest level visitors board a small train for the quarter-mile journey to a recreated work site. In the early 1900s miners worked twelve-hour shifts by candlelight, hacking at the ore face with pickaxes and shovels; by 1963, when high production costs shut down the mine, they were using electric lamps and air-powered, carbide-tipped drills.

MN 169 continues north along the Vermilion Iron Range, roller coasting through dense stands of aspen, birch, spruce, fir, and pine atop the Precambrian rocks of the Canadian Shield. Outcrops of granite and gneiss thrust from the undergrowth beside the road. Openings in the forest offer glimpses of cattail marshes and deep, cold lakes devoid of development. At one point, 16 miles north of Tower, the road sweeps close to four lakes in rapid succession: Armstrong, Clear, Robinson, and Deadman (no word on how the last lake acquired its name). The rounded, heavily wooded hills become even higher and more rugged as you approach Ely's brightly hued water tower. Road cuts along this stretch have exposed layers of greenstone, an uncommon gray-green rock that formed at the bottom of a primeval ocean 2.7 billion years ago.

Sheridan Street in Ely (see Drive 17) is chockablock with canoe outfitters, cafes, and other businesses that cater to weekend *voyageurs* from the Twin Cities. There's no industry of any kind, unless you count canoe building and mukluk manufacturing. But Ely, like Tower and the cities of the Mesabi, has a long, rich mining history. Iron ore was discovered here in 1886, and in the 1930s Ely was considered the capital of the Vermilion Range, with three underground mines employing 1,500 men. The rusting skeletons of lift towers overlooking a pit lake north of downtown mark the location of the mines. Pioneer Road, an extension of Central Avenue, winds through young stands of aspen and birch to the ruins of the Pioneer Mine, across the road from a Holiday Inn. Cave-ins and settling created the lake after the mine closed in 1967.

The drive ends here. Ely is the starting point for two other drives: Drive 16 along the Echo Trail, and Drive 17 to the North Shore via Minnesota Highway 1.

16

The Echo Trail

Ely to Orr via St. Louis County Road 116

General description: A 72-mile roller coaster ride on asphalt and gravel through the untrammeled wilderness of the Superior National Forest and Kabetogama State Forest. Numerous trailheads and canoe portages along the Echo Trail provide access to the Boundary Waters Canoe Area Wilderness (BWCA). A sidetrip presses north to the resort village of Crane Lake, a gateway to Voyageurs National Park.

Special attractions: Unmatched views of sharply rolling forest, lakes, wetlands, rivers, and granite crags in one of the most remote areas in the Continental U.S.; canoeing, fishing, cross-country skiing, snowmobiling, and primitive camping in the Superior National Forest and Boundary Waters; opportunity to see wildlife such as bald eagles, ospreys, moose, bears, and beavers; blueberry picking and wildflower viewing.

Drive route numbers: Minnesota Highway 169; St. Louis County Roads 88, 23, 24, 116 (the Echo Trail).

Location: Northeast Minnesota. The drive begins in Ely, gateway to the BWCA, and ends in Orr, a resort village on Pelican Lake.

Travel season: Trekking the Echo Trail, a genuine wilderness road, is inadvisable in winter and early spring unless you have four-wheel drive. Wildflowers show their best in May and June, while prime blueberry-picking season is July to August.

Camping: Fall Lake and Silver Rapids campgrounds near Ely; Fenske Lake, Lake Jeanette, and Echo Lake national forest campgrounds; Beddow's Campground in Crane Lake; Pine Acres Resort and Lakeside RV Park in Orr.

Services: Gas, food, and lodging in Ely, Crane Lake, and Orr; nothing at all on the Echo Trail, so stock up (and check your oil and coolant) before you leave Ely.

Nearby attractions: Guided boat tours and snowmobiling in Voyageurs National Park; long-distance hiking and canoe routes into the Boundary Waters; outstanding fishing on Vermilion Lake southeast of Orr; Minnesota's oldest and deepest underground mine at Tower Soudan State Park south of Ely; Voyageurs National Park Area Information Center south of Orr.

Drive 16: The Echo Trail

Ely to Orr via St. Louis County Road 116

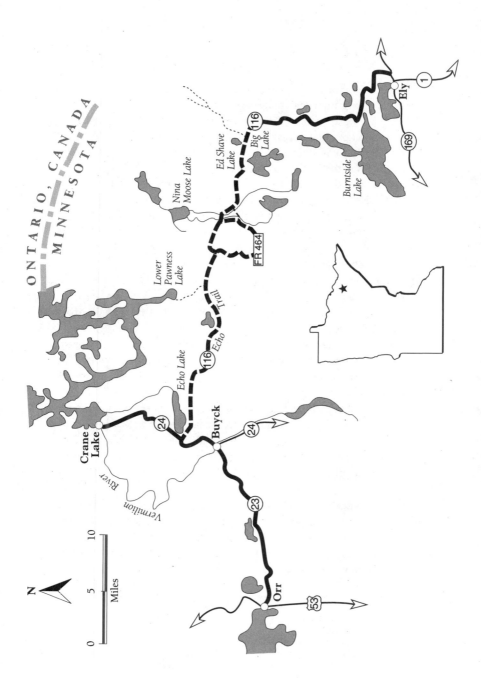

 # The drive

You're in for a true wilderness experience on this drive between the far northern outposts of Ely and Orr. No stoplights. No SuperAmericas. No ex-urban ramblers. Just mile after mile of forest, marsh, conifer bog, and lakeshore draped over the ancient, glaciated bones of the Canadian Shield. Much of the 72-mile route traverses the Echo Trail, built by the Civilian Conservation Corps (CCC) in the 1930s to move men and supplies through what was then a trackless wilderness. Gravel for much of its length, the road skirts the Boundary Waters Canoe Area Wilderness—1.1 million acres of nirvana for outdoor enthusiasts. Dozens of pull-offs and side roads provide access to lakes, hiking trails, and primitive campgrounds in the Boundary Waters and adjacent Superior National Forest. Wildlife abounds along the Echo and county roads linking the trail to Orr and Crane Lake; if you're lucky you may catch a glimpse of a white-tailed deer, beaver, loon, or bald eagle, and hear the spine-tingling howl of the timber wolf.

The drive begins in Ely (see Drive 17), a bustling resort center and a jumping-off point for expeditions into the Boundary Waters. Follow Minnesota Highway 169 north, past the junction with Minnesota Highway 1 and the International Wolf Center, then turn left on St. Louis County Road 88. The road curves around the irregular, piney shore of Shagawa Lake for 2 miles, meeting the Echo Trail (St. Louis County Road 116) at the foot of a high, bare ridge of granite topped by evergreens and young aspen. The trail heads to the right and immediately plunges into dense coniferous forest, lurching and dipping over bedrock laid bare by glaciers during the last Ice Age. Large outcrops of granite, whale-like with their encrustations of lichen, thrust out of the undergrowth. Gravel roads lead to boat accesses, hiking trails, and resorts on clear, cold fishing lakes such as Little Long, Bass, and Hobo.

After about 8 miles the narrow, shoulderless road sweeps close to the shore of Burntside Lake, a big, beautiful lake stretching 9 miles to the west. Tall white spruce, balsam fir, and red and white pine cling to rock ledges at the waterline and several small islands—just a sampling of the more than 100 islands scattered about the lake. The source of Ely's water, Burntside brims with lake trout, northern pike, and walleye; signs point the way to nearby boat ramps.

As the trail bores deeper into the Superior National Forest, flanked on both sides by the BWCA, the going gets even bumpier and more tortuous; you'll find yourself gripping the steering wheel with both hands as the road clambers over glacial ridges and whips around gaunt masses of granite, gneiss, and schist. In the spring and early summer wild roses, columbine, fire weed, marsh marigold, and other wildflowers bloom along the roadside.

A high, weathered ridge of granite marks the entrance to the Echo Trail outside Ely.

Fenske Lake is the first of three U.S. Forest Service campgrounds along the trail. They're nothing fancy; water comes out of a hand pump, and the toilets are the kind that don't flush. But what these campgrounds lack in modern amenities they make up for in scenic beauty and solitude. Fenske Lake has a swimming beach, picnic pavilion, fishing pier, and boat landing. To get a taste of the Boundary Waters without having to apply for a permit, put your canoe in here; a canoe trail winds through a small chain of lakes linked by portages. Two-tenths of a mile past the campground entrance, look for a narrow track to your right; a short hike brings you to the site of a CCC camp, one of dozens that put thousands of jobless men to work on reforestation and construction projects during the Great Depression. The stone fireplaces from the original buildings are still standing.

The Echo forges on, passing tall stands of white, red, and jack pine planted by the CCC and expanses of marsh thick with cattails, reeds, and sedges. Soon the asphalt ends, and the resorts drop away; only canoe accesses and trailheads lie at the end of narrow gravel roads snaking off into the forest. BWCA permits are required to hike and canoe to the towering cliffs above North Hegman Lake, emblazoned with centuries-old Indian pictographs, and take in the panoramic lake views along the Angleworm Trail. Along the shore of Ed Shave Lake, 2 miles beyond the Angleworm trailhead, you get an idea of the prodigious effort expended on this road 60 years ago. The face of a cliff towering 50 feet above the water has been blasted away, leaving just enough room for a car to scramble up and around, poised between rock and thin air. Take care on this vertiginous climb; there's a sharp blind corner at the top.

West of Big Lake, a popular canoeing lake with island campsites, the hills subside into undulating woodland and swaths of conifer bog laced with slow-moving streams. Shrub swamp—a type of wetland dominated by speckled alder, willow, and water-loving sedges and ferns—embraces the Moose River as it flows under a narrow wooden bridge. Farther from the river, their roots anchored tenuously in boggy soil, black spruce and tamarack cut a jagged profile against the sky. Several readily accessible hiking trails branch off from the Echo in this area, skirting the bogs and winding through rolling uplands of red, white, and jack pine to remote lakes.

The 5-mile Devil's Cascade Trail (look for the sign just before the Little Indian Sioux River) ascends a steep ridge overlooking Lower Pawness Lake, ending at a dramatic, rocky gorge known as the Devil's Cascade. Backtrack from the Moose River to National Forest Road 464 to reach the starting point of the Big Moose Trail, a 2-mile trek through the forest and along the craggy shores of Big Moose Lake. You'll need to fill out a BWCA day-use permit, available at the trailhead, for both of these trails. For a short hike not requiring a permit, try the Fire and Ice Trail. From the trailhead just east of the Little Indian Sioux River, this 10-minute interpretive loop runs along the bluffs of a glaciated valley, passing an 85-ton boulder deposited by the retreating ice and overlooks of broad swaths of forest scorched by fire in

Burntside Lake on the Echo Trail near Ely.

1971. Sun-bleached snags (dead trees) are prime roosting spots for bald eagles and ospreys.

More evidence of the fire, which raged for three days, consuming 15,000 acres of forest, can be seen along the Echo as it continues past Meander Lake and the Little Indian Sioux River. Tall pine snags rise out of a dense understory of aspen and birch, always the first species to colonize a burned area. The big pine and spruce return at Lake Jeanette, an island-strewn, picture-perfect lake with a national forest campground on the right. The road runs barely 15 feet from the shore, close enough to make out the patterns of green and orange lichen on boulders at the water's edge. Swinging close to the forested bluffs of Pauline Lake, the Echo descends into the broad, marshy valley of the Hunting Shack River. Bog reed, cattails, and black spruce in the lowlands give way to birch, balsam fir, and pine on a high ridge to the left. Canoeists can park by a wooden bridge and paddle down the river to Pauline and its neighbor, Astrid Lake. Because neither lake is in the BWCA, you don't need a day permit.

The route follows the sluggish, meandering river for several miles, then climbs out of the valley and heads due west, passing the Timberwolf Point Resort, a hint that civilization is nigh. Look for beaver meadows—the washed-out remains of abandoned lodges and dams—along a creek as you approach the turnoff to the Echo Lake campground. This is your last opportunity to stretch your legs on a wilderness trail; trailheads at the campground and a parking area near Picket Creek provide access to 13 miles of trails that loop through dense stands of aspen, birch, and spruce—habitat for deer, woodcocks, and ruffed grouse.

The Echo Trail ends just ahead, at the junction with St. Louis County Road 24, the main road in and out of the resort town of Crane Lake. If you're looking for a place to stay, or just want to take a gander at one of the state's largest and most alluring resort lakes, turn right; it's 8 miles through rolling forest and wetlands to Crane Lake, a chain of resorts and campgrounds strung along the rocky lakeshore. A marina and public boat ramp on St. Louis County Road 425 is the departure point for waterborne excursions on Crane and dozens of other lakes in Voyageurs National Park. A 1.5-mile hiking trail leads from the Voyagaire Lodge to a dramatic overlook where the Vermilion River surges between sheer granite walls into the lake. The site of a wintering camp used by fur-trading voyageurs in the 1700s and early 1800s is a short distance downstream.

The last leg of the drive runs southwest through a rugged landscape of marsh, bog, and soaring granite ridges crowned with pine, spruce, and fir. From the Echo Trail, turn left on CR 24; in 4 miles the road crosses the Vermilion River, once an important link in the chain of lakes and streams that allowed fur traders to paddle between Crane Lake and the Mississippi River. In the early

1890s, the riverside hamlet of Buych was a rest stop for prospectors on the way to gold fields on Rainy Lake; today the Vermilion River Tavern, appropriately painted red, offers succor to motorists and canoeists.

Bear right on St. Louis County Road 23, entering the Kabetogama State Forest. The woods rear up into high ridges on both sides of the road as you approach Myrtle Lake, rimmed with evergreens and giant outcrops of granite. The road parallels the shore for 2 miles, then crosses the leisurely, reed-bound Pelican River into gentler, more open woodland sprinkled with meadows and farmsteads. Finally, CR 24 coils down a hill and across some railroad tracks into Orr, a two-block resort village on Pelican Lake. The Orr General Store & Mercantile Co., three motels, a supermarket, and a cafe cater to fishermen, boaters, and travelers speeding by on U.S. Highway 53, the main road to International Falls. A wayside rest with a fishing pier offers a splendid view of Orr Bay and the high, forested bluffs of Indian Point. The Voyageurs National Park Area Information Center is a mile south of the village on US 53.

17

Minnesota Highway 1
Ely to Crystal Bay

General description: Bisecting the rugged, heavily forested Arrowhead region, Minnesota Highway 1 runs for 68 miles between the North Woods outpost of Ely and Crystal Bay on Lake Superior. Trails and public lake accesses in Superior National Forest and Finland State Forest provide plenty of opportunities for hiking, fishing, cross-country skiing, and bird watching.

Special attractions: International Wolf Center and Dorothy Molter Museum in Ely; sharply rolling forest, coldwater streams, and pristine lakes in Superior National Forest and Finland State Forest; glorious views of Lake Superior from the Laurentian Highlands; hiking, canoeing, trout fishing, cross-country skiing, snowmobiling, and primitive camping in the forest and two state parks; loons, bald eagles, ospreys, bears, beavers, and other wildlife; blueberry picking and wildflower viewing on the roadside and along hiking trails.

Drive route numbers: MN 1.

Location: Northeast Minnesota. The drive begins in Ely, gateway to the Boundary Waters Canoe Area Wilderness, and ends on the North Shore of Lake Superior at Crystal Bay.

Travel season: Paved for its entire length, MN 1 is passable all year, but you may have trouble getting through to off-highway trailheads and campgrounds in the early spring or after heavy snowfalls. If you travel in the winter, be sure to carry emergency food and extra blankets in case of a breakdown. Wildflowers are at their peak in May and June, while prime blueberry-picking season is July to August.

Camping: Fall Lake and Silver Rapids campgrounds near Ely; Kawishiwi Lake, Little Isabella and McDougal Lake national forest campgrounds; Wildhurst Lodge and Campground near Finland; Eckbeck and Finland state forest campgrounds on the Baptism River; George H. Crosby–Manitou and Tettegouche state parks.

Services: A full array of motels, bed and breakfasts, restaurants, and filling stations in Ely; limited food and gas in Isabella and Finland. The nearest town of any size on the North Shore is Beaver Bay, 10 miles south of Tettegouche.

Nearby attractions: Outstanding scenery and historic towns along the North Shore of Lake Superior; long-distance hiking and canoe routes into the Boundary Waters Canoe Area Wilderness north of Ely; wilderness hiking and camping at George H. Crosby–Manitou State Park; Minnesota's oldest and deepest underground mine at Tower Soudan State Park south of Ely on Minnesota Highway 169.

Drive 17: Minnesota Highway 1

Ely to Crystal Bay

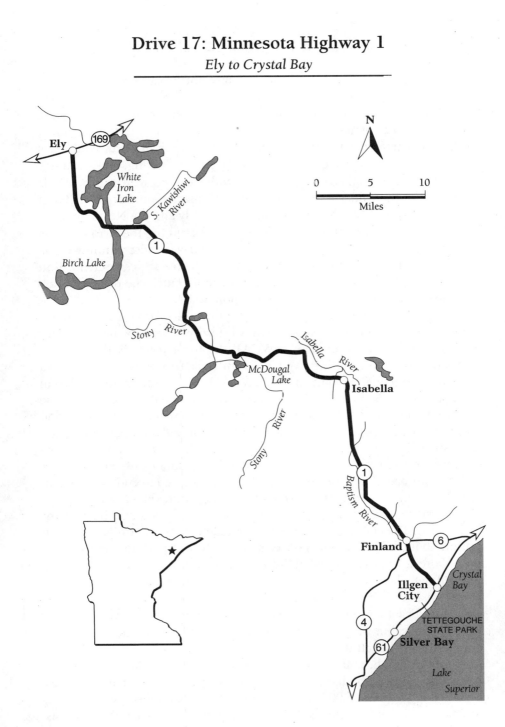

 # The drive

The forest rules the Arrowhead region of northeast Minnesota. A century after logging companies decimated the white and red pine, a diverse tapestry of aspen, birch, spruce, fir, and pine covers thousands of square miles of the vast triangle that extends from Duluth north to the Canadian border. The Arrowhead's rocky terrain and multitude of clear, cold lakes and streams makes it a sporting paradise, laced with hiking, cross-country skiing, and snowmobile trails, and flush with fish and wild game. MN 1, carved out of the wilderness by the Civilian Conservation Corps (CCC) in the 1930s, slices across the Arrowhead between Ely and the North Shore of Lake Superior. Its 68 miles offer a little bit of everything the Arrowhead is famous for: endless, rolling stretches of forests and wetlands; stunning views of Lake Superior and interior lakes; and the chance to leave civilization completely behind on a backwoods trail or canoe route. The route can easily be driven in reverse, from the North Shore to Ely.

Ely, once a rough mining and logging town (see Drive 16), promotes itself today as Canoe City, U.S.A. The western gateway to the Boundary Waters Canoe Area Wilderness (BWCA), the town teems with outfitters who will rent you everything you need for a daytrip on nearby Shagawa Lake or an extended sojourn in the BWCA. Ely is the hometown of Will Steger and Paul Schurke, members of an international expedition to the North Pole by dogsled in 1986. You can buy Steger-brand mukluks, and every other imaginable outdoors accessory, on Sheridan Street, Ely's main retail strip. The International Wolf Center, a modern facility on Minnesota Highway 169 east of town devoted to research and public outreach, features award-winning exhibits on an animal that has managed to endure in northeast Minnesota despite decades of bounty hunting. More than 1,500 wolves—the largest population in the lower 48—roam the forests and bogs of the Arrowhead. The center also dispenses Boundary Waters permits and information about hiking, cross-country skiing, and camping in Superior National Forest. For a taste of what life was like in the North Woods before TV and cellular phones, visit the nearby Dorothy Molter Museum. Known as the "Root Beer Lady" to generations of canoeists who dropped by her remote island cabin, Molter was the last resident of the BWCA. After she died in 1986, the cabin was transported log by log to Ely, reassembled, and furnished just as she left it.

MN 1 branches off from MN 169 west of the Molter Museum. Follow it through rolling woodland and marsh into Superior National Forest, established in 1909 on 36,000 acres of cutover land abandoned by the logging companies. Today Superior is the largest national forest east of the Mississippi River, embracing 3.7 million acres of woods, wetlands, and water. Thick

*Golden aspen and evergreen pine along Minnesota Highway 1
in the Superior National Forest.*

stands of aspen, birch, balsam fir, white spruce, and red and white pine crowd the roadside as MN 1 curves around the southern tip of White Iron Lake (a gravel side road leads to a boat access) and crosses Birch Lake Dam, a popular fishing hole.

Another 2.5 miles brings you to the South Kawishiwi River, a lovely reach of water flowing serenely between bluffs draped in aspen, fir, and tall, wispy-crowned white pine. Bulrushes and smooth granite boulders line the riverbank by a steel-truss bridge, one of many erected in the Arrowhead by Depression-era CCC work crews. Many of them have been replaced by modern concrete spans, but this one survives, an elegantly functional tracery of beams and cross braces. On the other side of the bridge there's a boat ramp and a rustic campground with five riverside sites.

Conifer bog sprawls as far as the eye can see on both sides of the road as MN 1 burrows deeper into Superior National Forest. Virtually all the trees, up to 100 years old but stunted by the acidic, water-logged soil, are black spruce and tamarack. In the fall the saffron, downswept boughs of tamarack—the only conifer that drops its leaves—stand out boldly against a backdrop of dark green spires. The terrain quickly becomes more rugged as the route enters a region of forested ridges, rock-bottomed lakes, and heaves of bare granite, schist, and gneiss—bedrock formed 2.7 billion years ago, when northeast Minnesota was the scene of active mountain building. Some outcrops, gouged and polished by the passage of glaciers, are as big as a house; spruce and cedar trees cling to them, their roots curling like vines into the thin soil.

The road bucks, dips, and weaves through the forest, a dense tangle of birch, aspen, spruce, and balsam fir. Scattered white and red pines, some of them survivors of the logging era, soar above the canopy, their upturned branches bathed in sunlight. Occasionally the wall of greenery parts to reveal a cattail marsh, or a kettle lake that probably looked the same one hundred years ago, or five hundred years ago. One such lake, too small to have a name, suddenly appears to the left at the bottom of a steep hill; clear, still water in the lake's center gives way to waving reeds and sedges around the shore, which in turn yield to stands of black spruce, birch, and aspen on the bluffs above. More reeds rim the banks of the Stony River, fed by a chain of wilderness lakes and streams stretching to the east. Rough forest roads (four-wheel- drive is recommended, especially in the spring) twist and jounce through the forest to several canoe entry points.

The gravel road to McDougal Lake, 7 miles ahead on the right, won't bust your axles, and the views along the way are well worth a brief detour. The entrance to a beautiful national forest campground is 0.75 mile from MN 1, on the right. Waterfront campsites offer sweeping vistas of the completely undeveloped lake, ringed with birch and spruce. A 1-mile hiking

Matted reeds and sedges on a small lake south of Ely on Minnesota Highway 1.

trail loops through the woods close to shore. The narrow, winding forest road keeps going, following the course of the aptly named Stony River, tumbling over rocks and pebbles 50 feet below. But after less than a mile the road deteriorates into a primitive logging road; you'll want to return to MN 1 to continue on to the hamlet of Isabella. On the way you pass swaths of young aspen—early colonizers of clear-cut areas—and another national forest campground on the Little Isabella River.

Isabella consists of a gas station, a cafe (open only during the warm months), a canoe rental operation, and a tiny wooden chapel. The village's largest employer is the Isabella Ranger Station, which dispenses information on hiking, canoeing, and camping in this part of the national forest. Turn left on Forest Road 172 to reach two lakes with national forest campgrounds, good fishing, and hiking trails that give you a taste of the wilderness without leading you too far astray. Divide Lake, 5 miles east of Isabella, features a wheelchair accessible fishing pier and a 2.5-mile lakeside trail. Hogback Lake, 5 miles farther up FR 172, also has a barrier-free pier where you can fish for trout (state trout stamp required) or just watch loons and osprey fish for their dinner. Designed for the semi-tough, a 6-mile hiking trail explores the granite-rimmed shore of Hogback and several other lakes with primitive campsites.

MN 1 continues south, crossing the Laurentian Divide in 4.5 miles.

Following the crest of a mountain range that once extended from southwest Minnesota to the St. Lawrence River, this invisible line separates waters flowing north to Hudson Bay from those draining towards Lake Superior. It also separates the mature, upland forests of the interior from a more open, varied landscape of woods, shrub swamp, marsh, and conifer bog. Expanses of water-loving alder, willow, and cattails alternate with dense stands of black spruce, white cedar, and mountain ash. About 6 miles south of Isabella the highway descends into the valley of the Baptism River, bouncing over a series of forested ridges. You've just entered Finland State Forest, one of the largest tracts of state-owned woodlands in the Arrowhead.

Finland, as the name suggests, was founded by Finnish lumbermen who settled on the Baptism at the turn of the century. Their descendants sell stained glass, wood carvings, and felt purses and gloves at Old School Artisans, a gallery housed in a former schoolhouse next door to the Finland Co-op. The co-op, a gas station, and a restaurant across the river cater to motorists heading inland on MN 1, and to travelers on the North Shore State Trail, a snowmobile and horseback route that runs for 146 miles between Duluth and Grand Marais. St. Louis County Road 7 splits off to the left here, following the richly wooded valley of the Baptism's east branch 8 miles to George H. Crosby–Manitou State Park. The park, quiet and uncrowded on even the busiest summer weekends, has 24 miles of moderate-to-strenuous hiking trails in and around the steep gorge of the Manitou River.

From Finland, MN 1 drops rapidly towards Lake Superior, coasting over tilted lava flows formed a billion years ago, when the North American continent began to split along a great rift stretching to present-day Kansas. After about 3 miles the highway crosses the main channel of the Baptism River, framed by aspen and conifers as it rushes over granite boulders and logs carried downstream by spring floods. Eckbeck, a state forest campground on the left, offers an alternative to state parks along the North Shore, which can be tough to get into on summer and fall weekends.

Rounded hills cloaked in aspen, birch, and fir—an explosion of gold flecked with green in the fall—cascade down the last 3 miles to U.S. Highway 61. On clear days you can see the wavy outline of the Apostle Islands, 40 miles away. As the big lake rushes up, look for a pull-off on the right. The Superior Hiking Trail, one of the country's premier long-distance walking paths, crosses the road here and disappears into the woods. It's a 1.5-mile hike to the High Falls, a spectacular 50-foot cataract on the Baptism River. The drive ends on US 61 at Crystal Bay, the site of a feldspar quarry in the early 1900s. The Minnesota Mining & Manufacturing Company (3M) used the hard mineral to make sandpaper—still a leading product for the Twin Cities-based company.

The entrance to Tettegouche State Park, one of the largest and most popular parks on the North Shore, is a mile south on US 61. Seventeen miles of hiking and cross-country ski trails wind through a rugged, mini-Alpine landscape with four inland lakes, offering glorious views of the Sawtooth Mountains (see Drive 19) and Lake Superior. A short trail accessible from a parking lot off the highway follows the rocky shore of the lake out to Shovel Point, a 170-foot-tall mass of basaltic lava protruding into the lake like the prow of a great battleship.

18

The North Shore

U.S. Highway 61 from Duluth to the Canadian Border

General description: Hugging the rugged shoreline of Lake Superior for 150 miles, U.S. Highway 61 serves up some of the most spectacular scenery in the country—richly wooded hills, rock-bound bays and inlets, and the limitless horizon of the world's largest lake. The view from Split Rock Lighthouse and the nautical atmosphere of Duluth, Two Harbors, and Grand Marais will have you humming "The Wreck of the *Edmund Fitzgerald.*"

Special attractions: Stunning views of Lake Superior and the Sawtooth Mountains; Canal Park, Glensheen mansion, and Skyline Drive in Duluth; strolling, shopping, dining, and lake watching in Grand Marais and Two Harbors; spectacular waterfalls at Gooseberry, Cascade, Judge C. R. Magney, and Grand Portage State Parks; historic Split Rock Lighthouse; agate hunting and trout fishing at the mouths of numerous coldwater streams; Grand Portage National Monument, a reconstructed eighteenth century fur-trading post; hiking, rock-climbing, kayaking, fishing, cross-country and downhill skiing.

Drive route numbers: US 61; Cook County Road 17.

Location: Northeast Minnesota. The drive begins in Duluth and ends at Grand Portage State Park on the Canadian border.

Travel season: Traffic on US 61, always fairly heavy, can reach Excedrin levels on summer weekends. For a quieter drive—and a better chance of finding vacant campsites and resort/motel accommodation—consider driving the Shore during the week or in the fall. State parks remain open throughout the winter, but many resorts, bed and breakfasts, and tourist attractions are either closed or keep limited hours.

Camping: Duluth Tent & Trailer Camp; Gooseberry, Split Rock, Tettegouche, Temperance, Cascade, Judge C. R. Magney, and Grand Portage state parks; Burlington Bay Campground in Two Harbors; Tourist Recreation Park in Grand Marais.

Services: No shortage of gas stations, restaurants, and hotel accommodation in Duluth, Two Harbors, and Grand Marais. Most lakeshore villages boast at least a gas station and a convenience store. North of Grand Marais, amenities are fewer and farther between.

Nearby attractions: Jay Cooke State Park and the scenic St. Louis River gorge, south of Duluth on Minnesota Highway 210; walking on the Superior Hiking Trail in the Sawtooth Mountains; Isle Royale National Park, accessible by ferry from Grand Portage; sidetrips into Superior National Forest on MN 1 and the Sawbill and Gunflint Trails (see Drives 17 and 19); city of Thunder Bay and Sibley Provincial Park in Ontario.

Drive 18: The North Shore

U.S. Highway 61 from Duluth to the Canadian Border

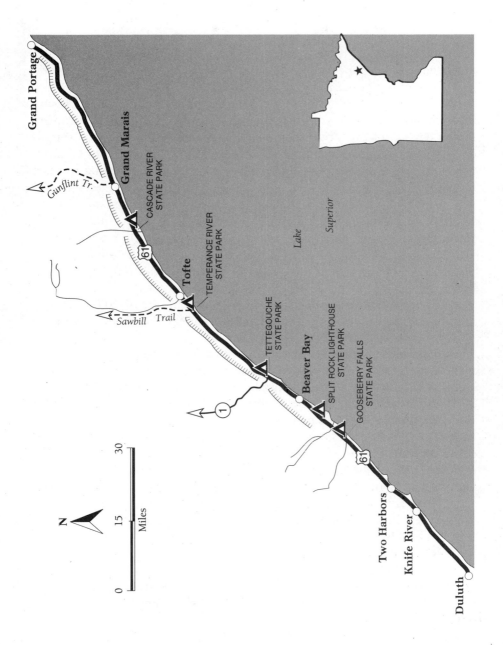

The drive

US 61 along the North Shore of Lake Superior is *the* drive to many Minnesotans. Clinging to the edge of the largest body of fresh water in the world, the highway offers phenomenal views reproduced in millions of postcards: 300-foot-high, wave-battered cliffs; waterfalls cascading down deep, mossy gorges; and Superior herself, sunny and azure or windswept and iron-gray, depending on her mood. From Duluth, an international port with a colorful, revitalized waterfront, US 61 pushes north for 150 miles, passing through villages and towns whose names—Grand Marais, Castle Danger, Beaver Bay—evoke two centuries of exploration and exploitation. Fur traders, lumbermen, fishermen, and lighthouse keepers wrested a living from the North Shore in the past; today the area supports a booming tourism industry.

You'll want to take your time on this drive. Experiencing many of the North Shore's scenic splendors, such as Split Rock lighthouse and Palisade Head, requires short detours off the highway. And historic towns such as Two Harbors and Grand Marais are tailor-made for strolling and lakeside picnicking. Plan on two or three days for the entire trip to the border and back.

The gateway to the North Shore is Duluth, a city of 86,000 that in moments of unbridled civic pride fancies itself the San Francisco of the Midwest. Like San Francisco, Duluth has hills, old brick buildings, gulls, and a photogenic bridge: the Aerial Lift, which rises dozens of times a day to make way for the iron ore carriers and ocean-going freighters that drive Duluth's economy. In Canal Park (take the Lake Avenue exit off Interstate 35) you can watch the parade of ships, share your lunch with the gulls, wander around upscale shops and eateries, and soak up the maritime ambience. The Canal Park Marine Museum features artifacts, ship models, and exhibits on the history of shipping on the lake, including the sinking of the ore carrier *Edmund Fitzgerald* in 1975, an event immortalized in a song by Gordon Lightfoot. A visitors center on Lake Place Drive (next door to the Canal Park Inn) can direct you to other nearby attractions, such as Park Point (great beaches) and Depot Square, a renovated railroad depot with four levels of living-history and arts exhibits.

Two alternate routes lead to the North Shore from downtown; to take the low road, follow I-35 or Superior Street north until you see the signs for US 61 and London Road. A stately boulevard lined with elm trees and expensive homes, London Road parallels the lakeshore for 6 miles, emerging onto the open lake at the mouth of the Lester River. One of the houses you pass is Glensheen, a 39-room Jacobean-style mansion built in 1905 by mining magnate Chester A. Congdon. Guided tours of the house and formal gardens make no mention of a celebrated murder at Glensheen in 1977; in a case right out of *Mystery!*, impatient heirs smothered 83-year-old Elisabeth Congdon to death with a satin pillow.

The high road, on scenic Skyline Drive, arcs across the roof of the city more than 500 feet above the lake. Follow Lake Street up a steep bluff, bear right on Mesaba Avenue, and look for the green and white Skyline Drive signs. They'll lead you along the ancient shoreline of Glacial Lake Duluth, through hillside neighborhoods with to-die-for views of the harbor, downtown, and the lake. An overlook at Hawk Ridge offers a spectacular vista of Superior stretching to the shadow of Wisconsin on the horizon. In the fall the skies above the ridge fill with migrating hawks, eagles, and peregrine falcons, wheeling on the thermals rising from the uplands. Looping back and forth over heavily wooded Amity Creek, Skyline Drive descends to US 61 at Lester Park.

The Lester River is the first of dozens of swift, cold streams that cascade down from the heavily forested hills rimming Superior. There's a tourist information booth just across the river, and a wonderful view of downtown Duluth from the beach—actually a shelf of glacier-polished rock covered with ruddy boulders and pebbles. There are no sandy beaches on the North Shore, which is just as well, because Superior is not kind to swimmers; the water stays a bracing 40 degrees F. all year. But the lake's red-

Ocean-going freighter passing beneath the Aerial Lift Bridge in Duluth.

pebble beaches are well trodden by rockhounds on the lookout for agates, Minnesota's official gemstone. You can try your luck here or at Brighton Beach, just ahead on the right; a gravel track descends to a rocky strand with shaded picnic tables.

The highway splits within half a mile of the river; turn right onto North Shore Scenic Drive, a section of US 61 that takes it slow and easy up to Two Harbors. For 14 miles the highway follows a relatively flat, winding course close to the lake, past bait shops, motels, and small family resorts. Wayside rests let you pull over to take in views of headlands thick with aspen and birch, rock-bound coves, and the bluffs of Wisconsin gradually receding to the south.

The hamlets that dot the shore, founded in the days when steamships and dogsleds were the only mode of travel, would surely fade from the map altogether if not for the custom of fishermen and tourists. In French River, founded by would-be copper miners in the 1840s (they never found the mother lode), a state fish hatchery raises salmon, splake, and three species of trout for the pleasure of anglers who can often be seen casting at the mouths of ice-cold streams. Knife River, another mining settlement that later switched to commercial fishing and logging, is renowned for its sports fishing and smoked Lake Superior trout. You can try this local delicacy, served with cheese, at Russ Kendall's Smokehouse, on the left just across the river.

A mile or two north of Knife River the road pulls back from the shore, paralleling the former route of the Duluth & Iron Range Railroad—now plied by scenic train tours between Duluth and Two Harbors—through dense stands of aspen and birch. After 6 miles the Scenic Drive rejoins the main highway; turn right by Lou's Fish 'n' Cheese House into Two Harbors, an old iron-ore and fishing port that makes the most of its picturesque setting on a point between two bays. A bustling commercial strip with several restaurants and a modest shopping mall runs through town on US 61. Turn right on Waterfront Drive to reach the historic waterfront on Agate Bay.

The *Edna G.*, the last coal-burning tugboat on the Great Lakes when she retired in 1981, lies moored in the lee of a mammoth ore dock, still used to load taconite from the Iron Range (see Drive 15) into 1,000-foot-long ore carriers. Nearby, a historical museum housed in a 1907 railroad depot has exhibits on railroads, lumbering, commercial fishing, and the Samuel P. Ely, a schooner-barge that foundered on the sharp rocks offshore in 1896. Multiple admission tickets, available at the museum, will also admit you to Minnesota's last operating lighthouse and the 3M/Dwan Museum, possibly the world's only museum dedicated to sandpaper.

About 4 miles north of Two Harbors a tunnel bores through Silver Cliff, a 300-foot high mass of basaltic rock that marks the beginning of the elemental North Shore. From here on the coastline grows craggier, the road more steeply rolling, the rivers that flow from the highlands more turbulent. Nowhere is the work of water on land more dramatic than at Gooseberry River State Park, 2 miles beyond the hamlet of Castle Danger. A deep gorge cut through red volcanic rock guides the Gooseberry River over two waterfalls and a series of cascades and rapids to the lake 250 feet below. It's no longer possible to park by the bridge, a recent replacement for the 1925 original; turn right into the park to reach Gooseberry's new interpretive center, a handsome structure of black granite, cedar, and redwood overlooking the gorge. Trails wind through groves of birch, fir, and cedar to both the Upper and Lower Falls and Agate Beach, a favorite spot for paddling and rock-scrambling.

Seven miles north of Gooseberry, the road curves around the rocky, foam-tossed crescent at the mouth of the Split Rock River and drops down a steep hill to the entrance to Split Rock Lighthouse State Park. Perched atop a 170-foot cliff, Split Rock epitomizes the wild, harsh beauty of the North Shore. From 1910 until 1969, when it was decommissioned, the lighthouse flashed a warning at 10-second intervals to ore boats criss-crossing the shipping lanes. A staircase spirals up to the top, where a seven-ton glass lens turns by clockwork on mercury bearings. For a classic view of the lighthouse, walk past the keeper's house down to a broad pebble beach, a launching spot for kayakers exploring islets and caves along the shore.

US 61 presses on to Beaver Bay and Silver Bay, the oldest and youngest towns, respectively, on the North Shore. In Beaver Bay, established in 1856 as a logging center, an Indian cemetery contains the bones of John Beargrease, a legendary musher who delivered mail along the Shore in the early 1900s. His feats of endurance are repeated each January in the John Beargrease Sled Dog Marathon, a 500-mile race from Duluth to Grand Portage and back. Silver Bay didn't exist until 1954, when the Reserve Mining Company built houses and a small commercial strip on the hill above the highway. Today the hulking taconite processing plant and ore docks by the lake are operated by the Northshore Mining Company.

The Lake Superior palisades, a line of cliffs formed from molten lava pouring from a continental rift a billion years ago, extend for 40 miles east of Silver Bay. One of the most imposing of these crags is Palisade Head, 2.5 miles up the shore. An extremely narrow road winds up and up through birch, fir, and spruce forest to the top, stripped of soil and polished by glacial ice. You'll want to keep small children in hand as you gaze at the lake and Shovel Point, another starkly eroded palisade to the north; it's a sheer drop of 348 feet to the water. According to local legend, Indian braves in canoes at the cliff's base once tested their strength by attempting to shoot arrows onto the top. You can walk out onto the tilted lava flows of Shovel

Point at Tettegouche State Park, 3 miles ahead near the junction with Minnesota Highway 1 (see Drive 17).

The tough basalts and rhyolites of the palisades presented a formidable obstacle to engineers constructing US 61 in 1923-24; walls of fractured rock tower beside the road as you hurtle down a steep, winding hill, then ascend another mount, its bald top mottled with lichen. The highway shadows the coastline for the next 25 miles, a thin black ribbon uncoiling around richly forested hills and rock-bound bays studded with tiny islands. More rivers—Little Marais, Manitou, Caribou, Two Island, Cross—boil down from the highlands to the left, carving out deep gorges and mini-waterfalls visible from the road. Small wooden signs advertise family-run resorts, motels, and bed and breakfasts tucked into the woods between the highway and the lake.

In Taconite Harbor, home of LTV Steel Mining Co., a 0.3-mile gravel road leads to an observation area where you can watch ore trains trundle down a gigantic trestle extending into the harbor. Evergreens bristle on the knobby backs of Gull and Bear Islands, a haven over the years for ships caught in Superior's violent storms. A lakeside monument near the village of Schroeder, 3 miles up the shore, commemorates one particular tempest in 1846. Just beyond the Cross River, look for a sign on the right pointing the way to Father Baraga's Cross. A Catholic priest named Frederic Baraga— the "Apostle of the Ojibwe"—landed his canoe here after a harrowing, storm-tossed crossing from Wisconsin. Giving thanks for his safe passage, Baraga nailed a small wooden cross to a tree. A granite cross now stands at the mouth of the river that the Ojibwe named *Tchibaiatigo-zibi* or "Wood of the soul river" in his honor. Footpaths wander along the river gorge with its series of short cascades.

Temperance River State Park is a mandatory stop on this section of the drive. Sure, there's a great view from the highway bridge of the river foaming through a dark-walled canyon to the lake; but wait until you see the gorge upstream, accessible from trails that leave from the parking lot. The Temperance—so named because there's no sandbar at its mouth—rips an impossibly narrow channel through bedrock, cascading over cedar-framed ledges and whirling through a series of cauldrons formed by the grinding action of pebbles caught in the maelstrom.

Between the resort village of Tofte (see Drive 19) and Cascade River State Park, US 61 rides high above the shore, following a prehistoric beach of Glacial Lake Duluth. Thick stands of birch and aspen slope down to the lake, parting momentarily to allow glimpses of the water where a creek or stream dashes under the road. Lutsen Resort, on the right 7 miles north of Tofte, is one of the most luxurious resorts on the North Shore. In business since 1885, the resort features a massive, many-gabled lodge, lakeside townhouses, a conference center, and golf on both a private course and nearby Superior National, a public course famed for its lake views. Just ahead, Cook County Road 36 heads for the hills around Eagle Ridge, one of the Midwest's premier downhill ski resorts. More than 50 runs plummet from the summits of Moose, Eagle, Mystery, and Ullr mountains to the valley below.

The road sidles up to Superior again at Cascade River State Park; after an exhilarating descent over a series of waterfalls—accessible from roadside trailheads—the river surges through a wide, boulder-strewn gorge into the lake. On the beach at Good Harbor Bay, 4 miles beyond the park entrance, you can hunt for nuggets of Thomsonite, a pinkish semi-precious stone that formed in gas bubbles trapped in the lava flows. It's 9 miles to Grand Marais, roller-coasting over immense, stony swells draped in evergreens and hardwoods. On one particular steep down-grade, a pull-off to the right offers a magnificent view of the Sawtooth Mountains, a series of basaltic knobs and ridges that have resisted millions of years of weathering.

The residents of Grand Marais, tongues firmly in cheek, call their town "the Scandinavian Riviera." Nestled at the foot of a high, forested ridge on the shore of a natural harbor, Grand Marais ("big marsh" in French) is easily the most photogenic community this side of Duluth. Drawn by its dramatic setting and the natural air conditioning provided by the lake, painters, writers, and artisans flock to the village during the summer, helping to double its year-round population of 1,200. Artist's Point, a wooded peninsula behind the Coast Guard Station, offers windblown serenity and a marvelous view of the Sawtooths, which burn with gold and crimson in the fall. The town has an art gallery, a community theater, eight motels, and several good restaurants specializing in grilled Superior lake trout and herring. The tourist information center is on Broadway, next to City Hall.

Confined to a narrow band of undulating woodland between the Sawtooths and the lake, US 61 continues north across the Devil Track and Kodunce Rivers into Grand Portage State Forest. Dense stands of birch, aspen, balsam fir, and white spruce sweep down from the hills as you approach the Brule River and Judge C. R. Magney State Park. From the bridge, a half-mile path ascends the river gorge to a riverside picnic area on the site of a Depression-era work camp. Farther upstream the Brule rages through mysterious Devil's Kettle Falls; part of the river plunges into a huge pothole and, according to local legend, disappears forever. Ahead on the right is Naniboujou Lodge, built in 1929 as a private club by a group of Jazz Age investors that included Babe Ruth, boxer Jack Dempsey, and writer Ring Lardner. The Lodge stills serves afternoon tea (3-5 P.M.) and dinner in the Great Hall, decorated with striking, colorful designs drawn from Indian mythology.

The Sawtooths form a suitably alpine backdrop for Hovland, a hamlet named after a village in Norway. The road descends a steep hill, clambers around the shoulder of a tall peak draped in evergreens, then curves around Big Bay, guarded by naked sentinels of basaltic lava. More vistas of forested scarps, scalloped shoreline, and distant islands open up as the highway enters the Grand Portage Indian Reservation, home to 400 Ojibwe who earn a living from fishing, traditional crafts, and casino operations. Topping a rise after a long uphill climb, US 61 drops down to Grand Portage, headquarters of the reservation and the northernmost settlement on the North Shore.

Half a mile past Grand Portage Lodge and Casino, turn right on Cook County Road 17. The road spirals down to the richly wooded shore of Grand Portage Bay, cradled by high hills that taper to a distinctively shaped promontory known as Hat Point. A gnarled white cedar believed to be 400 years old clings to the eastern shore of the point. The Witch Tree, held in reverence by the Ojibwe, isn't visible from the road; the casino offers guided tours to the site during the summer.

Two centuries ago the Witch Tree was a welcome sight to fur traders arriving at Grand Portage after months of arduous travel by land and water. From 1784 to 1803 the Scottish North West Company maintained a fur-trading post here, the center of an empire that stretched 3,000 miles from Montreal to Lake Athabaska in the Canadian Northwest. It was built on the backs of *voyageurs*—small, wiry men from Montreal who could paddle a birchbark canoe and tote 250-pound packs for 14 hours a day. Each spring, *voyageurs* who had spent the winter in the wilderness trading with Indians would make their way east to swap their beaver pelts for goods brought by canoe from Montreal. Most of the journey could be accomplished by canoe, via the border lakes, but over the last 9 miles the *voyageurs* would have to slog over the *grand portage* ("great carrying place"), a foot trail around treacherous waterfalls and rapids.

At Grand Portage National Monument, just ahead on the right, you can almost hear the *voyageurs* singing and swearing as they trot the last few yards to their goal. A rebuilt stockade of white-cedar surrounds faithful replicas of the post's Great Hall, kitchen, and lookout tower. Inside the Hall, with its two cavernous fireplaces and long table laid with antique china, costumed guides act as though it's still 1797 and they've got important business to conduct over Madeira and cigars. To get an idea of what the place was like in full swing, visit on the second week in August, when Ojibwe from the area and latter-day voyageurs convene for an annual Rendezvous Days/Pow Wow celebration. A wooden dock on the lakeshore is the departure point for ferry trips to Isle Royale National Park, 22 miles offshore. Black bears, moose, and wolves inhabit this roadless wilderness, a mecca for backpackers and campers.

The village of Grand Portage, up the hill on Cook County Road 73, consists of a tribal government building, a few wood-frame houses and the

The Union Jack still flies outside the Great Hall at Grand Portage National Monument.

Grand Portage Trading Post, a combination post office, convenience store, and gas station. Paralleling the Grand Portage trail—still open for hiking and cross-country skiing—the road intersects US 61 in less than 0.25 mile.

The North Shore saves the best for last; the final 6 miles to the border offer the most spectacular scenery of the entire drive. Vistas of the Sawtooths and Teal Lake—round and ringed by hills, like a flooded volcanic crater— appear to the left as the road scales the forested slopes of Mount Josephine. Then you're barreling downhill through towering road cuts shot through with veins of quartz, hundreds of feet above Lake Superior. Two waysides afford glorious views of Pigeon Point and the Susie Islands, a small archipelago that falls just within U.S. waters. US 61 flattens out and becomes a divided highway as you approach the Canadian border, marked by a row of customs booths. Just as you're beginning to think about declaring your fruits and vegetables, a left turn provides an escape route into Grand Portage State Park. One of Minnesota's newest state preserves, the park contains the highest waterfall in the state, the High Falls of the Pigeon River. After a short hike to the 70-foot cascade, you'll understand why those *voyageurs* took the easy way out, shouldering their canoes down to Grand Portage.

The drive ends here, unless you're continuing to Thunder Bay, Ontario, 40 miles farther up the shore. Otherwise, turn around and head downshore. Drive 19, which can easily be done in reverse, emerges onto US 61 at Grand Marais.

19

The Sawbill Trail
*Tofte to Grand Marais through
the Laurentian Highlands*

General description: Rising rapidly from the Lake Superior shore into the Laurentian Highlands, this 56-mile circuit arcs through a rugged landscape of forests, lakes, wetlands, and streams, passing the highest point in the state. Beautiful lakeside campgrounds and trails suitable for hiking, mountain biking, cross-country skiing, and snowmobiling abound along the famed Sawbill and Gunflint Trails. Mostly gravel but well-maintained, the route ends in the picturesque resort town of Grand Marais.

Special attractions: Views of the Sawtooth Mountains, lakes, rivers, wetlands, and sharply rolling forest in a wilderness setting; commercial fishing museum in Tofte; trail to Eagle Mountain, highest point in Minnesota; canoeing, fishing, mountain biking, cross-country skiing, snowmobiling, and camping in the Superior National Forest; opportunity to see bald eagles, ospreys, moose, beavers, and other wildlife; spectacular Lake Superior overlook at Pincushion Mountain near Grand Marais.

Drive route numbers: Cook County Roads 2 (the Sawbill Trail), 12 (the Gunflint Trail), 8, 27; Superior National Forest Road 170.

Location: Northeast Minnesota. The drive begins in the resort village of Tofte on the shore of Lake Superior and ends in Grand Marais, 30 miles farther up the shore.

Travel season: Year-round, but portions of the route may demand four-wheel drive after a heavy snowfall or in the early spring. Wildflowers show their best in May and June, while prime blueberry-picking season is July to August.

Camping: Temperance River State Park, just south of Tofte on U.S. Highway 61; Cascade River State Park near Grand Marais; national forest campgrounds at Temperance River and Baker, Crescent, and Two Island lakes; Tourist Recreation Park in Grand Marais.

Services: Restaurants, gas, and resort/motel accommodation in Tofte and Grand Marais; nothing at all in between.

Nearby attractions: Dramatic river gorges and waterfalls at Temperance River and Cascade River state parks; beachcombing for Thomsonite at Good Harbor Bay (see Drive 18); downhill skiing at Lutsen Mountains; long-distance hiking and canoe routes into the Boundary Waters Canoe Area Wilderness; Artist's Point, fresh seafood, and shopping in Grand Marais; afternoon tea in the Great Hall at Naniboujou Lodge.

Drive 19: The Sawbill Trail
Tofte to Grand Marais through the Laurentian Highlands

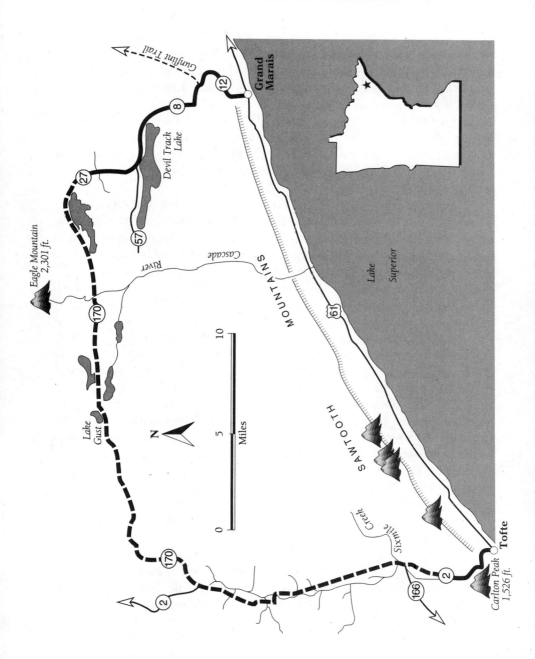

The drive

A vast hinterland of rugged hills, granite-rimmed lakes, and turbulent streams stretches inland from the North Shore of Lake Superior. Black bears, moose, and timber wolves live here, and outdoor enthusiasts come to visit, drawn by the incredible beauty of a land that has been barely touched by modern civilization. This 56-mile route, ideal for a half-day outing, follows the Sawbill Trail deep into the Laurentian Highlands, then swings east, crossing the wild Temperance River several times and skirting dozens of pristine lakes and wetlands in Superior National Forest. Virtually every lake has a boat or canoe access, and waysides provide access to hiking, cross-country ski, snowmobile, and horseback trails. The drive returns to the North Shore on the Gunflint Trail, offering splendid vistas of Lake Superior and the town of Grand Marais.

The drive begins in Tofte, a lakeside village founded in 1896 by settlers from Norway. At one time the local economy revolved around fishing and logging, but a disastrous forest fire claimed the sawmill in 1910, and fishing declined in the 1930s. Today the scattered residents of Tofte make a living from tourists streaming up US 61 (see Drive 18). There's a gas station, a bakery and deli, a Holiday Express motel, and Bluefin Bay Resort, a plush complex perched on the rocky shore. A bright red, wood-frame building by the roadside doubles as a visitor center and commercial fishing museum. A restored Mackinaw fishing boat, equipment displays, and the taped recollections of early residents recall the days when fishermen set out daily to snare Lake Superior trout and herring for sale in Duluth. For Superior National Forest trail guides and maps, stop in at the Tofte Ranger Station, on the left just south of the village.

The Sawbill Trail (Cook County Road 2) is clearly marked off US 61. The road climbs rapidly, turning sharply to the left and winding through stands of young birch and aspen—regrowth after that 1910 forest fire. More birch and aspen interspersed with fir, spruce, and pine drape the rounded crowns of hills rising in the distance. These are the Sawtooths, the result of selective erosion of lava flows that poured from a continental rift a billion years ago. Only the hardest knobs and ridges of basaltic rock have resisted eons of weathering by water, wind, and ice.

One of those survivors is Carlton Peak, rearing up out of the forest to the left. An outcrop of iron-tough anorthosite named after an early mining entrepreneur, the mountain soars 924 feet above Lake Superior. Yes, the view from the top is breathtaking, but you have to sweat to enjoy it; a wayside sign indicates a 1.5-mile foot path that grows progressively steeper with each step. The path is part of the Superior Hiking Trail, a long-distance route from Two Harbors to Hovland that *Backpacker* magazine has lauded

Wooden bridge over the Temperance River on Maple Leaf Drive,
a forest road branching off the Sawbill Trail.

as one of the 10 best hiking trails in the country.

In 2 miles, CR 2 turns to gravel and enters the broad valley of the Temperance River, one of the many swift, cool streams that rush to Lake Superior along the North Shore. Mixed stands of evergreens, birch, and aspen—a variegated quilt of dark green and saffron in the fall—cascade down 400-foot bluffs on both sides of the road. Riding a terrace above the valley floor, the road steadily rises into thickly wooded uplands, the eroded core of a mountain range that once towered as high as the Rocky Mountains. More than 2.6 billion years later, the Laurentians have been reduced to a granite ridge separating the Lake Superior and Hudson Bay watersheds. After 3 miles on the gravel, Maple Leaf Drive (Forest Road 166) splits off to the left. Pull off and walk out onto a one-lane, wooden bridge for a view of the Temperance, tumbling darkly over rock ledges and boulders. Phalanxes of fir, spruce, and cedar press up to the high riverbank, ripped raw by the passage of meltwater in the spring.

The North Shore State Trail, a snowmobile and horseback route that runs for 146 miles between Duluth and Grand Marais, crosses the road just ahead. A parking lot provides access to this trail and a cross-country ski trailhead on the far side of Sixmile Creek, a tributary of the Temperance.

The Sawbill Trail (sawbill is a local nickname for a merganser, by the way), rolls on through undulating spruce, aspen, and jack pine forest, spanning three more rock-bottomed creeks and passing Temperance River Campground, a U.S. Forest Service facility with nine riverside campsites. Fishing for brook trout lurking in pools and under rock ledges is the main attraction here. The terrain becomes noticeably hillier and wilder north of the campground; crossing the Temperance, the road clambers over a series of ridges cloaked in almost impenetrable stands of fir and spruce. This section was widened and straightened in 1996, but enough sweeping bends remain to keep you alert. Ditches cavernous enough to swallow a tank straddle the steeply cambered roadbed.

A sign near the junction with Superior National Forest Road 170 marks the site of a Civilian Conservation Corps (CCC) camp, home to two hundred men from 1933 to 1940. Given room and board and paid $30 a month, men who would otherwise be unemployed built roads and bridges and planted pine seedlings that stand 50- to 60-feet tall today. The Sawbill Lake camp is an empty forest glade now, its concrete foundations obscured by undergrowth and a thick mat of pine needles.

Turn right on FR 170, a gravel road that follows an abandoned railbed plied by logging trains until the late 1930s. A large swamp, part marsh and part conifer bog, yawns on the left. Belying their small stature, many of the black spruce ringing the marsh are more than one hundred years old; soggy, acidic soil slows their growth to a crawl. In the next 5 miles more marshes and tamarack-black spruce bogs appear, sunlit oases in a jungle of spruce, fir, jack pine, and mountain ash. Twice more the road crosses the Temperance, much narrower now and overhung with willow and speckled alder.

Marsh Lake is the first in a chain of deep, mountain-rimmed lakes that FR 170 passes as it meanders eastward, following the grain of the Laurentians more than a thousand feet above Lake Superior. Marsh Lake is aptly named: wedges of cattails and sedges thrust out from the near shore. On the opposite side, a dark band of spruce runs along the water's edge at the foot of a high, rounded bluff. A quarter-mile ahead on the left, a side road leads to Baker Lake, a portal into the 1.1 million-acre Boundary Waters Canoe Area Wilderness (BWCA). Permits (available at U.S. Forest Service ranger stations and many outfitters) are required for overnight stays in the Boundary Waters during the summer months.

The parade of clean, beautiful, completely undeveloped lakes continues for 8 miles as FR 170 winds through the forest, following the path of Ice Age glaciers that gouged depressions into the bedrock. Close by the shore of Nelson Lake, light filters through a scrim of birch and aspen, revealing the crest of a high ridge cloaked in birch, aspen, and evergreens. Islands clad in pine, cedar, and spruce dot the brilliant surface of Crescent Lake, renowned for its muskie, walleye, and northern pike fishing; a turnoff leads to a boat

Cattails, reeds, and sedges thrive along the shore of Marsh Lake on Superior National Forest Road 170.

ramp and a national forest campground with waterfront sites and a handicapped-accessible fishing pier. At Gust Lake, 6 miles farther on the left, a long spit juts out into the water, spruce and fir clinging to its mottled granite spine.

Eagle Mountain, the highest point in the state, can be reached on foot from a trailhead half a mile beyond the Cascade River, serene and broad here as it weaves through reed beds and alder thickets. A small parking lot with a vault toilet and water pump serves as base camp for the assault on the mountain top, 2,301 feet above sea level. Actually, the 3.5-mile path through dense jack pine, aspen, and birch forest and over three beaver streams isn't that difficult, although protruding rocks and tree roots can make the going tricky. You'll be rewarded with an amazing panorama of forested hills and lakes in the national forest and BWCA.

The route passes two more lakes, barely visible through the trees, before coming to a T-junction in about 5 miles. Turn right on Cook County Road 27, passing Two Island Lake Campground on the right. Frequented by anglers in pursuit of walleye, small-mouth bass, and northern, the campground has a boat launch and thirty-eight campsites with picnic tables and fire grates. Waves of aspen, fir, birch, and spruce roll by as CR 27 heads south towards Lake Superior; here and there big red and white pines—mere saplings when the logging companies came through eight or ninety years ago—poke their bottle-brush crowns above the forest canopy.

After about 5 miles, bear left onto Cook County Road 8. You're back on asphalt now, hugging the shore of Devil Track Lake, one of the largest lakes on the North Shore. A 20-mile mountain bike and snowmobile trail circumnavigates the lake, following CR 8 and Cook County Road 57 west along the northern shore and then striking into the bush on old logging roads. For the first time in 50 miles, roadside mailboxes reveal the presence of lake homes secreted behind a screen of aspen, fir, and spruce. Rounding the eastern end of the lake, CR 8 crosses the Devil Track River (named for the violent rapids and waterfalls that roil its surface downstream) and makes a sharp left turn, meeting Cook County Road 12 in about a mile. CR 12 is better known as the Gunflint Trail, another CCC-built route that arcs for 60 miles through the Superior National Forest and the BWCA.

Turn right and check your brakes; the remaining 4.5 miles of the drive flash by quickly as the Gunflint spirals downward to the North Shore at Grand Marais. You can savor the view at the Pincushion Mountain overlook, down a gravel road to the left. Some 500 feet below, sailboats bob at anchor in the marina at Grand Marais. Beyond the breakwater and Artist's Point, Lake Superior stretches out to a perfectly even horizon, broken only by the occasional passage of an ore freighter. Hiking, mountain biking, and cross-country ski trails loop around the mountain, a national forest recreation area. For more outstanding views of the lake and the Sawtooth Mountains, walk along the Superior Hiking Trail, which crosses the parking lot en route to Sawtooth Bluff, 2 miles to the south.

CR 12 continues to Grand Marais, tacking across the forested hillside in great S curves. The Gunflint Trail, and the drive, end on the North Shore at US 61. For a description of Grand Marais and nearby attractions such as Cascade River State Park, Lutsen Mountains, and Naniboujou Lodge, see Drive 18.

20

The St. Croix River Valley
Hastings–Stillwater–Taylors Falls

General description: A National Scenic Riverway, the lower St. Croix River winds along the Minnesota-Wisconsin border, hemmed in by wooded bluffs and rocky escarpments. This drive rambles along the alternately wild and pastoral St. Croix for 60 miles, visiting three state parks and picturesque river towns such as Hastings, Afton, Stillwater, and Taylors Falls.

Special attractions: Wonderful views of the forested bluffs and islands of the St. Croix River; historic river towns of Hastings, Afton, Stillwater, Marine-on-St. Croix, and Taylors Falls; Northern Vineyards and Alexis Bailly wineries; dramatic Dalles of the St. Croix and glacial potholes at Interstate State Park; hiking, canoeing, cross-country skiing, and birdwatching at three state parks and Carpenter-St. Croix Valley Nature Center; antique shopping, riverside picnicking.

Drive route numbers: U.S. Highways 61, 10; Minnesota Highway 95; Washington County Road 21.

Location: Eastern Minnesota. The drive begins in Hastings southeast of the Twin Cities and ends at Taylors Falls on the St. Croix River.

Travel season: Year-round. Autumn color peaks from late September to mid-October, but so do the crowds in Stillwater and Taylors Falls. Later winter and spring—prime time for eagle and osprey watching on the river—are considerably less hectic.

Camping: Greenwood Campground, south of Hastings off US 61; Golden Acres RV Park, north of Stillwater on Partridge Road; William O'Brien State Park near Marine-on-St. Croix; Interstate State Park in Taylors Falls; Wildwood Park, west of Taylors Falls on U.S. Highway 8.

Services: No shortage of gas stations, restaurants, and motel/bed and breakfast accommodations in Hastings and Stillwater. Bed and breakfasts and more limited dining opportunities in Afton, Marine-on-St. Croix, and Taylors Falls.

Nearby attractions: Swedish cuisine and crafts in Lindstrom, west of Taylors Falls on US 8; Wild Mountain Water Park and Alpine Slides, north of Taylors Falls on Chisago County Road 16; North West Company Fur Post, a reconstructed nineteenth century trading post near Pine City; Carlos Avery Wildlife Area, west of Lindstrom; biking on the Cannon Valley Trail between Cannon Falls and Red Wing (see Drive 1).

Drive 20: The St. Croix River Valley
Hastings–Stillwater–Taylors Falls

The drive

The beauty of the St. Croix Valley has enthralled visitors for hundreds of years. In *Bring Warm Clothes*, a collection of historical letters and photos by Peg Meier, George Nelson recalls his youth as a clerk in the St. Croix fur trade during the early 1800s:

> ... *Whenever this country becomes settled how delightfully will the inhabitants pass their time. There is no place perhaps on this globe where nature has displayed & diversified land & water as here. I always felt as if invited to settle down & admire the beautiful views with a sort of joyful thankfulness for having been led to them.* ...

A land of high, rolling bluffs and deeply wooded ravines watered by small streams, the valley was one of the first areas of Minnesota to be settled. Yankee lumbermen set up camp here in the 1840s, founding river towns such as Taylors Falls, Marine-on-St. Croix, and Stillwater. With their nineteenth century buildings converted into antique shops, restaurants, and bed and breakfasts, those towns still exude character and charm. And their inhabitants—joined by large numbers of daytrippers from the Twin Cities—do indeed pass the time delightfully, on land and water.

The Lower St. Croix, a federally protected wild and scenic river, is unpolluted and easily navigable by canoes and powerboats. Three state parks attract hikers, cross-country skiers, mountain bikers, fishermen, and rock climbers. The valley even boasts local wines made from cold-hardy grapes. Plan on at least half a day, preferably a full day, for this 60-mile drive up the valley to Taylors Falls and the dramatic Dalles of the St. Croix.

The drive begins in Hastings, a town of 16,000 on the Mississippi River southeast of the Twin Cities. Only thirty minutes from St. Paul on US 61, Hastings retains a distinct identity as one of the state's oldest communities. Architectural treasures in the historic district include City Hall, an imposing structure that blends Gothic, French Renaissance, and neoclassical styles; and the LeDuc-Simmons Mansion, the Gothic Revival home of a Civil War general. Second Street, lined with brick and limestone storefronts and warehouses, has remained virtually unchanged since 1895. A self-guided walking tour of the town is available from the Chamber of Commerce on the corner of Third Street and Vermilion (US 61). On the waterfront you can watch barges, cabin cruisers, and sailboats plying the broad Mississippi, the setting for a boat parade, water-ski show, hot air-balloon lift, and other events during Rivertown Days on the third weekend in July.

South of town, off US 61 (turn right on 180th Street), Alexis Bailly Vineyard produces award-winning vintages from vines that must be buried in the winter to survive 40-below temperatures. Winemaker Nan Bailly is a descendant of Alexis Bailly, one of the four original founders of Hastings.

A bright blue steel truss bridge leads the way out of Hastings on US 61. At the top of the hill, turn right on U.S. Highway 10, the road to Prescott, Wisconsin. The highway rides along the blufftop for 2.5 miles, passing an apple orchard and grand views of the Mississippi River and downtown Hastings. The St. Croix River joins the Mississippi at Prescott; just before US 10 begins its descent to the water, turn left on Washington County Road 21 (the St. Croix Trail). Scaling the precipitous, thickly wooded bluff in a series of hairpin turns, the road quickly emerges into rolling, lightly wooded cropland. Stone pillars flanked by pines mark the entrance to Carpenter–St. Croix Valley Nature Center, a former country estate with 15 miles of hiking and snowshoe trails through blufftop prairie, wooded ravines, and bottomland forest. Great blue herons, bald eagles, and red-tailed hawks frequent the nature center.

CR 21, originally a military road used to supply Fort Snelling in St. Paul, parallels the St. Croix River for the next 10 miles, roller coasting over open hills and intimate, wooded valleys. To the right, cropland dotted with scattered houses on the ex-urban fringe slopes down to the St. Croix, flowing unseen at the foot of 150-foot bluffs. Corn silos gleam atop wooded bluffs on the Wisconsin side of the river. Apples, strawberries, and raspberries thrive in the relatively mild climate of the valley, drinking up the sun on south-facing slopes; keep your eyes peeled for roadside stands and signs showing the way to apple orchards and U-pick berry farms. The countryside gradually becomes more wooded as you approach Afton State Park, at the crest of a hill with a sweeping view of the valley and Wisconsin bluffs. In the distance, on the far side of a golf course, you can see the chair lifts of Afton Alps, a downhill ski area.

The terrain of Afton State Park can hardly be called alpine, but this patch of wildness on the edge of the metro area does offer fetching views from its 18 miles of hiking and cross-country ski trails. Narrow ravines cloaked in oak, aspen, birch, and cherry drop 300 feet to the river from uplands that are being restored to native prairie. Most of the park is accessible only on foot, but an interpretive center and blufftop picnic area are located near the main parking lot. To enter the park, turn right on Washington County Road 20.

The roller coaster keeps going on CR 21, swooping down into the deeply shaded defile of Trout Brook, then climbing back up into rolling meadows and woodland. After 2 miles, just past a hilltop farmstead with a picture-postcard red barn, the road descends a long hill, curving between towering walls of fractured limestone. The village of Afton, named after a poem by Robert Burns, nestles at the bottom of the hill.

It's obvious why the place is a favorite stop for bicyclists and classic car collectors touring the St. Croix Valley; Afton evokes a simpler, more sedate era with its shady main street lined with white wood-frame buildings. The Afton House Inn, a two-story clapboard structure on the right, was built in 1867; a clothing store across the street occupies an 1841 house built by an Irish lumberman. Other old buildings house a tiny post office, an ice cream parlor, and Lerk's Bar, renowned for its hamburgers. Walk down to the village marina (directly behind the Afton Inn) for a great view of the river, hemmed in by high forested bluffs.

The St. Croix Trail joins Minnesota Highway 95 in Afton. The riverbank between here and Stillwater, 12 miles upstream, is cluttered by residential and commercial development creeping out from the metro core. But north of Interstate 94, sweeping vistas of Lake St. Croix make up for the incipient sprawl. Formed by a natural dam of sand and silt at the mouth of the St. Croix, this wide bulge in the river gives cabin cruisers, sailboats, and stern-wheeling riverboats room to roam. During the summer hundreds of pleasure craft tie up at the Bayport Marina, a large complex with a restaurant, gas dock, tennis court, and swimming pool. The town of Bayport, 1.5 miles farther on, is dominated by a sprawling Andersen Windows factory and the tall smokestack of Northern State Power's Alen S. King Plant in nearby Oak Park Heights.

Blufftop panorama of Stillwater and the frozen St. Croix River.

Another 2 miles takes you around sheer limestone cliffs into Stillwater, the hub of the St. Croix River Valley. Stillwater—the name refers to the tranquil waters of Lake St. Croix—teems with tourists on summer weekends. For your sanity, find a place to park and explore this grand old lumber town on foot. The wealth of King Pine built the more than thirty brick and limestone buildings that spill down the bluff to the waterfront, including the Freight House (1833), Warden's House (1853), and the Washington County Courthouse (1867-70). Staples Mill, a towering edifice of limestone and corrugated iron at the north end of Main Street, has been converted into a three-story antique mall. Northern Vineyards Winery, a cooperative run by area grape growers, occupies space on the ground floor, next door to an espresso bar and ice cream shop.

Lowell Park on the riverfront, with a view of the town's aerial lift bridge and Wisconsin's wooded bluffs across the river, is a popular picnic spot. A long flight of stone steps behind Vittorio's Restaurant leads up to a blufftop panorama of the historic district and the river coiling away to the northeast.

Passing the Minnesota Zephyr depot on the right—the departure point for 1940s-style train tours of the valley—MN 95 scales a forested bluff, scraping past deep cuts blasted into the limestone hillside. A wayside rest on the right offers a spectacular view of the Stillwater marina and Lake St. Croix, dotted with wooded islands at its northern end. Great blue herons nest in the treetops in the early spring, taking flight above the recently thawed river to hunt for fish. Nearby is the St. Croix boomsite, a clearinghouse for millions of pine logs in the late 1800s. Logs cut along the Upper St. Croix and its tributaries were sorted and clumped together in rafts for the journey to sawmills in Stillwater and towns farther downstream.

North of this point the St. Croix becomes the domain of canoeists and kayakers. Cabin cruisers and sailboats turn around, unable to negotiate a narrow channel constricted further by sandbars, islands, and sloughs. For a glimpse of this younger, thinner St. Croix, turn right on a gravel road at the top of the hill; the Arcola Trail winds past expensive homes, under a wooden railroad trestle, and along the densely wooded riverbank before rejoining the highway in 4 miles. Otherwise, stay on MN 95 as it veers away from the river through sharply rolling woodland and pasture. Square Lake County Park, 2 miles up the hill on Washington County Road 59, has a swimming beach and a picnic area sloping down to the lake. Scuba divers from the Twin Cities frequent Square Lake's deep, limpid waters on weekends.

Swinging back toward the river, the highway rises and dips over the feet of bluffs cloaked in maple, oak, pine, and fir. Turn right on Washington County Road 7 (Judd Street); a narrow, wooded lane winds past riverside homes and over a brook into Marine-on-St. Croix, a village that rivals Afton in bucolic charm. The Marine-on-St. Croix General Store and Village Hall, modeled on the elegantly simple wood-frame buildings of New England, anchor the oldest civilian community in the state. Minnesota's first commercial sawmill operated here from 1839 to 1885, powered by the rushing waters of Marine Falls. Today the falls still tumble into the woods behind Village Hall, but the mill has crumbled into a pile of moss-covered rubble. A two-minute walk through the woods leads to an overlook above the mill site and the banks of the St. Croix. Up the street, an outdoor cafe serves homemade soups, sandwiches, and desserts.

MN 95 continues north through William O'Brien State Park, a rolling expanse of maple-basswood-oak forest, lakes, marshes, and meadows. Mr. O'Brien was an ex-lumberman who bought much of the cutover land once owned by the logging companies; in 1945 a bequest of 180 acres from his daughter became the nucleus of a park that now covers over 1,300 acres. Eleven miles of hiking and cross-country ski trails loop through uplands and along the river. Canoes can be rented for the short paddle out to Greenberg Island, a haven for mink, beaver, deer, fox, songbirds, and other wildlife. A mile beyond the park entrance you pass a modest wood-frame building on the right: Crabtree's Kitchen, a culinary institution on the St. Croix since 1949. The restaurant's December special is lutefisk (cod cured in lye) with Swedish meatballs and sausage; on weekends, horse-drawn sleigh rides aid the digestion.

The land becomes progressively more rural as MN 95 dips and rolls through lush woodland and pasture into Chisago County. Barns replace scattered houses on the urban fringe, and sheep and dairy cattle graze by the roadside. This area has become popular with ex-urbanites pursuing alternative lifestyles. After the highway makes a sharp right turn towards Taylors Falls, you'll see an unusual crop sprouting from a patch of native prairie: giant wooden and metal sculptures. Franconia Sculpture Park, billed as "the only high-profile, work/residence outdoor sculpture park in the Midwest," is open daily from March through November.

The precipitous descent into Taylors Falls on MN 95/U.S. Highway 8 is one of the most exhilarating stretches of pavement in the state. As the road curls around a sheer sandstone cliff, a magnificent vista of the St. Croix and soaring bluffs draped in oak, maple, fir, and tall red pine opens up to the right. A shallow pull-off to the right offers an excellent view of the St. Croix Dalles, a deep, ruddy canyon gouged out by an immense torrent of meltwater at the end of the last Ice Age. Rock climbers can often be seen inching their way up the 200-foot basalt cliffs; on summer weekends kayaks and canoes dot the aquamarine waters below. The Dalles are protected from development by state parkland on both sides of the river. On the Minnesota side of Interstate State Park, a self-guided interpretive trail loops around potholes, giant cauldrons, and other geologic oddities carved into rock ledges high above the river. Turn

The Dalles of the St. Croix River at Taylors Falls.

right at the bottom of the hill to reach the trailhead and an interpretive center. Riverboat tours of the Dalles leave from a dock just below the bridge.

Lumbermen from New England founded Taylors Falls in the 1840s, harnessing their sawmills to falls which are now covered by a dam. Many buildings remain from the village's golden age, including the 1884 county jail, now a bed and breakfast, and the William H. C. Folsom House, a masterpiece of Greek Revival architecture built in 1855. The Folsom House, open for tours from late May to mid-October, is located in the Angel Hill historic district, a slice of New England perched atop a high wooded bluff behind the town.

The drive ends here. Continue over the bridge to reach St. Croix Falls, Wisconsin and the eastern unit of Interstate State Park. US 8 to Interstate 35 via Lindstrom is the most direct route back to the Twin Cities.

21

The Grand Round
Minneapolis to St. Paul via the Chain of Lakes and Minnehaha Parkway

General description: A 20-mile promenade of parklands and historic neighborhoods in Minneapolis and St. Paul. The route traces the shores of four lakes and the wooded banks of Minnehaha Creek and the Mississippi River before making a grand entrance into downtown St. Paul on Summit Avenue.

Special attractions: Vistas of Minneapolis's Chain of Lakes, the Mississippi River gorge, and both downtowns; Guthrie Theater, Walker Art Center, and Minneapolis Sculpture Garden; elegant turn-of-the-century mansions on Mount Curve Avenue in Minneapolis and Summit Avenue in St. Paul; Lake Harriet Bandstand, Rose Garden, and streetcar ride; swimming beach at Lake Nokomis; Minnehaha Falls and Stevens House Museum at Minnehaha Park; walking, biking, in-line skating, wind surfing, people watching.

Drive route numbers: Kenwood Parkway, Minnehaha Parkway, and parkways around Lake of the Isles, Lake Calhoun and Lake Harriet in Minneapolis; West River Parkway and Mississippi River Boulevard; Mount Curve, Summit Avenue, and other residential streets.

Location: Central cities of Minneapolis and St. Paul. The drive begins at the Guthrie Theater near downtown Minneapolis and ends at the St. Paul Cathedral on Summit Avenue.

Travel season: All-year. Leaf color peaks in early to mid-October. You'll enjoy better views of Minnehaha Creek and the Mississippi—and lighter traffic on the parkways—after the leaves have fallen. Lakes and streams freeze over in the winter, creating a dramatic arctic landscape in the midst of the city.

Camping: No campgrounds on this drive.

Services: Hotel accommodation is concentrated in both downtowns. For a quick bite to eat on the drive, try Lake Street in Uptown, 44th and Sheridan in Linden Hills, or Grand Avenue a block south of Summit. The Mel-o-Glaze Bakery at the corner of Minnehaha Parkway and 28th Avenue sells doughnuts and pastries, and espresso on weekends.

Nearby attractions: St. Anthony Falls and historic riverfront north of downtown; major-league baseball and football at the Hubert H. Humphrey Metrodome; State Capitol, Minnesota History Center, Minnesota Science Museum, and Children's Museum in downtown St. Paul; restored frontier post and hiking trails at Fort Snelling State Park; top-notch shopping and dining in downtown Minneapolis, Uptown, and along Grand Avenue in St. Paul.

Drive 21: The Grand Round

Minneapolis to St. Paul via the Chain of Lakes and Minnehaha Parkway

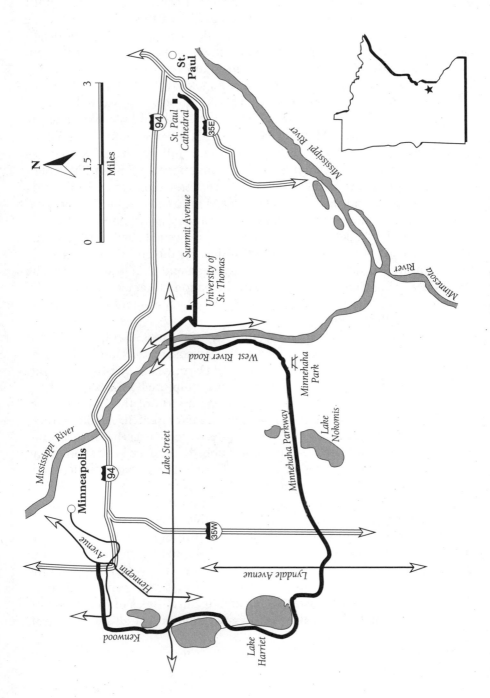

The drive

Minneapolis is justifiably famous for its park system, a "Grand Round" of lakes, streams, and parkways arcing across the city from downtown to the Mississippi River. Some of the Twin Cities's oldest and most prestigious neighborhoods are strung along this necklace of water and greenery, created out of swampland at the turn of the century. And the Chain of Lakes is the metro area's most popular playground, a huge draw for walkers, bicyclists, in-line skaters, canoeists, and boaters. This 20-mile drive between the downtowns of Minneapolis and St. Paul traces the shores of four lakes and the richly wooded banks of Minnehaha Creek and the Mississippi. The final 4.5 miles follow Summit Avenue, a boulevard of magnificent mansions that was once home to railroad tycoon James J. Hill and novelist F. Scott Fitzgerald.

Begin the drive on Vineland Place, across Hennepin Avenue from Loring Park. This is the cultural nerve center of Minneapolis. A modernist complex on the left contains not one but two great artistic institutions: the Guthrie Theater and the Walker Art Center. The Guthrie, established in 1963 by the distinguished British director Tyrone Guthrie, is the country's premier regional theater, a showcase for classic American and European drama. The Walker's austere galleries house one of the nation's foremost collections of twentieth century art, featuring works by Roy Lichtenstein, Andy Warhol, and Deborah Butterfield.

The Walker extends outdoors, into the Minneapolis Sculpture Garden across the street. Eleven acres of lawn, hedged courtyards, and linden trees provide a contemplative setting for forty-odd large-scale sculptures, including *Spoonbridge and Cherry*, a giant fountain-sculpture by Claes Oldenburg and Coosje van Bruggen. In the background a vista of the Basilica of St. Mary and the downtown skyline rises behind a curtain of Black Hills spruce.

Turn left on South Bryant Avenue, a steep ascent past the Guthrie onto Lowry Hill. A sinuous glacial moraine dubbed "the Devil's Backbone" by early settlers, it was renamed in honor of Thomas Lowry, a real estate developer and street railway entrepreneur. The hilltop, with its stunning views of the sculpture garden, Loring Park, and downtown, has been the home of Minneapolis movers and shakers for more than a century. The parade of grand residences begins as you make a right turn onto Groveland Terrace, and continues on Mount Curve Avenue, the first right at the top of the hill. Many of the big, two- and three-story houses on Mount Curve date to the 1890s and early 1900s, when the city's elite spared no expense in demonstrating their wealth and taste. All the architectural styles of the era are on display: Classical Revival, Italian Renaissance, Prairie School, Tudor Revival, Queen Anne.

Bear right at a traffic island and follow Mount Curve around to the left as it twists and dips over glacial hummocks and ridges. Massive elms, maples, and oaks arch overhead, partly obscuring the handsome facades set off by well-tended lawns and flower beds. Mount Curve veers to the left and meets Kenwood Parkway in about 0.5 mile. Turn left, winding along the edge of Kenwood Park, 20 wooded acres on the flanks of the Devil's Backbone. A tall brick monolith thrusts skyward on the right: Kenwood's landmark water tower, built in 1910. Long since run dry, the octagonal, Romanesque tower contains city communications equipment.

Kenwood, almost as prestigious as Mount Curve, was an upper middle-class suburb in the 1890s, linked to distant downtown by electric trolley lines. Lovely brick and wood-frame houses with turrets, leaded-glass windows, and wide front porches line the parkway as it spirals gently downhill. An oak-shaded Queen Anne at number 2104 was the TV home of Mary Richards on *The Mary Tyler Moore Show*. Kenwood Parkway ends at Lake of the Isles, one of several Minneapolis lakes formed from huge ice blocks left imbedded in the earth by the retreating glaciers.

Turn right onto Lake of the Isles Parkway, passing Peavey Fountain, a knob of ruddy granite that may be the world's only monument dedicated to horses killed in battle. The stone and brick mansions along the lake's 4-mile shoreline are younger than those in Kenwood, built between World War I and 1930. In the early 1900s, Lake of the Isles wasn't a pleasant place to live; swarms of malaria-carrying mosquitoes rose nightly from extensive marshlands along the shore. A herculean dredging and filling project transformed the swamp into the beautiful wooded parkland that rings the lake today. The parkway, built atop dredged fill in the 1920s, winds around the lake's west shore, crossing a narrow channel to Cedar Lake, the least developed of the city's five major lakes. Two densely wooded islands to the left are sanctuaries for egrets and great blue herons, off limits even to canoes. Behind the islands you can see the skyscrapers of downtown Minneapolis, only 2.5 miles distant but a world away from this urban oasis.

The parkway forks in 1 mile; bear right, passing under a concrete railroad bridge. The channel on your right is Kenilworth Lagoon, dredged in 1911 to allow canoes and pleasure boats to pass between Lake of the Isles and Lake Calhoun. Its banks are a favorite spot for anglers casting for smallmouth bass, bluegill, crappies, and sunfish. A couple of stoplights orchestrate heavy traffic on Lake Street, a major east-to-west thoroughfare. This is your chance to pick up a cafe latte or Evian to go; Uptown, an area of chic restaurants and shops, is up the hill to the left. Go straight through the intersection onto East Lake Calhoun Parkway. A concessions building on the right sells hot dogs and ice cream, and rents canoes by the hour. Small sailboats rock at city-owned buoys offshore.

The Lake Harriet Bandstand, a popular venue for concerts on summer evenings.

Lake Calhoun is the largest of Minneapolis's lakes, and the deepest, with a maximum depth of 90 feet. Oval and windswept, the lake attracts hordes of walkers, bikers, in-line skaters, sunbathers, and sailboarders on summer weekends. Thick foliage permits only glimpses of the water for four or five blocks; then the parkway emerges into the open at 36th Street, kitty corner from Lakewood Cemetery. Landscaped in the romantic Victorian manner, with leafy glades and flower-bedecked knolls, the cemetery contains the graves of many famous Minnesotans, including Hubert H. Humphrey, Thomas Lowry, and former Governor Floyd B. Olson. There's a parking lot on the right where you can take in the view and watch the human parade on the biking and walking paths. A file of Lombardy poplars leads the way down the shore to the south end of the lake, a popular venue for wind surfing; when the wind is blowing multi-hued sails flit over the water like butterflies.

Turn left on William Berry Parkway, a half-mile jog through the woods and over a hill to Lake Harriet. A masterpiece of architectural whimsy dominates the shore: the Lake Harriet Bandstand, the site of classical and popular music concerts on summer evenings. Pennants flutter from corner turrets out of Gothic romance, and a glass wall at the rear of the stage lets the audience watch waves and clouds dance to the strains of Bach or Duke Ellington. On the right, a small wooden depot houses a gift shop and interpretive displays on Minneapolis's streetcar system, scrapped in the 1950s. The trolleys aren't completely dead, however; from May through October you can board a restored streetcar for a 1-mile ride to Lake Calhoun and back on the old Como-Harriet line. The street spanning the tracks leads to Linden Hills, another upscale neighborhood with a lively mix of shops and eateries at 44th and Sheridan.

Continue along the high, densely wooded shore on West Lake Harriet Parkway, a one way-loop. Large brick and stucco homes sit well back from the road in the shade of mature hardwoods and evergreens. Flocks of Canada geese, mallards, herring gulls, and American coots congregate along this stretch of shoreline, lingering into early winter to take advantage of hand-outs from residents and passersby. Look to your left as you round the bot-tom of the lake for a long-distance perspective on the bandstand and down-town, an emerald city on the horizon. Turn right on West Minnehaha Park-way opposite Harriet Beach. If you want to see the Lake Harriet Rose Gar-den, with its spitting-turtle fountain and hundreds of varieties of roses and other flowers, you'll have to go around the lake again. Alternatively, you can park and walk; the gardens are about 200 yards ahead on the right.

Winding past 100-year-old stands of elm and maple, Minnehaha Park-way meets the creek of the same name in half a mile; bear right at an elementary school and follow the one-way, narrow road along the Minnehaha's wooded banks. Two-story houses of stucco and brick, many of them sporting the red, Hacienda-style roofs popular in the 1920s and 1930s, line the parkway to the right. Their counterparts on the creek's northern bank are barely visible during the summer, masked by a wide band of parkland criss-crossed by walking and biking paths. In the spring, when the flow eastward from Lake Minnetonka is highest, canoes and kayaks can often be seen floating downstream, weaving their way past weed beds and under wooden footbridges.

Lyndale Avenue is the first of several major thoroughfares that cross the parkway on its 6-mile ramble across south Minneapolis. Beyond this busy in-tersection the creek sinks into a deep gorge, taking the walking and biking paths with it. The neighborhood on the other side of the creek is coveted for its hilly terrain and maze of crooked streets—a departure from the city's standard grid. To tour Tangletown, turn off the parkway and cross the creek on Nicollet Avenue. Otherwise, continue on the parkway, under the Nicollet and Interstate 35W overpasses. Designated East Minnehaha Parkway now, the road traces the northern bank of the creek for 2 more miles to Lake Nokomis, the last in the Minneapolis Chain of Lakes. Expansive parkland surrounds the lake, the site of a hotly contested milk-carton boat race during the Aquatennial festival in July. There's a swimming beach with a lifeguard, changing rooms, and conces-sions to the right, on Lake Nokomis Parkway. To the left, a golf course abuts much smaller Lake Hiawatha.

If you detect a pattern in these names, you're right; all are characters from Henry Wadsworth Longfellow's epic poem *The Song of Hiawatha*. Nokomis was the Indian hero's grandmother, and Minnehaha was his bride. Veering away from the creek, the parkway heads straight for the source of Longfellow's inspiration: Minnehaha Falls. Crab apple trees and lilacs—a fantasia of mauve and purple in the spring—line the median in a neighborhood of relatively modest houses and corner shops. The parkway ends at Hiawatha Avenue, a four-lane highway; go straight through the stoplights onto Godfrey Parkway, passing a yellow two-story house on the right—a replica of Longfellow's Colonial home in Boston. You're in Minnehaha Park, established in 1889 to protect the falls, a majestic cataract dropping 53 feet into a steep-walled gorge. In the winter, when Minnehaha Creek freezes, a curtain of iridescent ice drapes over the falls like candle drippings.

Longfellow actually never saw the falls, basing his poem on the accounts of explorers and traders. But its publication in 1855 made the "laughing water" famous, and since then countless pilgrims—including naturalist Henry David Thoreau, composer Antonin Dvorak, and President Lyndon Johnson—have made their way to the falls. You can make your own pilgrimage from a parking lot on the right. Near the falls there is a life-size bronze sculpture of Hiawatha carrying Minnehaha across the creek, by artist Jacob Fjelde. A stone bridge leads to the Stevens House, the first house erected west of the Mississippi River, and trails that wind down the bluff and along the wooded creek bottom.

Stay on Godfrey Parkway, passing the Minnesota Veterans Hospital and slipping under the approaches to the Ford Bridge. A pull-off ahead offers a view of the bridge arching over the Mississippi to St. Paul; just beyond it the river plunges off the edge of the Ford Lock and Dam, built in 1917 to provide power for the Ford Motor Company assembly plant in Highland Park. A hydroelectric plant on the east bank still feeds electricity into Northern State Power's regional grid. The lock, down the hill to the right, has an observation platform where you can watch barges and pleasure boats rising and falling on an artificial tide. Continue north on West River Parkway, atop steep bluffs cloaked in burr oak, maple, and basswood. Like the Minneapolis lakes, the Mississippi River gorge is a legacy of the Ice Age: a vast torrent of glacial meltwater tore through the Twin Cities area about ten thousand years ago, exposing layer after layer of Platteville limestone, shale, and sandstone. On the far side of the river a band of bare, chalky rock runs beneath the foundations of houses perched on the blufftop. The parkway follows the river for 2 miles, edging two-story, pre-World War II homes set back behind spacious front lawns.

An exit ramp to the left leads up to the Lake Street Bridge, and a stunning panorama of the river flowing between richly wooded bluffs. On the

Mississippi River Boulevard near the Lake Street Bridge in St. Paul.

other side, make an immediate right, then a left onto Mississippi River Boulevard. Eastcliff, a Colonial manse that is the official residence of the president of the University of Minnesota, sprawls down the hill to the left. Rounding a sharp bend, the parkway scales the bluff, then doubles back on itself, hugging the contours of a deep, wooded ravine. The road straightens out again at Summit Avenue; to the right an overlook by a World War I memorial offers a splendid vista of the river gorge, the Lake Street bridge, and distant downtown Minneapolis.

Summit Avenue, the best-preserved boulevard of grand Victorian mansions in the country, stretches 4.5 miles from the river to the edge of downtown St. Paul. Ornate houses built by the city's merchant princes in the era of the horse and carriage march shoulder to shoulder down the avenue, divided by a grassy median sprouting century-old oaks, elms, and maples. Monumental churches, synagogues, and colleges add gravity to a streetscape that has changed little since the 1920s. Entire books have been written about Summit Avenue. A sampling of its architectural treasures:

- The Governor's Residence (1006), a three-story, English-Tudor mansion built in 1910 for a local lumber baron.
- House of Hope Presbyterian Church (797), one of the country's best examples of Gothic Revival style with its arched windows and crenellated bell tower.

- The F. Scott Fitzgerald House (599), the red-sandstone rowhouse where F. Scott Fitzgerald rewrote *This Side of Paradise* in the summer of 1919, pinning drafts to the curtains.
- The James J. Hill Mansion (240), a Richardsonian Romanesque fortress with 32 rooms, 22 fireplaces, and a dining table that seats 40.

For a respite from Summit's grandeur, drive one block south to Grand Avenue, a strip of cafes, restaurants, and fashionable retail stores. Fairview, Snelling, Lexington, and Victoria all lead to bustling neighborhood business districts. Summit angles to the left at Ramsey Street, passing the University Club and a small blufftop park on the right. The drive ends at the St. Paul Cathedral, an imposing edifice of granite crowned by a green copper dome. The cathedral commands a hill with a panoramic view of the Minnesota State Capitol, the Minnesota History Center, and the modern high-rises of downtown St. Paul.

22

Lake Minnetonka Loop

General description: Lake Minnetonka, the largest lake in the Twin Cities, is beloved of wealthy residents, boaters, and nature lovers alike. A 40-mile circle tour of Minnetonka's beauty spots and historic towns, with sidetrips through Carver Park Reserve and the Minnesota Landscape Arboretum.

Special attractions: Marvelous views of woods, wetlands, and expensive real estate on Lake Minnetonka; hiking and bird watching at Lowry Nature Center and Carver Park Reserve; scenic 3-mile drive around Minnesota Landscape Arboretum; lake views and gardens at Noerenberg Memorial County Park; lake cruises on the steamboat *Minnehaha*; shopping and fine dining in Wayzata and Excelsior; boating, water-skiing, biking, people watching.

Drive route numbers: Minnesota Highways 7, 5, 101; Hennepin County Roads 15, 51, 125, 110, 92, 19; Carver County Roads 11, 117, 16, and various residential streets.

Location: Far-western suburbs of Minneapolis. The drive begins and ends in the upscale suburb of Wayzata on Lake Minnetonka.

Travel season: All-year. Every season has its attractions: blooming plants at the Arboretum and Noerenberg Gardens in the spring; non-stop boating action throughout the summer; vivid leaf color in early October; and dramatic views of a snow-covered, frozen lake in the winter.

Camping: Are you kidding? Campgrounds would drive down property values on the lake. But rustic camping is available at Lake Auburn Campground in Carver Park Reserve.

Services: You're rarely more than a couple of minutes away from a gas station, restaurant, or hotel on Lake Minnetonka. Wayzata, Mound, and Excelsior are the biggest towns on the lake.

Nearby attractions: Morris T. Baker and Lake Rebecca Park Reserves, north of Lake Minnetonka; Mystic Lake Casino and Canterbury Park horse racing near Shakopee; biking on the Luce Line State Trail through Wayzata and Orono; Planes of Fame Air Museum in Eden Prairie.

Drive 22: Lake Minnetonka Loop

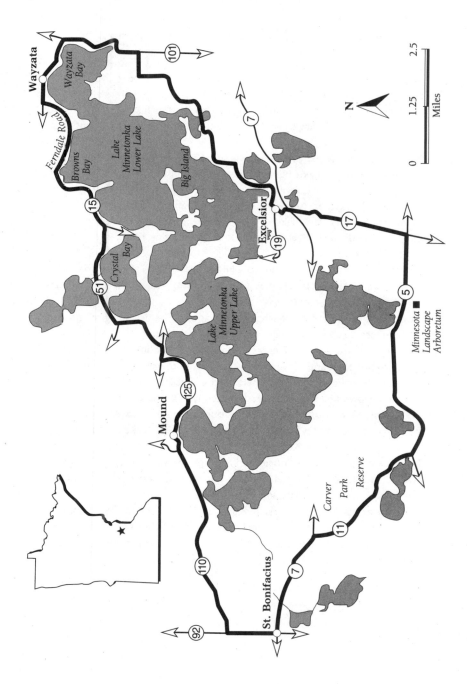

The drive

Two 17-year-old boys on a canoe trip from Fort Snelling in 1822 were the first white men to see the big, sprawling lake the Dakota Indians called *Me-ne-a-ton-ka* ("Big Water"). They'd be amazed at its transformation if they visited Lake Minnetonka today. Luxurious homes, upscale shops and restaurants, and marinas filled with expensive boats line the shore of the metro area's largest lake. But development has not spoiled the beauty of Lake Minnetonka, a maze of bays, straits, capes, and points formed by irregular melting of glacial debris at the end of the last Ice Age. Much of the shoreline remains heavily wooded, and land in the vicinity has been set aside for parks, gardens, and wildlife preserves. Lake Minnetonka's split personality—ritzy playground and sylvan retreat—is revealed on this 40-mile drive around its convoluted shore and out into the countryside to the southwest.

The drive begins in tony Wayzata on the north shore of the lake (take Interstate 394 west from Minneapolis). Art galleries, restaurants, and specialty shops line Lake Street, a pleasant promenade on the waterfront. Wayzata—the name is derived from a Dakota word meaning "god of the north"—rapidly developed as a summer resort at the turn of the century. The Wayzata Depot at the west end of Lake Street was the end of the line for street trolleys bringing heat-weary Minneapolitans out for a concert on Big Island, or a stroll along the beach at Excelsior. Today the renovated depot houses the Chamber of Commerce and old photos of daytrippers in flannels and boaters.

A lakeside park behind the depot offers a sweeping view of Wayzata Bay, ringed with oak, maple, elm, fir, and pine; the rest of the lake remains out of sight, beyond Lookout Point. During the summer the steamboat *Minnehaha*, a restored 1906 passenger ferry, embarks on roundtrip excursions to Excelsior from a wooden dock in the park.

You pass Minnetonka Boat Works, a large powerboat marina, and the Gothic-flavored First Star Bank on the way out of town on Lake Street. After half a mile turn left on Ferndale Avenue South, crossing some railroad tracks and keeping straight up a slight rise. Ferndale, one of the most visually alluring residential lanes on the lake, curves past palatial homes hidden behind impeccably trimmed hedges and high stone walls. To the right, willow trees overhang expanses of cattail marsh that come alive with swallows and redwing blackbirds in the spring.

Entering Orono, one of nine small municipalities that ring Lake Minnetonka, Ferndale meets Hennepin County Road 15 (Shoreline Drive) in 2.5 miles. Turn left and follow this busy road close along the shore of Browns Bay. There's a wayside on the left where you can pull off and take in

View of Lake Minnetonka over expensive greensward on Ferndale Avenue South.

a park-like vista of water lapping at the feet of mature oaks, maples, and willows. In the spring and fall it's not unusual to see flocks of migrating waterfowl—Canada geese, coots, canvasback ducks—diving for fish in the bay. CR 15 crosses a narrow isthmus straddled by two marinas and sweeps into Smiths Bay, the next big bite out of Minnetonka's scalloped shoreline. Here, for the first time, the lake unfolds to its full breadth; thickly wooded Big Island partly obscures the southern shore at Deephaven, 3 miles away. On summer weekends white sails fleck the main channel, vying for honors in club regattas.

Watch closely for the turnoff to North Shore Drive (Hennepin County Road 51); it's the second major road on the right. Turning away from the water, CR 51 slices through a large cattail marsh on the way to Noerenberg Memorial County Park, once one of Lake Minnetonka's grandest estates. The entrance is on the left, shaded by a stand of tall Norway spruce and Scotch pine. A beautiful garden in the English Landscape style—groomed greensward, beds overflowing with flowers, ornamental grasses, and shrubs—slopes down to the shore of Crystal Bay.

At the turn of the century this was the private paradise of Frederic and Johanna Noerenberg, one of the first families to establish a permanent residence on the lake. Frederic, a wealthy Minneapolis brewer, spared no expense on his enormous Queen Anne-style house and the magnificent gardens that surrounded it, filled with trees and plants from all over the world. Today the mansion is gone, replaced by a classical colonnade in a grove of 100-year-old elms. But the Noerenberg's gazebo/boathouse, styled after a Chinese pagoda, still invites visitors to take their ease by the lake.

North Shore Drive continues through the park and along a narrow spit of land separating Crystal Bay from two bodies of water almost completely cut off from the lake: Maxwell Bay and the North Arm. Narrow channels allow passage for powerboats only; sailboat masts can't clear the low bridges. There's a public boat ramp ahead on the right, a low-cost alternative to mooring your 35-foot pleasure craft at a marina. Turn left on Hennepin County Road 51/19 (Shadywood Road), the main highway linking the north and south shores of Lake Minnetonka. After you cross the bridge over another boat channel, follow CR 51 around to the right. Just ahead is Lord Fletcher's of the Lake, a faux-Tudor restaurant complex frequented by the powerboat crowd. In the summer the action centers on The Wharf, a spacious outdoor deck where you can order a drink and watch an endless parade of cabin cruisers burbling past the dock.

At this point in the drive you're in the middle of Lake Minnetonka, on an archipelago of interconnected capes, points, and islands. Turn right on CR 15 into the city of Spring Park, then left on Hennepin County Road 125 (Interlachen Road). Vistas of water, sky, and wooded shoreline spread out on both sides of the road as it crosses a causeway with parking spots for photographers and fishermen. Bear right on Wilshire Boulevard, passing relatively modest homes and two lagoons thick with cattails, reeds, and pondweed. Another large marsh appears on the right as CR 125 veers to the right on Bartlett Boulevard. Minnesota's rigorous wetland protection laws prevent marshes like these—sitting atop some of the priciest real estate in the metro area—from being filled for residential development.

Turn left on Hennepin County Road 110 in the city of Mound, named for the multitude of ancient Indian burial mounds found in the area. Like Wayzata and Excelsior, Mound had an independent existence as a farming and resort center before the suburbs engulfed Lake Minnetonka. Mound's red-brick, rather nondescript downtown is half a mile to the right. You're back on *terra firma* now; take a last look at Lake Minnetonka to the left as CR 110 heads west into open farmland on the ex-urban fringe. Scattered new homes share the rolling landscape with serried ranks of corn, dairy cows, and red wooden barns. After 5 miles, turn left on Hennepin County Road 92 into St. Bonifacius, once a thriving center for beekeeping, led by a Catholic priest at St. Bonifacius Church. Almost all of the headstones in the cemetery across Main Street bear the names of settlers from Germany and their descendants; today the village's Teutonic heritage is fading as new families move into a burgeoning subdivision on the hill.

The gazebo/boathouse at Noerenberg Memorial County Park.

Continue down the hill through St. Bonifacius's one-block downtown and turn left on Minnesota Highway 7. It's 2.5 miles over gently rolling woodland and pasture to Carver Park Reserve, one of three large tracts of parkland in the Minnetonka area. Turn right into the park on Carver County Road 11. Offering a complete change of pace from the manicured beauty of Lake Minnetonka, the road twists and rolls for 2.75 miles through oak woods and meadows dotted with lakes and small wetlands. The entrance to Lowry Nature Center is on the left. A narrow road winds past a shorebird sanctuary frequented by Canada geese, buffle-head ducks, and trumpeter swans to an interpretive building with kid-friendly displays on wildlife and native plants. Six miles of turf trails and boardwalks loop through woodland, prairie, cattail marsh, and tamarack swamp.

CR 11 leaves the park along the reed-bound shore of Lake Auburn and quickly joins Minnesota Highway 5. Turn left, following the highway east through farmland that is steadily giving ground to the expanding suburb of Victoria. Executive homes overlook Lake Minnewashta, a large lake ringed with marsh. Across the road on the right, the Minnesota Landscape Arboretum contains 905 acres of wooded hills, ponds, and wetlands dedicated to the improvement of nature. The Haralson apple, Princess Kay plum, and many other winter-hardy fruits, flowers, and vegetables have been developed over the years at the Arboretum's Horticultural Research Center. A 0.25-mile drive winds past the gatehouse (admission charge) to an administration building with a conservatory, library, and tearoom. From there a 3-mile, one-way loop tours the gardens, a constantly evolving panorama of flowers, grasses, shrubs, and ornamental trees. Along the way, strategically placed benches invite contemplation of the gardens and surrounding woods and meadows.

The route stays on MN 5 for 1.5 mile, then turns left at the second stoplight, Galpin Road (Carver County Road 117). Heading north towards Lake Minnetonka over sharply rolling terrain, the road snakes past patches of marshland and luxurious homes secreted in the woods, meeting MN 7 in about 3 miles. Turn right, then immediately left on Hennepin County Road 19 (Oak Street). You're back on the shore of the big lake in Excelsior, a town of 2,600 founded in the 1850s by pioneers from New York City who came west to grow apples, peaches, plums, cherries, and pears. Turn right on Water Street, a handsome nineteenth-century thoroughfare lined with antique stores and specialty shops, to reach the waterfront on Excelsior Bay. Extensive parkland and docking facilities for the *Minnehaha* and other excursion boats stretches along the shore. Across the harbor, a lone Ferris wheel spins on the site of the old Excelsior Amusement Park, now a restaurant and marina complex.

Follow Lake Street and Excelsior Boulevard around the harbor, crossing the Southwest Regional LRT Trail, a 27-mile bike path from Victoria to Hopkins along the south shore of Lake Minnetonka. Turn left on Minnetonka Boulevard; the road slips between Excelsior Bay and St. Alban's Bay and winds through the leafy, prestigious enclaves of Greenwood and Deephaven. The route seems complicated, with frequent turns and distracting cul-de-sacs, but Minnetonka Boulevard is clearly sign-posted. After 3 miles, turn left on Minnesota Highway 101 and head downhill to the lakeshore. A causeway separates Wayzata Bay from Gray's Bay, the outlet for Minnehaha Creek (see Drive 21). Splendid views of wooded shoreline and distant Wayzata open up as the road crosses the water and veers to the right up a steep hill. At the top, turn left on Hennepin County Road 16 (McGinty Road), which curves past the Wayzata Yacht Club and into downtown Wayzata.

The drive ends here. Drive 5 begins in Chaska, 7.5 miles south of Excelsior on Minnesota Highway 41.

Appendix
For More Information

*For more information about public lands and community events,
please contact the following organizations.*

General information about Minnesota:

Minnesota Office of Tourism
100 Metro Square
121 Seventh Place East
St. Paul, MN 55101
(800) 657-3700 or 296-5029
in the Twin Cities

World Wide Web: http://
www.tccn.com/mn.tourism/
mnhome.html

Minnesota Department of
  Natural Resources
P.O. Box 40, 500 Lafayette Road
St. Paul, MN 55155
(800) 652-9747 or 296-6157
in the Twin Cities

Drive 1

Red Wing Convention
  and Visitors Bureau
418 Levee Street
Red Wing, MN 55066
(612) 385-5934

Winona Convention
  and Visitors Bureau
67 Main Street, P.O. Box 870
Winona, MN 55987
(800) 657-4972

Wabasha Area
  Chamber of Commerce
257 West Main Street, P.O. Box 105
Wabasha, MN 55981
(612) 565-4158

Frontenac State Park
29223 County Road 28 Boulevard
Lake City, MN 55041
(612) 345-3401

Whitewater State Park
Route 1, Box 256
Altura, MN 55910
(507) 932-3007

Drive 2

La Crescent Chamber of Commerce
P.O. Box 132
La Crescent, MN 55947
(800) 926-9480

Rushford Area Business Association
P.O. Box 430
101 North Mill Street
Rushford, MN 55971
(507) 864-2444

Lanesboro Tourism Office
P.O. Box 20
Lanesboro, MN 55949
(800) 944-2670

Forestville/Mystery Cave State Park
Route 2, Box 128
Preston, MN 55965
(507) 352-5111

Nerstrand Big Woods State Park
9700 170th Street East
Nerstrand, MN 55053
(507) 334-8848

Drive 3

Harmony Tourist Information
P.O. Box 141
Harmony, MN 55939
(800) 247-MINN or
(507) 886-2469

Spring Grove City Hall
P.O. Box 218
118 First Avenue NW
Spring Grove, MN 55974
(507) 498-5221

Beaver Creek Valley State Park
Route 2, Box 57
Caledonia, MN 55921
(507) 724-2107

Drive 5

Le Sueur Area
  Chamber of Commerce
500 North Main Street, Suite 106
Le Sueur, MN 56058
(612) 665-2501

Mankato Area Convention
  and Visitors Bureau
P.O. Box 999
Mankato, MN 56001
(800) 657-4733

Minneopa State Park
Route 9, Box 143
Mankato, MN 56001
(507) 389-5464

Drive 4

Northfield Area
  Chamber of Commerce
500 Water Street South
P.O. Box 198
Northfield, MN 55057
(800) 658-2548

St. Peter Chamber of Commerce
101 South Front Street
St. Peter, MN 56082
(800) 473-3404

Faribault Chamber of Commerce
P.O. Box 434
530 Wilson Avenue
Faribault, MN 55021
(800) 658-2354

Drive 6

Pipestone Chamber of Commerce
117 Eighth Avenue Southeast,
P.O. Box 8
Pipestone, MN 56164
(507) 825-3316

Luverne Area
  Chamber of Commerce
102 East Main
Luverne, MN 56156
(507) 283-4061

Blue Mounds State Park
Rural Route 1
Luverne, MN 56156
(507) 283-4892

Wilder Museum/Visitor
  Information
P.O. Box 58WG
Walnut Grove, MN 56180
(507) 859-2358 or 2155

Drive 7

New Ulm Convention
  and Visitors Bureau
P.O. Box 384
1 North Minnesota Street
New Ulm, MN 56073
(507) 354-4217

Granite Falls Area
  Chamber of Commerce
155 West Seventh Avenue
Granite Falls, MN 56241
(320) 564-4039

Montevideo Area
  Chamber of Commerce
110 North First, Suite 2
Montevideo, MN 56265
(800) 269-5527

Fort Ridgely State Park
Route 1, Box 65
Fairfax, MN 55332
(507) 426-7840

Laq Qui Parle State Park
Route 5, Box 74A
Montevideo, MN 56265
(320) 752-4736

Drive 8

St. Cloud Area Convention
  and Visitors Bureau
P.O. Box 487
St. Cloud, MN 56302
(800) 264-2940

Little Falls Tourism
  and Convention Bureau
200 First Street Northwest
Little Falls, MN 56345
(800) 325-5916

Sauk Centre Area
  Chamber of Commerce
1220 South Main Street,
  P.O. Box 222
Sauk Centre, MN 56378
(612) 352-5201

Charles A. Lindbergh State Park
P.O. Box 364
Little Falls, MN 55951
(320) 632-9050

Drive 9

Alexandria Lakes Area
  Chamber of Commerce
206 Broadway
Alexandria, MN 56308
(800) 235-9441

Pelican Rapids Area
  Chamber of Commerce
P.O. Box 206
Pelican Rapids, MN 56572
(800) 545-3711

Fergus Falls Convention
  and Visitors Bureau
P.O. Box 868 City Hall
Fergus Falls, MN 56538
(800) 726-8959

Maplewood State Park
Route 3, Box 422
Pelican Rapids, MN 56572
(218) 863-8383

Drive 10

Garrison Commercial Club
P.O. Box B
Garrison, MN 56450
(800) 346-7646

Mille Lacs Indian Museum
Star Route, Box 195
Onamia, MN 56359
(320) 532-3632

Mora Area Chamber of Commerce
20 North Union Street
Mora, MN 55051
(800) 291-5792

Mille Lacs Kathio State Park
15066 Kathio State Park Road
Onamia, MN 56359
(320) 532-3523

Drive 11

Brainerd Lakes Area
  Chamber of Commerce
124 North Sixth Street
Brainerd, MN 56401
(800) 450-2838

Nisswa Area
  Chamber of Commerce
124 North Sixth Street
549 Main Street, P.O. Box 185
Nisswa, MN 56468
(800) 950-9610

Cuyuna Country
Crosby-Ironton-Deerwood
P.O. Box 23
Crosby, MN 56441
(800) 950-2898

Drive 12

Park Rapids Area
  Chamber of Commerce
Box 249, Highway 71 South
Park Rapids, MN 56470
(800) 247-0054

Bemidji Area Information Center
  and Convention Bureau
P.O. Box 850
Bemidji, MN 56601
(800) 458-2223

Leech Lake Area
  Chamber of Commerce
Box 1089
Walker, MN 56484
(800) 833-1118

Itasca State Park
HCO 5, Box 4
Lake Itasca, MN 56460
(218) 266-2124 or 266-2100

Chippewa National Forest
Route 3, Box 244
Cass Lake, MN 56633
(218) 335-8600 or (218) 335-8632

Drive 13

International Falls
  Chamber of Commerce
301 Second Avenue
International Falls, MN 56649
(800) 325-5766

Voyageurs National Park
3131 Highway 53
International Falls, MN 56649
(218) 283-9821

Lake of the Woods Area
  Tourism Bureau
P.O. Box 518
Baudette, MN 56623
(800) 382-3474

Northwest Angle &
  Island Chamber of Commerce
P.O. Box 68
Angle Inlet, MN 56711

Zippel Bay State Park
HC 2, Box 25
Williams, MN 56686
(218) 783-6252

Drive 14

Grand Rapids Visitors
  and Convention Bureau
One Northwest Third Street
Grand Rapids, MN 55744
(800) 472-6366

Itasca County Resort
  and Tourism Association
P.O. Box 33
Marcell, MN 56656
(800) 472-6366

Chippewa National Forest
Marcell Ranger District
HC1 Box 600
Marcell, MN 55657

Scenic State Park
HCR 2, Box 17
Bigfork, MN 56628
(218) 743-3362

Drive 15

Ely Chamber of Commerce
1600 East Sheridan Street
Ely, MN 55731
(800) 777-7281

Superior National Forest
Isabella Work Station
2759 Highway 1
Isabella, MN 55607
(218) 323-7722

George Crosby Manitou State Park
474 Highway 61 East
Silver Bay, MN 55614
(218) 226-3539

Drive 16

International Wolf Center
1369 Highway 169
Ely, MN 55731
(800) 359-9653 or (218) 365-4695

Superior National Forest
Kawishiwi Ranger District
118 South Fourth Avenue East
Ely, MN 55731
(218) 365-7600 or 7601

Crane Lake Visitors
  and Tourism Bureau
Handberg Road
Crane Lake, MN 55725
(800) 362-7405

Orr Tourist Information Center
Highway 53
Orr, MN 55771
(218) 757-3932

Drive 17

Hibbing Chamber of Commerce
211 East Howard Street,
P.O. Box 727
Hibbing, MN 55746
(800) 4-HIBBING

Virginia Chamber of Commerce
P.O. Box 1072
Virginia, MN 55792
(800) 777-7395

Town of Embarrass
7528 Levander Road
Embarrass, MN 55732
(218) 984-2672

Soudan Underground
  Mine State Park
Highway 169
Soudan, MN 55782
(218) 753-2245

Drive 18

Duluth Convention
  and Visitors Bureau
Endion Station
100 Lake Place Drive
Duluth, MN 55802
(800) 4-DULUTH

Lake County
  Visitor Information Center
8 Highway 61 East
Two Harbors, MN 55616
(800) 554-2116

Grand Portage Tourist Association
P.O. Box 307M
Grand Portage, MN 55605
(800) 232-1384

Gooseberry Falls State Park
1300 Highway 61 East
Two Harbors, MN 55616
(218) 834-3855

Tettegouche State Park
474 Highway 61 East
Silver Bay, MN 55614
(218) 226-6365

Drive 19

Lutsen-Tofte Tourism Association
P.O. Box 2248
Tofte, MN 55615
(218) 663-7804

Superior National Forest
Tofte Ranger District
Tofte, MN 55615
(218) 663-7981

Grand Marais
  Chamber of Commerce
P.O. Box 1048
Grand Marais, MN 55604
(800) 622-4014

Drive 20

Hastings Area
  Chamber of Commerce
119 West Second Street, Suite 201
Hastings, MN 55033
(612) 437-6775

Stillwater Area
  Chamber of Commerce
Brick Alley Building
423 South Main Street
Stillwater, MN 55082
(612) 439-7700

Taylors Falls
  Chamber of Commerce
350 Government Road
Talors Falls, MN 55084
(612) 462-7550

Afton State Park
6959 Peller Avenue South
Hastings, MN 55033
(612) 436-5391

Interstate State Park
P.O. Box 254
Taylors Falls, MN 55084
(612) 465-5711

Drive 21

Minneapolis Park
  & Recreation Board
400 South Fourth Street
Minneapolis, MN 55415
(612) 661-4800

Greater Minneapolis Convention
  and Visitors Association
4000 Multifoods Tower
33 South Sixth Street
Minneapolis, MN 55402
(612) 348-7000

St. Paul
  Convention and Visitors Bureau
102 Norwest Center
55 East Fifth Street
St. Paul, MN 55101
(800) 627-6101 or 297-6985
in the Twin Cities

Drive 22

Greater Wayzata
  Chamber of Commerce
402 East Lake Street
Wayzata, MN 55391
(612) 473-9595

Excelsior Area
  Chamber of Commerce
P.O. Box 32
Excelsior, MN 55331
(612) 474-6461

Noerenberg Gardens
2840 North Shore Drive
Wayzata, MN 55391
(612) 475-0050

Lowry Nature Center
P.O. Box 270
Victoria, MN 55386
(612) 472-4911

Minnesota Landscape Arboretum
3675 Arboretum Drive
Chanhassen, MN 55317
(612) 443-2460

Suggested Reading

Bray, Edmund C. *Billions of Years in Minnesota: The Geological Story of the State*. St. Paul, Minn.: The Science Museum of Minnesota, 1977.

Condon Johnston, Patricia. *Minnesota: Portrait of the Land and its People*. Helena, Mont.: American Geographic Publishing, 1987.

Federal Writers' Project of the Works Progress Administration. *The WPA Guide to Minnesota*. St. Paul, Minn.: Minnesota Historical Society Press, 1985.

Fritzen, John. *Historic Sites and Place Names of Minnesota's North Shore*. Duluth, Minn.: St. Louis County Historical Society, 1974.

Hallberg, Jane King. *Minnehaha Creek Living Waters*. Minneapolis: Cityscapes Publishing Company, 1995.

Johnson, Elden. *The Prehistoric Peoples of Minnesota*. St. Paul, Minn.: Minnesota Historical Society Press, Rev. 3rd. ed., 1988.

Lanegran, David, and Sandeen, Ernest R. *The Lake District of Minneapolis: A history of the Calhoun-Isles Community*. St. Paul, Minn.: Living Historical Museum, 1978.

Lass, William E. *Minnesota: A History*. New York: W.W. Norton & Company, Inc., 1977

Meier, Peg. *Bring Warm Clothes: Letters and Photos from Minnesota's Past*. Minneapolis: Minneapolis Star & Tribune Company, 1981.

Olsenius, Richard. *Minnesota Travel Companion: A guide to the history along Minnesota's highways*. Wayzata, Minn.: Bluestem Productions, 1982.

Sandeen, Ernest R. *St. Paul's Historic Summit Avenue*. St. Paul, Minn.: Living Historical Museum, 1978.

Shepard, John G. *Minnesota Backroads*. Helena, Mont.: American Geographic Publishing, 1990.

Minnesota: Off the Beaten Path. Chester, Conn.: The Globe Pequot Press, 1989.

Tester, John R. *Minnesota's Natural Heritage*. Minneapolis: University of Minnesota Press, 1995

Waters, Thomas F. *The Streams and Rivers of Minnesota*. Minneapolis: University of Minnesota Press, 1977.

Index

About the Author

Phil Davies moved to Minnesota in 1982. A freelance journalist with a strong interest in the outdoors and in regional history, he rarely passes up an opportunity to seek out new places to bike, hike, cross-country ski, and soak up local atmosphere. His travel articles have appeared in a number of regional and national publications, including the *St. Paul Pioneer Press,* the *Dallas Morning News, Bicycling Guide, U.S. Art, France,* and *British Heritage.*

Born in England, Davies spent much of his childhood in warm climates, living at various times in Australia, New Guinea, Florida, and the U.S. Virgin Islands. He quickly came to grips with winter at the University of Minnesota in Minneapolis, where he earned an M.A. in creative writing. Today, equipped with Sorel boots and eight pairs of gloves, he lives in St. Paul with his wife Lydia. This is his first book for Falcon Press.

FALCON GUIDES ® are available for where-to-go hiking, mountain biking, rock climbing, walking, scenic driving, fishing, rockhounding, paddling, birding, wildlife viewing, and camping. We also have FalconGuides on essential outdoor skills and subjects and field identification. The following titles are currently available, but this list grows every year. For a free catalog with a complete list of titles, call FALCON toll-free at 1-800-582-2665.

SCENIC DRIVING GUIDES

Scenic Driving Alaska and the Yukon
Scenic Driving Arizona
Scenic Driving the Beartooth Highway
Scenic Driving California
Scenic Driving Colorado
Scenic Driving Florida
Scenic Driving Georgia
Scenic Driving Hawaii
Scenic Driving Idaho
Scenic Driving Michigan
Scenic Driving Minnesota
Scenic Driving Montana
Scenic Driving New England
Scenic Driving New Mexico
Scenic Driving North Carolina
Scenic Driving Oregon
Scenic Driving the Ozarks including the
    Ouchita Mountains
Scenic Driving Texas
Scenic Driving Utah
Scenic Driving Washington
Scenic Driving Wisconsin
Scenic Driving Wyoming
Back Country Byways
National Forest Scenic Byways
National Forest Scenic Byways II

HISTORIC TRAIL GUIDES

Traveling California's Gold Rush Country
Traveler's Guide to the Lewis & Clark Trail
Traveling the Oregon Trail
Traveler's Guide to the Pony Express Trail

WILDLIFE VIEWING GUIDES

Alaska Wildlife Viewing Guide
Arizona Wildlife Viewing Guide
California Wildlife Viewing Guide
Colorado Wildlife Viewing Guide
Florida Wildlife Viewing Guide
Idaho Wildlife Viewing Guide
Indiana Wildlife Vewing Guide
Iowa Wildlife Viewing Guide
Kentucky Wildlife Viewing Guide
Massachusetts Wildlife Viewing Guide
Montana Wildlife Viewing Guide
Nebraska Wildlife Viewing Guide
Nevada Wildlife Viewing Guide
New Hampshire Wildlife Viewing Guide
New Jersey Wildlife Viewing Guide
New Mexico Wildlife Viewing Guide
New York Wildlife Viewing Guide
North Carolina Wildlife Viewing Guide
North Dakota Wildlife Viewing Guide
Ohio Wildlife Viewing Guide
Oregon Wildlife Viewing Guide
Tennessee Wildlife Viewing Guide
Texas Wildlife Viewing Guide
Utah Wildlife Viewing Guide
Vermont Wildlife Viewing Guide
Virginia Wildlife Viewing Guide
Washington Wildlife Viewing Guide
West Virginia Wildlife Viewing Guide
Wisconsin Wildlife Viewing Guide

■ *To order any of these books, check with your local bookseller or call FALCON® at **1-800-582-2665**.*

Visit us on the world wide web at:
www.falconguide.com

get
FALCON GUIDED

HIKING GUIDES

Hiking Alaska
Hiking Alberta
Hiking Arizona
Hiking Arizona's Cactus Country
Hiking the Beartooths
Hiking Big Bend National Park
Hiking Bob Marshall Country
Hiking California
Hiking California's Desert Parks
Hiking Carlsbad Caverns
   and Guadalupe Mtns. National Parks
Hiking Colorado
Hiking the Columbia River Gorge
Hiking Florida
Hiking Georgia
Hiking Glacier & Waterton Lakes National Parks
Hiking Grand Canyon National Park
Hiking Glen Canyon
Hiking Great Basin National Park
Hiking Hot Springs
   in the Pacific Northwest
Hiking Idaho
Hiking Maine
Hiking Michigan
Hiking Minnesota
Hiking Montana
Hiker's Guide to Nevada
Hiking New Hampshire
Hiking New Mexico
Hiking New York
Hiking North Cascades
Hiking North Carolina

Hiking Northern Arizona
Hiking Olympic National Park
Hiking Oregon
Hiking Oregon's Eagle Cap Wilderness
Hiking Oregon's Three Sisters Country
Hiking Shenandoah
Hiking Pennsylvania
Hiking South Carolina
Hiking South Dakota's Black Hills Country
Hiking Southern New England
Hiking Tennessee
Hiking Texas
Hiking Utah
Hiking Utah's Summits
Hiking Vermont
Hiking Virginia
Hiking Washington
Hiking Wisconsin
Hiking Wyoming
Hiking Wyoming's Wind River Range
Hiking Yellowstone National Park
Hiking Zion & Bryce Canyon National Parks
The Trail Guide to Bob Marshall Country

BEST EASY DAY HIKES

Beartooths
Canyonlands & Arches
Best Hikes on the Continental Divide
Glacier & Wateron Lakes
Glen Canyon
North Cascades
Olympics
Shenandoah
Yellowstone

■ *To order any of these books, check with your local bookseller*
or call FALCON® at **1-800-582-2665**.

Visit us on the world wide web at:
www.falconguide.com

get
FALCON GUIDED

BIRDING GUIDES
Birding Arizona
Birding Minnesota
Birder's Guide to Montana
Birding Texas
Birding Utah

FIELD GUIDES
Bitterroot: Montana State Flower
Canyon Country Wildflowers
Great Lakes Berry Book
New England Berry Book
Plants of Arizona
Rare Plants of Colorado
Rocky Mountain Berry Book
Southern Rocky Mtn. Wildflowers
Tallgrass Prairie Wildflowers
Western Tree
Wildflowers of Southwestern Utah
Willow Bark and Rosehips

FISHING GUIDES
Fishing Alaska
Fishing the Beartooths
Fishing Florida
Fishing Maine
Fishing Michigan
Fishing Montana

PADDLING GUIDES
Floater's Guide to Colorado
Paddling Montana
Paddling Oregon

HOW-TO GUIDES
Bear Aware
Leave No Trace
Mountain Lion Alert
Wilderness First Aid
Wilderness Survival

ROCK CLIMBING GUIDES
Rock Climbing Colorado
Rock Climbing Montana
Rock Climbing New Mexico
  & Texas
Rock Climbing Utah

ROCKHOUNDING GUIDES
Rockhounding Arizona
Rockhound's Guide to California
Rockhound's Guide to Colorado
Rockhounding Montana
Rockhounding Nevada
Rockhound's Guide to New Mexico
Rockhounding Texas
Rockhounding Utah
Rockhounding Wyoming

WALKING
Walking Colorado Springs
Walking Portland
Walking St. Louis

MORE GUIDEBOOKS
Backcountry Horseman's
  Guide to Washington
Camping California's
  National Forests
Exploring Canyonlands &
  Arches National Parks
Exploring Mount Helena
Recreation Guide to WA
  National Forests
Touring California & Nevada
  Hot Springs
Trail Riding Western
  Montana
Wild Country Companion
Wild Montana
Wild Utah

■ *To order any of these books, check with your local bookseller*
*or call FALCON® at **1-800-582-2665**.*

Visit us on the world wide web at:
www.falconguide.com

FALCON®

WILDERNESS FIRST AID

By Dr. Gilbert Preston M.D.

Enjoy the outdoors and face the inherent risks with confidence. By reading this easy-to-follow first-aid text, all outdoor enthusiasts can pack a little extra peace of mind on their next adventure. *Wilderness First Aid* offers expert medical advice for dealing with outdoor emergencies beyond the reach of 911. It easily fits in most backcountry first-aid kits.

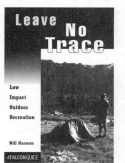

LEAVE NO TRACE

By Will Harmon

The concept of "leave no trace" seems simple, but it actually gets fairly complicated. This handy quick-reference guidebook includes all the newest information on this growing and all-important subject. This book is written to help the outdoor enthusiast make the hundreds of decisions necessary to protect the natural landscape and still have an enjoyable wilderness experience. Part of the proceeds from the sale of this book go to continue leave-no-trace education efforts. The Official Manual of American Hiking Society.

BEAR AWARE

By Bill Schneider

Hiking in bear country can be very safe if hikers follow the guidelines summarized in this small, "packable" book. Extensively reviewed by bear experts, the book contains the latest information on the intriguing science of bear-human interactions. *Bear Aware* can not only make your hike safer, but it can help you avoid the fear of bears that can take the edge off your trip.

MOUNTAIN LION ALERT

By Steve Torres

Recent mountain lion attacks have received national attention. Although infrequent, lion attacks raise concern for public safety. *Mountain Lion Alert* contains helpful advice for mountain bikers, trail runners, horse riders, pet owners, and suburban landowners on how to reduce the chances of mountain lion-human conflicts.

Also Available

• **_Wilderness Survival_** • **_Reading Weather_** • **_Backpacking Tips_**
• **_Climbing Safely_** • **_Avalanche Aware_**

To order check with your local bookseller or

call FALCON® at **1-800-582-2665.**

www.falconguide.com